"*The 99 Percent Economy* is not just a compelling indictment of capitalism run amuck. Adler makes a clear and convincing case for economic planning, expanded public investment, and greater social ownership and democratic management of productive enterprises. His book will be an essential educational tool for activists in labor and on the left."

—**Steve Early**, former International Representative for
the Communications Workers of America and author
of *Refinery Town: Big Oil, Big Money,
and the Remaking of an American City*

"In this insightful and highly readable volume, Paul Adler shows how we can define a shared purpose in the face of environmental and economic catastrophe. His prescription is both optimistic and practical—a must-read for our times that demand radical innovation in the way we organize our society . . . together."

—**John August**, Scheinman Institute, ILR School,
Cornell University, and former Executive Director,
Coalition of Kaiser Permanente Unions, 2006–2013

The Clarendon Lectures in Management Studies are jointly organized by Oxford University Press and the Saïd Business School. Every year a leading international academic is invited to give a series of lectures on a topic related to management education and research, broadly defined. The lectures form the basis of a book subsequently published by Oxford University Press.

CLARENDON LECTURES IN MANAGEMENT STUDIES:

THE 99 PERCENT ECONOMY

How Democratic Socialism Can Overcome the Crises of Capitalism

Paul S. Adler

OXFORD
UNIVERSITY PRESS

Oxford University Press is a department of the University of Oxford. It furthers
the University's objective of excellence in research, scholarship, and education
by publishing worldwide. Oxford is a registered trade mark of Oxford University
Press in the UK and certain other countries.

Published in the United States of America by Oxford University Press
198 Madison Avenue, New York, NY 10016, United States of America.

CIP data is on file at the Library of Congress
ISBN 978-0-19-093188-9

9 8 7 6 5 4 3 2 1

Printed by Sheridan Books, Inc., United States of America

CONTENTS

The 99 Percent Economy

INTRODUCTION

The Argument

In recent years, we have seen the eruption of several progressive and surprisingly radical movements, most notably Occupy, the 2016 Bernie Sanders campaign, the Fight for Fifteen, Black Lives Matter, the People's Climate March, and #MeToo. Fueled by anger and hope, these movements gave voice to a widely shared passion for radical change—not just change in the personnel holding high positions, but change in the fundamental structures of power and privilege.

These movements have raised important questions that challenge the inevitability of those structures. Why is it that the Walton family alone, heirs to the Walmart fortune, has more wealth than 40% of American families combined, while the poorest quarter of the population have no net wealth at all?[1] Why is our government so unresponsive to people's need for affordable healthcare and quality public education? Why are the uncontrolled gyrations of financial markets allowed to throw millions out of their jobs and homes? Why are powerful corporate interests able to veto global efforts to address the looming climate crisis? Why do women have to endure discrimination, harassment, abuse, and violence at the hands of male bosses, clients, partners, and strangers? Why do poor and minority neighborhoods find themselves occupied by militarized police forces?

The emergence and urgency of such questions reflect a growing sense that we face multiple and deepening crises—in the economy, our workplaces, the political sphere, the natural environment, the social fabric of our communities, and our international relations.

We suffer from the growing irrationality of our economic system. This system generates obscene levels of inequality in wealth and income. It periodically stalls, throwing millions out of work. It produces much that we do not need and indeed much that poisons us and the planet. And on the other hand, so many products and services that we desperately do need are not profitable enough for business to produce and so we must go without.

We face a pervasive crisis of disempowerment in the workplace. People aspire to have a voice in the decisions that influence them, but as employees, we have little influence, if any, over the major decisions that affect our lives at work.

Our political system is unresponsive to the popular will. We have a system we call democracy, but it functions like a plutocracy—rule by the rich.

We are confronted with a mounting environmental crisis. Climate change is just one aspect of this crisis, but it is likely to disrupt profoundly civilization in the coming decades because we have failed to wean ourselves off fossil fuels.

We are suffering from a widening social crisis. In our gender and race relations; in our families, neighborhoods, cities, and regions; and in our systems of childcare, eldercare, justice, healthcare, housing, and education—our communities are constantly at war with business interests and with the government agencies supporting those interests.

And finally, our relations with other countries are rivalrous and domineering, when humanity so desperately needs international collaboration in resolving challenges such as climate change, war and the risk of nuclear conflagration, famine, and poverty.

The good news is: it doesn't have to be this way. The world has the resources and technological capabilities we need to offer everyone material comfort, human dignity, and opportunities for growth. But the social system that governs how this wealth is created and distributed leaves us insecure, fearful, and frustrated. We have a system that works for the one percent; but we could have one that works for the 99 percent.

Progressives in the United States—the "we" that I often refer to in this book—have engaged a debate on the origins of these crises and how best to address them. Some emphasize the need for more socially responsible leadership by the business sector. Some emphasize the role of government, advocating stronger social and environmental regulations, expanded welfare provisions, and limits on political campaign contributions. Some blame adversarial relations between business, government, and labor, and advocate Nordic-style social democracy. I argue that the origins lie deeper than these reforms can reach. These crises are endemic to capitalism itself, and as a result, while such reforms are surely worth pursuing, they cannot resolve our crises. If the root cause of these crises is capitalism, the solution is a more radical, democratic-socialist transformation.

Capitalism is a system of production for profit, not for people or for the planet. Yes, over the past decades and centuries capitalism has stimulated remarkable scientific and technological advances and has led to real improvements in the material conditions of many. But these improvements are only intermittent. They are shared very unequally. And they come with escalating social and environmental costs. Government is dependent on the profitability of the business sector for its legitimacy and resources and therefore cannot adequately address those costs. That's why we face a world in crisis.

If we are to overcome these crises and create an economy for the 99 percent, we need to change the way enterprises make decisions about investment, products, and work. These decisions need to be guided by the needs of people and the planet—not just by profitability considerations. They need to be made democratically, informed by deliberation and debate not only at the enterprise level, but also at the regional, industrial, and national levels—not made by CEOs and boards of directors doing the bidding of private investors. To make this happen, we need to replace private ownership of enterprise with socialized, public ownership. And this will enable us to shift from business-dominated government to a truly democratic political system. More modest reforms are worthwhile, but they are simply too limited to resolve the crises we now confront.

The goal of this book is to show why this socialist transformation is necessary and how such a society would work. This is not a blueprint for 21st-century socialism, let alone a step-by-step plan for getting there. Large-scale societal change doesn't work that way: it is by nature a zig-zagging, experimental process. But our efforts as progressives need to be guided—as is every human project—by a vision, a mental model, of the society we want to create. I argue that democratic socialism provides the most reliable guiding vision if we are to overcome the crises we face.

In making this case, this book focuses on the United States. The same general argument, however, applies in other countries. And the probability of success in overcoming these crises will be much greater if we engage this socialist transformation together.

There are many hurdles facing us if we want to move from capitalism to democratic socialism, and this book aims to help us overcome one of the most important—our lack of confidence that such a system could work.

To replace corporate hierarchy with democratic management within enterprises, and to replace market competition with democratic management of the entire economy, we will need to restore people's confidence in democracy—in our ability to make decisions together that benefit us collectively, that benefit the public good. But democracy has lost its luster.

The failure of successive administrations, both Republican and Democratic, to serve the interests of working people has created widespread cynicism about the very idea of democracy. Indeed, the support among working people for Donald Trump in the 2016 presidential elections showed the depth of the frustration they felt with the "elites" and with the empty democracy that these elites dominate. Hilary Clinton's campaign promises of stronger regulations and safety-net provisions rang hollow, and her support for foreign wars repelled many. In their frustration, working people turned to the candidate who seemed at least to recognize their predicament. If he sounded like an authoritarian populist, why would that deter them, when our country's vaunted democracy had failed them so abjectly?

But this cynicism is the most powerful weapon of the elites that rule today. This book aims to overcome that cynicism by sketching a world in which democracy—expanded and enriched—works for, rather than against, the public good.

I teach in a business school, and, yes, it is unusual to find a business-school professor advocating socialism. However, my research has given me the opportunity to study the management of some of our most sophisticated business enterprises, and this research has led me to two conclusions that both point toward democratic socialism.

First, while capitalist industry has been remarkably successful in many respects, it is impossible for the private-enterprise business sector to solve the big crises we face. In any society whose economy is based on competing, profit-seeking, capitalist firms, there are severe limits to what can be achieved by appeals for greater social and environmental responsibility on the part of business leaders, customers, or investors. Moreover, in any such society, national prosperity hinges on the profitability of the business sector, and as a result, there are also severe limits to the scope of government regulations, welfare programs, and international cooperation. To overcome the crises we face and to realize the better world that is within our reach, we need to find our way past those limits. We need a socialist transformation that allows us to decide democratically on our economic, workplace, political, environmental, social, and international goals, and to manage strategically our resources to pursue those goals.

Putting these two ideas together—*decide democratically* and *manage strategically*—may strike some people as incongruous. We are so accustomed to seeing management, strategic or not, as something done *to* us by people called managers—people over whom we have little influence and whose objectives are often quite antithetical to ours.

But management is far too important to be left to managers. To overcome the crisis of workplace disempowerment, we need to democratize the management of our enterprises. We need to put these enterprises under the control of boards representing workers, customers, and the broader community, and to replace top-down autocratic control with all-round participative management. Moreover, to overcome the other crises we face, we need to manage democratically not only each individual enterprise but also our society's overall economic activity. We can no longer afford to leave the direction of the economy to the roller-coaster market process, nor to rely on undemocratic agencies such as the Federal Reserve to moderate that process. We need to manage our economy to target our shared goals of well-being for people and sustainability for the planet.

The idea of such economy-wide strategic management for the public good—the idea that we could set goals, plan, organize, direct, coordinate, and evaluate and compensate performance for entire regions and industries, indeed for the economy as a whole—has been largely absent from recent discussions of alternatives to capitalism. Indeed, the idea of socialism rings alarm bells for many people because they do not see how such economy-wide strategic management (aka "government economic planning") could be democratic or effective, let alone both.

Socialism in the 21st century must be democratic. That's not only because the principle of equality is dear to us, but also because progress requires democracy. Authoritarian socialist planning may have been effective in forcing feudalistic Russia and China rapidly into the industrial age, but it came at a terrible cost. And today, in our postindustrial era, we can tackle the crises we face and assure the progress we need only if we mobilize widespread, creative problem-solving at every level in both our enterprises and our government. Democracy is an essential precondition for that active engagement.

But how can we ensure that our management of the economy is not only democratic but also effective? That is where the second conclusion from my research fits in. I have found that management innovations in some of our largest corporations show us how this combination can be assured. To coordinate their internal operations, many of these firms rely on strategic management, not on market competition between their subunits. And in some of these firms—in particular, the "high road" firms, those that try to create competitive advantage by engaging the creativity of their employees—strategic management is not a rigid, top-down process where top managers dictate a plan that tells everyone else what to do. It is rather an ongoing, highly participative dialogue about shared goals. Moreover, some of these high-road firms are truly massive—bigger than many smaller nations, employing sometimes millions of people in operations spanning the globe. If these high-road firms can manage so effectively and so participatively on such a massive scale, then we should be able to use similar strategic management practices to bring under democratic control the economic activity of enterprises, regions, industries, and the entire nation.

Employee participation in the strategic management of these high-road capitalist firms is, of course, limited and far from our democratic ideals. Participation by the wider community is even more limited. Even in these high-road firms, CEOs are still accountable primarily to investors, and employees are still essentially help for hire. In a socialist society, we would institutionalize much wider and deeper participation within enterprises, and we would use these democratic strategic management principles to guide our efforts to manage the economy at the wider levels. A radical socialist transformation is therefore not entirely a leap into the unknown. Capitalist industry is laying both technological and managerial foundations for democratic socialism.

To be sure, even with such foundations, the idea of democratic socialism has an inescapably utopian quality. Obviously, this transformation is not possible in the next election cycle, for example. But that should not deter us. Part of our challenge is to have the courage to believe that a better world is possible. As has often been said recently, it has become easier to imagine the end of the world than the end of capitalism.[2]

But capitalism is just the latest in the historical sequence of forms of society, and it is hard to believe that a system as flawed as capitalism represents the highest possible form of human civilization. The sketch of democratic socialism that I offer is thus a utopia—in Oscar Wilde's positive sense:

> A map of the world that does not include Utopia is not worth even glancing at, for it leaves out the one country at which Humanity is always landing. And when Humanity lands there, it looks out, and, seeing a better country, sets sail. Progress is the realisation of Utopias.[3]

The socialist utopia is an idea on which many have "landed" and toward which many have "set sail" over the past two centuries—ever since capitalism emerged as the basic structure of modern society and since its limitations became obvious. Over that period, each generation with a passion for social and economic justice has articulated its own vision of this utopia and its own strategies for how we might achieve it.

Looking back on the experiences of these earlier generations, I am struck by the fact that when the radical transformations they worked for did not happen in their own time or turned out to be disappointing, many activists gave up on the socialist vision, and quite a few even turned against it. I want to arm us against such despair. My message is at once urgent, hopeful, and optimistic.

Urgent: while the development of capitalism has brought many benefits, it also engenders crises, and these crises deepen and multiply over time. Given the suffering already created by this increasingly obsolete capitalist system, and given the very high likelihood that this suffering will be magnified in coming years—most notably, by climate change—socialist transformation is urgent.

Hopeful: even when prospects for radical change look slim, capitalism's failures fuel deepening and widening frustration, and this means that opportunities for a radical rupture might open at any moment, surprising us all. While there is a real danger that reactionary demagogues might capture these frustrations—the election of Donald Trump to the presidency in 2016 parallels similar events in several European countries—progressive activists can mobilize such frustrations to work toward a better world.

And optimistic: yes, we confront huge challenges, but we have means with which to meet them. Yes, this will require a fundamental change in our form of society, but we already have foundations on which this new form can be built. Yes, it is frustrating that this change has not happened yet, but over the longer term, capitalism's own development makes socialism progressively more feasible and more likely.

CHAPTER 1

Six Crises

The prevailing political-economic system—I call it neoliberal capitalism, but we could also call it financialized capitalism—is failing us.[1] In this system, most businesses compete to maximize profits while ignoring the social and environmental consequences of their activity. They employ people who accept management direction in exchange for a wage or salary, squeezing them ruthlessly, hiring and dismissing them at will as business conditions dictate—or they outsource responsibility for this to other firms. Government buttresses business interests through its statutes and legal system. It imposes the lightest possible taxation on the wealthy and minimal regulation on business. It facilitates the global mobility of capital while restricting the mobility of labor. It offers the bare minimum of collective services. And it outsources those services to the private sector as far as possible.

We have experienced nearly 40 years of this neoliberal system, since efforts to roll back progressive government regulation and welfare were inaugurated by Ronald Reagan in the United States and Margaret Thatcher in the United Kingdom. Before we diagnose the source of this system's failures or propose solutions, we should rapidly survey the damage.

ECONOMIC IRRATIONALITY

Let us not be distracted by the huge volume of books and articles on our irrationality as individuals: the irrationality of the economic system we will live under is far more consequential and far more dangerous. We have obscene levels of income and wealth inequality, far above anything plausibly related to productive contribution. Our economy is productive enough to provide amply for everyone; yet economic growth stalls periodically—at least once a decade—and when it does, millions of Americans are thrown out of work.[2] Our economy produces an extraordinary amount of goods and services we do not need and too little of what we do. Let's expand on each of those points in turn.

Inequality has come back into focus in recent years, partly because the trends have been so dramatic and partly because the Occupy movement was so successful in catalyzing discussion about it. Few deny that people who work harder or make bigger contributions to our well-being deserve some recognition and reward. But there is something profoundly offensive about the fact that eight people, six of them in the United States, now own as much in assets as the entire bottom 50% of the world's population.[3] In the United States, in 2010, the richest 1% held 48% of all stocks and mutual funds, 64% of all financial securities, and 61% of all business equity.[4]

At the other end of the spectrum, we find pervasive economic insecurity. In 2017, four out of 10 Americans could not cover an emergency expense of $400 without borrowing money or selling some of their possessions. Over one-fifth of American adults were unable to pay their current month's bills in full. Over one-fourth of all adults skipped necessary medical care because they were unable to afford the cost.[5] Over 12% of US households (some 41 million people, disproportionately African American and Hispanic) were "food insecure" at some time during 2016, uncertain of having enough food to meet their needs, or unable to get it.[6]

The risk of job loss haunts many working people, and that risk depends largely on forces outside our control—that is, on the roller coaster of the broader economy. When the economy slows down, people lose jobs, and we have had such slowdowns in at least one year in almost every decade since the government began keeping records in the mid-19th century. Work is not the only thing nor the most important thing in life, of course; but in a capitalist system, working is the main way people earn what they need to live. Which makes it so troubling that the proportion of people in the US labor force who were officially counted as unemployed reached close to 10% or exceeded it in the 1870s, 1890s, 1930s, early 1980s, and in the wake of the 2008 crisis.

Moreover, that official measure seriously understates the extent of unemployment. The undercount results from two factors. First, the official, "headline" unemployment figure ignores many people who should be counted. It does not count people who are forced to work part-time when they need full-time jobs, nor people who tell the government surveyors that they have given up looking for work because they were discouraged by the dearth of decent jobs. In mid-2018, for example, the official unemployment rate was unusually low, at 3.9%; but when you add in those two groups, the rate was 7.8%—nearly one in every 12 people.[7] Moreover, many people who struggle to find work eventually give up and no longer see themselves as part of the labor force. When we count all the working-age people who are not working, in school, or in prison, the true unemployment rate in 2018 was about 12%—nearly one in every eight people. We should also note that many people are forced into jobs that underutilize their capabilities. Estimates of the size of this group vary considerably, but in 2014, at least 25% of college-educated people were in jobs for which they were overqualified.[8]

Second, the unemployment rate measures only the proportion of people unemployed at a single point in time. In reality, about three times as many people experience unemployment at some time during any given year. With the recent growth in temporary "gig" work, that number is rising.[9] Moreover, the average duration of spells of unemployment has trended upward over the past half-century, reaching nearly 40 weeks in the wake of the 2008 crisis.

The suffering caused by such unemployment is deep. Even short periods of unemployment have long-term effects on people's earnings. And lengthy periods of unemployment—which have become so common in recent years—have huge negative consequences for people.[10] Unemployment is the single biggest cause of homelessness, and on any given night this year, over a half a million Americans are homeless, sleeping outside or in an emergency shelter or transitional housing program. (Notwithstanding the fact that at the same time, some 17 million homes are unoccupied.) Unemployment also increases the likelihood of cardiovascular disease, anxiety disorders, depression, and suicide. Unemployed people have poorer diet and fewer physician visits. They get less exercise, and they smoke, drink, and use drugs more, and their health is far worse.[11] Controlling for multiple other factors (including health conditions prior to losing employment), the risk of death is 63% higher for unemployed than for employed people, and this risk remains notably elevated for about a decade following a spell of unemployment.[12]

In economic down-cycles, it is not only people that end up underemployed but also productive resources like machinery, factories, and stores. Comparing the level of output that industrial buildings and equipment are physically able to produce—our economy's productive "capacity"—with what they in fact produce, the extent of capacity underutilization is appalling. The precise extent varies with the boom-and-bust cycles, but over the past 50 years, things appear to have progressively worsened.[13] In the best years since 2000, fully 20% of our economy's capacity was idle, and in the worst, an astounding 34%.[14] Yes, to respond to the environmental crisis, we will need to downscale material production; but that's not what's in play here. Yes, it makes sense to leave a little capacity "cushion"—otherwise, we would suffer a lot of shortages; but these rates are far higher than those needed for a cushion. Moreover, when they are left unused for more than a brief period, buildings are usually torn down and equipment is usually sent to the recycler or dump, if only to make sure that new investment does not have to compete with it. Consider all the effort invested in building that capacity. And consider the missed opportunity for meeting people's needs if this capacity had been put to good use. What waste!

The crisis of economic irrationality has a third, less visible face: our economy produces escalating amounts of goods and services we do not need. Products are designed to be thrown away rather than repaired, reused, or recycled. The result is an ever-growing quantity of waste, much of it destined for the landfill. Some 20 to 50 million metric tons of e-waste—much of it toxic—is generated worldwide every year, and the amount is growing rapidly. We generate over 1,500 pounds of municipal waste per person each year. And upstream, industry generates about the same amount too.[15] What an enormous amount of human effort and ingenuity, not to speak of natural resources, that is literally thrown in the trash!

Waste takes less visible forms too, with so much energy and creativity invested in economic activities that add nothing to our real well-being but afford industry nice profits. Junk food and cigarettes are Exhibit 1 for the argument that our individual irrationality is often induced by the irrationality of the system. Much of this waste is altogether outside our individual control. We pay private insurance companies for health insurance, when we know that if government were the single payer the country could save hundreds of billions of dollars each year.[16] And consider the waste created by companies rushing to offer me-too products, such as the many dozens of brands of breakfast cereals or toothpaste on the shelves of our supermarkets.[17]

A final facet of our crisis of economic irrationality is even less visible: we lack many necessities. Auto companies aggressively market their big SUVs as status symbols, even though most of us would be better off with more public transportation options and with smaller cars that have better mileage. Cures are developed for the ailments of rich and where profits promise to be high (such as cancer and heart disease), while the ailments of the poor (such as malaria and tuberculosis) are ignored.[18]

Numerous journalistic investigations have revealed how many people hate how they are treated in their jobs even if they enjoy the work itself.[19] Most of us have no real say or "voice" at work. Despite all the talk about modern management's embrace of employee involvement, only 45% of employees feel their employers listen to their ideas or concerns, and only 31% feel their employers "show concern for employees not just for the financial bottom line."[20]

Avenues for collective voice are even narrower. Only some 11% of employees today have any union representation—less than 7% in the private sector, and about 35% in the public sector—even though some 50% of nonmanagerial employees who are currently without any union representation say they want union representation.[21] In the absence of a union, some firms have management-run forums where employee representatives meet with management and talk about wages and benefits. But these forums are available for only about 34% of employees not already represented by a union, and it is hard to see employees speaking with much frankness in these forums if they lack union protection.[22] When it comes to the bigger decisions in the business, employees might have some influence in very small firms, but most people work in large firms, and very few such firms afford employees any significant influence. Among large firms in the United States, there are fewer than a dozen that have institutionalized employee participation in strategy setting, and many efforts at such "labor-management cooperation" do not last.[23]

It is hardly surprising then that people feel disengaged at work. The Gallup organization polls many employees on behalf of their employers, asking about engagement in terms of whether at work they feel they can do what they do best, their opinions count, they are committed to quality, they have opportunities to develop their skills, and so forth. The results show that the levels of employee engagement in US industry are on average startlingly low. In a 2016 survey, only one-third (33%) of US employees were "engaged" in this sense. Half of all employees (51%) were "not engaged." Another 16% were "actively disengaged." Other polls show that for fully 55% of private-sector employees, their job is "just what they do for a living," rather than something that gives them any sense of purpose or identity.[24]

If the term "crisis" seems exaggerated here, I think that is because we have grown habituated to this powerlessness. But the human cost of disempowerment is obvious. And its economic and social cost is massive. Gallup finds huge differences between the results of those business units that score in the top quartile of engagement as compared to those in the bottom quartile. Organizations in the top quartile have 70% fewer safety incidents, 40% fewer product defects, 17% higher productivity, and 21% higher profitability.[25]

UNRESPONSIVE GOVERNMENT

Disempowerment in the workplace is paralleled by disempowerment in the political sphere. Consider the big issues in politics in recent years: the dominance of business interests is all too obvious. Consider NAFTA—the North American Free Trade Agreement between the United States, Canada, and Mexico: it was opposed by a majority of Americans, but proceeded nevertheless.[26] Public opinion has long favored government action to ensure universal healthcare insurance (most supporters prefer a single-payer model, and some prefer a mixed public/private model), but instead, we got Obamacare—a very modest half-step forward.[27] Consider the repeated failure to raise the minimum wage sufficiently: public opinion has long supported a substantial increase, but business interests have prevailed here too over the preferences of the average American.[28] Or consider something that has never even made it to a vote—the Employee Free Choice Act, which would assure union recognition as soon as a majority of employees sign cards endorsing it. Measures like this that facilitate union recognition have been supported in public opinion polls for years, with absolutely no movement in Congress.[29] The political system is rigged in favor of big business, and that influence extends deep into the Democratic and Republican parties alike.

Indeed, our government is remarkably unresponsive to public opinion. In polling, Americans say they want more rather than less government intervention when it comes to energy (77%), environment (75%), healthcare (72%), and the economy and job growth (68%). A majority support more rather than less government action on initiatives such as providing a decent standard of living for the elderly (73%), ensuring food and drug safety (73%), ensuring access to affordable healthcare (73%), reducing poverty (69%), and ensuring clean air and water (67%). By a margin of 69% to 31% people say we need government to handle complex economic problems rather than relying solely on the market.[30] While it's true that such polls are hardly straightforward reflections of robust commitments, when we combine such data with the other evidence the conclusion seems inescapable: our preferences as citizens are systematically ignored by our legislators.

Given government's unresponsiveness, it is hardly surprising that so many people are so cynical about and so disengaged from politics.[31] In 2015, only 19% of Americans said they can trust the government always or most of the time. Only 20% described government programs as well run. Some 55% say "ordinary Americans" would do a better job of solving national problems than elected officials.[32] The Bernie Sanders campaign of 2016 showed that this cynicism does not necessarily lead to disengagement, but we are fighting an uphill battle. A 2014 study found that just 35% of adults in America regularly voted in elections, and just 22% of people under 30.[33] Only 8% had volunteered for any political campaign in the past two years.[34]

ENVIRONMENTAL UNSUSTAINABILITY

We are creating ever more stress on the planet's ecosystems through climate change, species extinction, and overexploitation of land and sea resources. By 1970, humanity had already exceeded the carrying capacity of the planet—our population was using more than the available natural resources could sustain. Today, humanity is using the planet's natural resources nearly 60% faster than they can be replenished. And here in the United States, we are consuming these resources seven times faster than the sustainable rate.[35] In the aggregate, humanity has, as a result, already crossed a number of "planetary ecological boundaries"—visible not just in accelerating climate change and forest destruction but also in the loss of biodiversity and disrupted nitrogen and phosphorus cycles.[36] We are killing off other species at an extraordinary rate. Between 1970 and 2012 alone, the populations of terrestrial species tracked by scientists fell about 38%. Marine populations fell by 36%. Freshwater animal populations fell by 81%. We are on the edge of a sixth mass extinction—this one caused by people, not by natural geological forces.[37]

Fearful of paralyzing potential supporters with anxiety, environmental activists often tone down their messages about collapsing ecosystems, disappearing ice, failing coral reefs, continued growth in greenhouse gas emissions, and so forth. But to talk straightforwardly: we are already over the precipice.[38] Climate change is already costing 400,000 lives a year globally—directly due to extreme weather, indirectly through the greater incidence of disease, and through civil wars and social strife created by crop failure and water scarcity.[39] Air pollution is already causing 5.5 million premature deaths annually.[40] And the road ahead looks much darker still. By 2100, unless carbon emissions are aggressively reduced, sea-level rises will likely displace one billion people worldwide, and between 13 and 20 million in the United States alone.[41]

To bring all this down to the city level, consider New York, for example. Higher sea levels will mean more floods like the inundation brought by Hurricane Sandy in 2012. That single storm caused nearly $20 billion in damage. It killed 43 people and injured many more. It shut down the city's airports, trains, subways, and highways. It incapacitated hospitals and wastewater treatment plants. It flooded electrical facilities and crippled cellphone systems. Sandy-scale floods used to happen about every 400 years; but with global warming, by the end of this century, they are likely to happen about every 23 years. The New York flood zone is expected to double in size, covering 99 square miles of the city.[42]

To be clear: to address this climate change threat requires much more than a shift to renewable energy. That would be a huge task in itself, but primary energy production accounts for less than a quarter of our CO_2 emissions. Most of our emissions come from transportation, agriculture, steel, cement, and chemicals. Vast swaths of our industrial system must be replaced.

SOCIAL DISINTEGRATION

We are experiencing a progressively widening set of interacting social crises in our gender and race relations, in our families, neighborhoods, cities, and regions, and in our systems of criminal justice, healthcare, childcare, eldercare, housing, and education.

Consider the #MeToo movement's revelation of pervasive abuse of women by men. In 2017, some 54% of American women reported receiving "unwanted and inappropriate" sexual advances.[43] This reflects the persistence of a deep power asymmetry between men and women in economic, social, and sexual relations. Harassment and abuse of women are commonplace in the workplace, where men are often in power positions as bosses, and where they use their power to abuse women, to cover up their crimes, and to force women to accept nondisclosure agreements that prevent them from alerting others to the danger. Child abuse and violence against LGBTQ people are also rampant.[44]

Consider the challenge women face in balancing work and nonwork. Pushed by the economic difficulties created by the stagnation in the earnings among nonsupervisory employees, and pulled by the social changes wrought by the women's movement, women (unmarried, married, with and without children) represent a growing proportion of the wage-earning labor force. But they still carry most of the burden of child rearing and housework. Many work part-time to deal with the resulting tensions.[45] But that makes it much more difficult to earn an adequate income, let alone build a career and assure some reasonable salary advancement. And part-time work itself has become more arduous, as businesses have demanded more flexibility in hours and greater availability outside working hours. So, for most working people—and for working women in particular—working hours are too long relative to home demands, and too short relative to their economic needs.[46]

Not surprisingly, stress has reached a pandemic level. The American Psychological Association surveys adults, asking them to rate their stress level on a 10-point scale, where 1 is "little or no stress" and 10 is "a great deal of stress." Respondents typically reported an average stress level of 5.1 as compared to the 3.8 level that they believe would represent a healthy state. Some 24% of adults reported extreme stress—a rating of 8, 9, or 10 on the 10-point scale. Women reported even higher stress levels than men—on average, 5.3 for women versus 4.9 for men in 2016. For both men and women, money and work were the biggest sources of stress. And many people reported mental health–related symptoms because of stress in the past month, such as feeling nervous or anxious (42%), feeling depressed or sad (37%), and constant worrying (33%).[47]

Consider our society's race relations. While real progress has been made since the days of Jim Crow, many white Americans are still very much attached to their privilege. And that attachment comes out in particularly ugly forms when economic growth stalls and, as a result, people fear that the advance of other groups jeopardizes their own economic chances.[48] Discrimination in the job and housing market is still rampant.[49] Poverty rates are far higher in minority communities, as are incarceration rates. While most white Americans express confidence that racial discrimination is a thing of the past, most African Americans feel its bite every day.[50] According to the FBI, of all the hate crimes in the United States between 2008 and 2012, fully one-third were directed against African Americans.

Consider our neighborhoods and regions. People are increasingly likely to live in economically and socially homogeneous neighborhoods. At the same time, people no longer know their neighbors: they have never even learned their names.[51] Minority-dominated neighborhoods are underfunded, with poorly maintained infrastructure, high crime rates, militarized policing, food deserts, and overcrowded housing. As a nation, we confront growing disparities of life conditions across regions. Rural areas and small towns are left in economic distress and young people desert them for the cities.[52]

Once-thriving cities like Detroit are allowed to slide into rubble when industries relocate.

Consider our criminal-justice system—widely acknowledged as a national disgrace. One out of 140 people are in prison in our country (as compared to 1 out of 531 in Canada), and another 1 out of 31 are on parole. With 4% of the world's population, we have 22% of the world's prisoners. And it is not that criminality is more frequent in the United States: we have about the same rate of victimization as many equally wealthy countries. Our system is just much more punitive. The average sentence for burglary is 16 months in the United States, compared to 5 months in Canada and 7 months in England. And much of this harshness is a result of racism. The racial inequities of our system beggar belief. For 20 years until 2010, distribution of 5 grams of cocaine in the form of crack (the cheaper form of cocaine, used disproportionately by poorer people and African Americans) carried a minimum 5-year federal prison sentence. But if the crime involved powder cocaine (the more expensive form, used disproportionately by richer people and whites) a 5-year sentence required 500 grams—100 times as much.[53] As a result of such inequities, we now find 4.7% of African Americans behind bars compared to 0.7% of whites. African Americans and Hispanics together account for about 30% of the population but 60% of the prison population. The vast majority of the people in prison are there for nonviolent crimes such as drug possession, or crimes against property, not against people. Once in prison, our fellow citizens encounter a world of violence and extortion, and opportunities for rehabilitation are rare. Not surprisingly, some 67% of prisoners released are rearrested within three years.

Consider our systems of care for the sick and the elderly. Men in suburban Maryland (wealthy, mainly white) live 17 years longer than men in directly adjacent Washington, DC (poorer, mainly minority). If they make it to the age of 35, men in Harlem live less long than men in Bangladesh.[54] These disparities reflect not only race but also education and income. Among both children (infant mortality, health status, activity limitation, healthy eating, sedentary adolescents) and adults (life expectancy, health status, activity limitation, heart disease, diabetes, obesity), poorer and less educated people are far less healthy, and those patterns hold both overall and within racial/ethnic groups.[55]

Consider housing. The for-profit housing market is failing us. Across the entire United States, there is not a single county that does not have a severe shortage of affordable housing. For every 100 extremely low-income households, there are only 29 rental units that are adequate, affordable, and available.[56] In the faster-growing cities, home ownership has become too expensive for most working people. The share of all renters forced to pay over 30% of their income on rent has doubled from 23% percent in the 1960s to 47% percent in 2016.[57] It is therefore heartbreaking but not surprising that on any given night in 2017, over 550,000 people were homeless in the United States. Of these, 21%, were children under 18 years old—114,000 children. And 35% of the total, some 192,000 people, were not in any shelter. Over the course of a year, somewhere between 2.3 million and 3.5 million Americans experience homelessness, and at least 7 million more have lost their own homes and are doubled up with others due to economic necessity.[58] And all this even though the number of vacant housing units is many times greater than the number of homeless people.

Consider too our education systems. Education is increasingly important to the economic future of both individuals and the country, and this leads to ever-higher demands on our schools and universities. Nevertheless, our primary and secondary schools are starved for resources, and our teachers are paid 35% less than their peers with comparable education working in other occupations. Not surprisingly, our 15-year-olds perform far worse on tests of their math, reading, and science ability than in many other countries that are poorer than us: in those fields, we rank 26th, 24th, and 25th, respectively.[59] Higher education is financially out of reach for many families. Those who take out loans to finance higher education find themselves deeply in debt, unable even to declare bankruptcy to avoid its crushing burden. Total student debt is now an astonishing $1.3 trillion, and as many of 40% of people with student debt are likely to default on that debt by 2023.[60]

INTERNATIONAL CONFLICT

Finally, we live in a world that cries out for international collaboration to address so many problems—climate change, wars, the risk of nuclear conflagration, the persistence of abject poverty, diminishing water resources, famines, migration, contagious diseases, to name just a few—but such collaboration is stymied by international rivalries.

And the United States is aggravating rather than helping. We are the most powerful nation and among the richest, but instead of helping heal the world, we are pursuing a nationalist, America-first policy. Our commitment to global cooperative efforts to combat climate change was only ever tepid—limited by worries that China might gain an economic advantage if we joined the Kyoto Protocol but they did not. And then President Trump announced his intention to pull the United States out of the 2015 Paris Agreement.

Even in the period when the United States was more actively engaged in multilateral efforts, our willingness to assert our "national interests" by violence has been monstrous. The record of our foreign military interventions since World War II is shameful, so many of them being in support of repressive regimes that happened to be useful allies.[61] In that period, we have helped overthrow at least 36 governments, interfered in at least 84 foreign elections, attempted to assassinate over 50 foreign leaders, and dropped bombs on people in over 30 countries. Some of this record can be attributed to Cold War conflict, but the trajectory since then is not much better. We still provide aid to three-quarters of the world's dictatorships.[62] We still maintain a network of over 800 military bases in over 70 countries.[63] Our nuclear arsenal remains on "hair-trigger" alert aimed at cities in Russia and China, risking nuclear catastrophe that would be just as devastating as the coming climate catastrophe.[64]

As concerns civilian assistance, our commitment to transcending national self-interest is just as shameful. During the 2010–2015 period, for example, we were the country with the biggest annual contribution to overseas nonmilitary development (roughly $30 billion a year), but as a share of our national income, we contribute less than 0.2%—that's not 2 cents in every dollar, but 2 cents in every 100 dollars—which is one-fifth the level of Sweden.[65] And over this same period, we were by far the biggest source of international arms sales, with Saudi Arabia as our biggest client—notwithstanding successive presidents' inspiring speeches about our commitment to human rights.

The good news—and at the same time, the saddest part of this story— is that so much of this suffering, alienation, and frustration is unnecessary. Our world has all the resources and technology we need. Yes, perhaps our species' capacity for greed and stupidity make some level of human suffering inevitable. But not this level, and not this systematically. If we suffer economic waste, frustrated desires for engagement at work, political dysfunction, natural resource devastation, and social and international conflict, these are not the results of our genetic inheritance. They reflect something terribly wrong with the way our society works.

CHAPTER 2
The Root Cause

If we are to overcome these crises, we need an accurate diagnosis of their root causes. Incompetence, greed, and short-sightedness are surely important contributing factors. But these factors are encouraged, and their impact is multiplied, by structural features of our current political-economic system.

Notwithstanding the considerable variety of forms in which capitalism appears—ranging from the currently prevailing neoliberalism to social democracies with stronger regulations and expanded welfare programs—these forms all share some basic features, and these features help to explain the six crises and why they appear so intractable.

To summarize the analysis presented in more detail in what follows: at root, the crisis of economic irrationality is the result of the fact that capitalism is based on a distinctive system of property—privately owned enterprises that compete for profits. Our workplace disempowerment reflects the fact that in a capitalist system, these enterprises employ people in exchange for wages. Government's unresponsiveness is a result of the fact that in any capitalist society, the political system—government—stands apart from the economy, and yet depends for its resources and its legitimacy on the profitability of the private-sector core of the economy. The environmental crisis is due primarily to the fact that in any capitalist system, firms must focus on their own profitable growth, and they therefore often behave irresponsibly toward the natural environment on which they and we all depend. The social crisis similarly stems in large part from the fact that firms' focus on profitability leads them to undertake actions that damage our communities. In a capitalist system, the maintenance of both the natural and the social environment of business becomes the responsibility of government—even though government is hamstrung in attending to this responsibility by the need to preserve private-sector business profitability. And the possibilities of international cooperation are similarly hobbled by rivalry because our government, like those of other capitalist nations, must support the interests of its own national businesses, which compete with those based in other nations.

This diagnosis is rather different from those offered by many progressive commentators today. Most highlight the contrast between the last 40 years of neoliberalism and the "glory years" of capitalism in the two or three decades following World War II. Back then, strong unions assured many employees regular pay raises, and many trends seemed pointed in the right direction: for example, the black/white pay gap shrank considerably between 1945 and 1970. Many progressives therefore trace the source of our ills today to the demise of the institutions that supported the gains of that period. But this diagnosis is too superficial. The six crises we face today have roots that go far deeper.

Other progressives highlight the failures of neoliberalism in comparison with the successes of countries where capitalism takes a more humane form, such as the Nordic social democracies. While there is much to admire in these countries, I will show later that there too the capitalist character of the economy blocks an effective response to those six crises.

In tracing these roots, we should also give credit where credit is due. Over the long term, and compared to the earlier systems that it replaced, capitalism has generated important benefits as well as costs for us. Our diagnosis of its failures will be more robust if we also keep in mind its benefits.

PRIVATE ENTERPRISE AND PRODUCTION FOR PROFIT

If our economic system behaves so irrationally, it is most fundamentally because it is a system based on private enterprise and production for profit.

In a capitalist economy, for the main part we do not produce for ourselves nor barter with others for what we need. Instead, we buy what we need from firms that produce it with the goal of selling it to make a profit. Of course, not all that we need comes from these firms. We also rely on the unpaid care that we offer each other in the home (most often, care that women provide men and children), on services provided by government, on natural resources such as air and water, and on various nonprofit organizations. But the bulk of the goods and services that we use as consumers and that enterprises rely on are produced by firms for profit.[1]

As private enterprises, capitalist firms make their own production and investment decisions. The overriding goal in making these decisions is profit. Moreover, that goal is made continually salient to corporate executives by competitive pressure to grow faster and more profitably than their peers. This pressure is not due fundamentally to the owners' greed: firms must grow or risk failure.[2] If a firm does not grow as fast and as profitably as its competitors, it risks being forced out of business. If it has outside investors, these investors might demand the replacement of the current managers. Or investors might move their funds to competitors, who can then purchase more advanced technology, increase their sales more rapidly, and crush the smaller and slower-growing firms.

Private enterprise and production for profit have been instruments of considerable progress. Historically, this system's growth imperative has pushed business into isolated communities, drawing them into commercial interaction, and in this way opened those communities to ideas and technologies from across the world. It has stimulated innovation, as firms rush to identify and create new needs and to develop better ways of satisfying existing needs. In doing so, capitalism has generated important improvements in the material standard of living of huge numbers of people in many countries. We are justified in our anger that the birth and expansion of this system have often been accompanied by terrible violence against both people and nature, that the system's benefits have been shared so unequally, and that there have been periods in which this progress has been temporarily reversed and other periods in which progress has only been achieved by dint of popular struggles.[3] But there is no denying that over the longer term and in broad aggregate, the overall material circumstances of most people's lives have been improved dramatically by capitalism's development. That can be seen in the starkest form if we look at mortality data: average life expectancy in the United States has increased from 40 years in 1880 to 79 years today. The global average has gone from 30 to 71 years over that same period.[4]

This private enterprise system's growth imperative, however, also has important costs—costs that together sum to a crisis of economic irrationality.

First, competition leads paradoxically to its opposite—concentration. Under the pressure of competition, the big fish eat the little fish, and the benefits of vigorous market competition are often overshadowed by the costs of monopoly. Where once almost all firms and farms were individual and family proprietorships, our economy is now dominated by big corporations relying on outside investors.

Indeed, notwithstanding the continued celebration of small business in American culture, big business has largely displaced small business across the board—in farming, manufacturing, and services. By 2012, the four largest firms captured over 25% of the market in nearly half of all industries in the United States. Indeed, in 14% of all industries, the four largest publicly traded firms claimed more than 50% of the market. Taken together, the four largest firms in each industry employed 30% of the US workforce and generated 40% of the economy's revenues.[5] Overall, while the US economy has a huge number of firms—some 5.5 million corporations, 2 million partnerships, 17 million nonfarm sole proprietorships, and 1.8 million farm sole proprietorships—most of these are very small. In 2015, firms with over 500 employees—which accounted for less than 0.5% of the total number of private-sector enterprises—accounted for over 52% of the entire private-sector workforce, and that proportion has been rising.[6] Most *firms* may be small, but most *people* work in large ones.

Competition leads to concentration through two intertwined mechanisms—technical efficiency and monopoly power. Consider first technical efficiency. Larger firms have often grown larger because they were more efficient, and larger size enables them to become even more efficient.[7] They enjoy economies of "scale" (they can share equipment and facilities as well as overhead administrative functions across a larger volume of output of any given product) and economies of "scope" (they can share these resources across a greater variety of products). Indeed, concentration is one way that capitalist development has augmented our society's material wealth.

However, in a capitalist economy, we don't get these benefits without suffering the corresponding costs, in the form of monopoly. Consider the example of Amazon. Amazon sells over 500 million different products in the United States alone, and 2 trillion worldwide. This single company now employs nearly 566,000 people and represents over 40% of all Internet retail sales in the United States, even as Internet sales themselves account for a rapidly growing share of all retail sales. Half of all online shopping searches start on Amazon. In 2016, its revenue from online sales in the United States totaled $63 billion, which is more than the sales of the 10 next biggest online retailers combined. Amazon represents 74% of all e-book sales. It is the largest online clothes retail outlet and will soon be the biggest apparel retailer in the country. And then there's all the rest that Amazon does: publishing the *Washington Post*, operating the largest cloud-computing platform, producing and distributing movies and television series, selling and delivering food. On the one hand, this enormous size and scope allows Amazon to rationalize, automate, and dramatically lower distribution costs. On the other hand, it also allows the company to use its monopoly power to drive down the prices of the retailers that sell through Amazon and to chase out competitors. It regularly wages price wars against innovative competitors, as it did with Quidsi, the parent company of Diapers.com—lowering prices so far that Quidsi was forced to sell out to Amazon, at which point, Amazon used its monopoly position to raise prices again.[8]

Monopoly has long been the object of popular anger in the United States. A century ago, the anger was directed at oil, steel, railroads, tobacco, and retail chain stores. Today, it is directed more often at technology, pharmaceuticals, cable service, health insurance, and airlines. But even if the targets change, the underlying concerns persist. Monopoly gives firms the power to dictate exorbitantly high prices. It gives them the power to drive competitors out of business or deter potential competitors from entering their markets by setting artificially low prices and then raising them again after the threat has been defeated. It allows firms to buy up potential competitors so as to stifle the emergence of new technologies that might render obsolete their existing business and replace it with one that is cheaper and better for consumers but might at the same time reduce profits. It allows firms to get away with offering poor-quality products and services. It allows firms to dictate low wages and bad working conditions even in a tight labor market. It gives firms inordinate influence over politicians in shaping legislation and over regulators in enforcing that legislation. As a result of this "capture," antitrust, environmental, and health and safety legislation are weak and weakly enforced.[9]

Moreover, the growing prevalence of monopoly power in the US economy is a major contributor to our growing economic inequality. Firms with monopoly power are far more profitable than the average firm, and the trend toward concentration has exacerbated that divergence. Whereas in the 1960s and 1970s the profitability of the average firm in a given industry was about half that of the firms in the 90th percentile of profitability, today it is only about one-fifth.[10] Since the ownership of share capital is also extraordinarily and increasingly concentrated—the wealthiest 1% now possess 38% of the nation's corporate stocks and the wealthiest 10% own 81%, while the bottom 80% own only 8%—this trend to monopoly in industry structure intensifies overall wealth inequality.

Looking beyond concentration, the growth imperative and the underlying basic private-enterprise structure of capitalism contribute to the crisis of economic irrationality in several other ways. In the capitalist private-property system, firms' decisions about what to produce and how to invest are driven primarily by "bottom-line" considerations, and that means their decisions are inevitably myopic in both time and space. Their decisions are myopic in time, focusing excessively on the short term, because under pressure from investors for returns, the firm is forced to severely discount longer-term benefits (such as from advanced R&D) and longer-term costs (such as those incurred when firms abuse their employees and lose their loyalty). Their decisions are myopic in space because they consider costs and benefits only for themselves and their trading partners: impacts on others outside that orbit—firms further removed from the trading parties, the local community, the natural ecosystem, etc.—are mere "externalities": that is, they are relevant only to the extent that they affect the costs experienced by one of the trading partners.[11] And the combination of the two forms of myopia is particularly damaging when our technologies are so powerful as to have effects on the natural world such as climate change. In these cases, the interests of future generations are simply ignored in the firm's strategic planning and in investors' decisions.[12]

The nearsightedness inherent in the private-enterprise system also makes our economy inherently unstable.[13] When economic investment and production decisions are made independently by competing firms, periods of growth and rising prosperity are inevitably followed by periods of recession and mass unemployment. Yes, fraud and mismanagement contribute to these crises—as we saw with the 2008 crash—but those factors are not the root cause of these crises, just aggravating factors. Let's clarify the connections.

Proponents of capitalism celebrate the ability of privately owned firms competing in their local markets—independently of each other and independently of government—to identify entrepreneurial opportunities. And they celebrate capitalism's reliance on market prices, which communicate superefficiently to firms how to adjust their plans to the actions of rival firms and to consumers' buying patterns. When prices rise, it is a signal to the firm that demand exceeds supply, so it is time to expand output. When prices fall, it is time to scale back output. This is the magic of what Adam Smith called the "invisible hand" of market coordination.[14]

But this invisible hand is a poor coordination mechanism in one key respect that is often overlooked by its admirers: the market process is not only decentralized, but also competitive. As a result, firms hide from each other at least one piece of critical information, namely, their production and purchasing plans. Each firm knows how its competitors have behaved in the past (that is, what products they offered, in what quantities, at what prices), but they do not know these competitors' plans for the future.

Given that each firm is under pressure to expand as fast as it can, and given that competitors hide their plans from each other, the firm's only rational choice is to bet on its own growth. But that same logic applies to all the competitors, and as a result, the capitalist market process typically leads to cycles of overproduction and crash.[15] These same pressures lead firms to expand faster than the available resources, in particular the labor supply, leading to cost pressures and a profit squeeze, to which firms respond by scaling back production, employment, and investment—which creates another pathway to recession.

The irrationality goes deeper, too. These recessions are not accidents that get in the way of economic growth: they are essential to the process of capitalist growth. Crises are a feature of capitalism, not a bug. Given that firms are driven to produce collectively more than the market can absorb, it is only by liquidating the excess products and productive capacity—and with them, millions of jobs—that opportunities for growth and investment can be renewed.[16] The reason is simple: firms invest when they see the possibility of a profitable return on their investment. Profitability, of course, is the ratio of net revenue to investment, so if you cannot increase the numerator (generate more net revenue), then all you can do is cut the denominator (write off the value of your investment). In practice, the only way large-scale liquidation happens is through economy-wide recessions . . . or war. It was the combination of these two that formed the foundation for the great boom after World War II. Indeed, without the war, the Depression would have continued even longer than it did. Absent such a massive wave of liquidation, a capitalist economy in serious recession is trapped in ever-lower profitability—and that is exactly what has been happening in many countries since the 1990s.

This instability in labor and product markets is compounded by instability in the financial markets. Periodic financial crashes lead to massive disruptions to industry, resulting in firms going bankrupt and employees losing their jobs, pensions, and savings. While the big investors in the United States and in those other countries generally regained the value of their investments after the 2008 financial crisis, many working people, especially older ones, suffered proportionately much larger and longer-lasting losses, which forced them to work into their older years or to live on considerably reduced incomes.[17] The rate of bankruptcy filings among Americans over 65 years of age has more than doubled since 1991, and among those over 75, it has more than tripled.[18]

If you read the business press, you might get the impression that this instability in financial markets was the result of the irrational "herd psychology" of investors or the incompetence of the Federal Reserve. More fundamentally, however, it is built into our capitalist system.[19] Here is how it works. A period of stability encourages investors to take more risk by borrowing money to make more speculative investments. The growth in investors' debt levels leads to cash-flow problems for these investors (because the cash generated by their investments is no longer enough to pay off the debt investors took on to acquire these investments). Seeing this growing problem, the people who lent to these investors get anxious and begin calling in their loans. This inevitably leads to a collapse of asset values. To repay their loans, the overindebted investors must sell assets— even assets that were less speculative. But by this point, it is hard to find buyers willing to pay the prices at which these assets were purchased. Now the market goes into a period of generalized panic, leading to a collapse in prices, a sharp drop in market liquidity, and a sharp increase in the demand for cash. When things stabilize again, the cycle restarts.

Alongside monopoly, inequality, insecurity, and crises, wastefulness is another hallmark of this private-enterprise system. Consider the finance sector, which sucked up about 15% of all corporate profits in the United States in the 1960s, 1970s, and 1980s, but now sucks up twice that share. There is no evidence that this growth was justified by improvements in our social well-being, or in greater profitability of the nonfinancial sector, or even in the enhanced effectiveness or stability of financial markets.[20] Or consider all the creative scientists working to find ways to make cigarettes and food more addictive.[21] Or the top-notch mathematicians working to develop algorithms so that Google and Facebook can help advertisers better target their ads. Or the talented psychologists working to determine what colors will make breakfast cereal advertising more effective to young kids watching TV.

Our system's wastefulness is exacerbated by the extension of capitalist property rights to the realm of ideas, in the form of "intellectual property rights" such as patents and copyright. The cost of assigning ownership rights to ideas rather than things is huge. In the United States, and looking at the pharmaceutical industry alone, we spend over $440 billion on drugs that would likely cost less than $80 billion without patent protections. The difference—going straight into the profits of the pharmaceutical companies—amounts to almost 2% of our national income.[22]

The counterargument—and the idea that motivates proponents of this strange institution of intellectual property—is that if inventors do not get the chance to profit from their ideas, they might not put as much effort into coming up with them. But this is a singularly weak counterargument. It overlooks the fact that the government funds much of the basic science that underlies corporate innovation and patenting. It overlooks all the creative efforts of inventors who are not motivated by profit, such as those working in academia.[23] It overlooks the way patents impede other innovation efforts: in the branches of industry that patent the most—pharmaceuticals, biotechnology, electronics—innovation and research have been slowed by the cost and practical difficulty of getting all the patent holders to agree on the use of their property.[24] And it overlooks the vitality of the rest of the economy, where innovation is not protected by patents but nevertheless thrives as a way to stay ahead of the competition. If patenting creates incentives for some firms to invest in innovation, that benefit is canceled out by the role of patenting in blocking access by other firms to fruitful new ideas. On balance, it turns out that patenting does nothing to accelerate the overall rate of innovation . . . but it does effectively siphon more wealth to the wealthy.[25]

WAGE EMPLOYMENT WITHIN FIRMS

If workplace disempowerment is so pervasive, it is at root because in a capitalist system most people work as employees in these privately owned firms.

In the earliest phase of capitalism in the United States, most people owned the resources (land, tools) necessary to produce what they consumed.[26] What they were not able to produce for themselves, they could get locally in exchange for what they produced and sold. The cobbler made shoes and sold them to buy food from the farmer. But this was destined to change, because, as we just saw, competition leads to concentration. Big farms and manufacturers used their efficiency, monopoly power, legal maneuvering, and sometimes violence to squeeze out their smaller rivals. As a result, the vast majority of people today cannot get most of what they need to live except by working for an employer. In exchange for a wage or salary, they accept the employer's authority to direct their work.[27] The proportion of truly independent producers in our labor force has long been falling, and it is now less than 10%.[28]

Work in such capitalist enterprises is not a joint effort to reach common goals, but primarily a means to an end. For investors, that end is profit. For employees, it is mainly income: work is the only way to earn the income they need to support themselves and their families. Many employees seek meaning in their work, but as we saw in the previous chapter, only a minority find it, and we all must work for someone whether or not we find much meaning in it. Whether employers squeeze employees ruthlessly (as in the neoliberal model) or treat them more kindly, employees are not partners in a cooperative undertaking where they decide democratically on production, pay, and investment.[29]

This capitalist employment relationship is an important factor in humanity's progress. As capitalist enterprises have grown in scale, their managers have developed impressively complex divisions of labor and systems for orchestrating the integration of these differentiated tasks. We are rightfully appalled by the narrow specialization and arbitrary management authority that many employees chafe under; but capitalist firms' ability to sustain productivity growth is undeniable, and often (although far from always) some of those productivity gains flow through to employees as higher wages.

Moreover, this employment relationship gives employees a freedom of movement that was not possible under feudalism, prior to capitalism's emergence. Whereas in feudal and slave systems peasants were tied to their land, often indentured to landowners, the capitalist employment relationship frees the employee to change their employer. This is progress, even if people are rarely able to work for themselves or able to participate in the big decisions that matter in their enterprises. In many countries where capitalism is less thoroughly diffused, large numbers of young people migrate to the cities to work in capitalist enterprises—even in poorly paid jobs in oppressive factories—in order to escape what they feel to be the constricted horizons of the precapitalist, traditionalistic social structures that dominate in their rural villages.[30] Capitalism's development encourages an ethos of individualism—a cultural shift away from forms of collectivism that engulf the individual in inherited tribal, village, or clan statuses and identities. The individualism of contemporary capitalist culture may be alienating; but it is a step forward compared to traditionalistic collectivism, allowing us more scope—admittedly, still too limited—to decide the course of our individual lives.

Notwithstanding these positive features, capitalist employment is fundamentally a relation of exploitation. Exploitation may seem like a harsh assessment, but it is not meant as a characterization of the attitudes of CEOs. Rather, it is a way of characterizing the structurally subordinate position of employees relative to employers. In any capitalist society, that society's productive resources are owned by a small minority, and those who are not part of this minority, lacking other ways of supporting themselves, must work as employees for an employer in this minority. Employees accept the direction of the employer in exchange for a wage, while the employer controls whatever profit is left after paying these employees their wages and after paying other business expenses such as interest on borrowed capital.

Under pressure to maximize enterprise profit, employers try to increase revenues and reduce costs. Sometimes profit can be increased by means that do not harm employees—for example, innovative products might be priced at a premium, and work might be reorganized to make it more efficient. But it remains management's prerogative to increase profits by means that are inimical to employees—laying off employees after replacing them with machines, pushing employees to work harder, limiting pay and benefits, stifling efforts to unionize, and seeking out sources of cheaper labor that can replace more expensive employees. Yes, firms need to pay employees enough and treat them well enough to attract and keep them. But most people have no way to support themselves except via an employment relation, and the employer therefore enjoys control over the profits created by the collective efforts of their employees.

Unions can mitigate this power imbalance to some extent, by bringing workers together rather than leaving them to compete against each other in the labor market, but their power is always limited. Over the past century, unions have helped push legislation that improved working conditions, and for several decades after World War II, unions helped ensure employees benefited from higher productivity with higher wages and benefits. Nevertheless, even when unions were at their strongest, the employer retained ultimate control over the disposition of the firm's profits, over investment decisions, and over products and work processes.

As individuals, some people have advanced professional skills and credentials that give them substantial bargaining power in this employment relationship, but such employees constitute a small minority. The great majority of us negotiate our pay and working conditions at a structural disadvantage, because we need the job more than the employer needs any one of us.[31]

Indeed, the capitalist market system is a marvelous mechanism for constantly undermining employees' bargaining power. First, this market system constantly renews the threat of unemployment that puts employees in competition with each other in the labor market and in a weak position relative to employers. This threat reflects an important asymmetry between the forces that lead firms to hire employees and the forces that lead firms to lay them off. The constant push for profits means that firms are always looking for ways to increase their productivity, and most firms, especially bigger ones, pursue deliberate programs of productivity improvement. However, unless the firm can increase its production output and sales revenue in corresponding proportion, the eventual result is layoffs. Of course, firms also pursue deliberate marketing and sales programs to drive up revenue. But their success in those marketing and sales efforts is far less predictable—revenue is decided by the chaotic process of market competition, not by the firm's executives. Combining a systematic, deliberate effort to increase productivity and a chaotic, competitive process that may or may not allow for increased revenue, the net effect is clear: capitalist industry is constantly throwing people out of work—sometimes faster, sometimes slower—so the threat of unemployment always lurks. Unemployment is not an unfortunate accidental outcome, but a permanent feature of capitalism.

Second, this asymmetry of bargaining power is aggravated by the capitalist business cycle. When business is booming, unemployment goes down, and the normal result is an increase in average wages and some reduction in employers' bargaining power. This cuts into private-enterprise profits, which in turn pushes some firms out of business and discourages business investment. As a result, employment falls, unemployment increases again, and employers regain their full bargaining power.[32]

The power asymmetry within the firm is the most basic reason for the inequality of wealth we see in capitalist societies. Where a few people own society's productive resources and everyone else must work for them in exchange for a wage, the few get wealthy by profiting from the efforts of the many. The people at the top of these huge corporations are among the top 1% of the distribution of wealth and income. And the increasing concentration of industry has contributed to the growth in inequality. But our attention to the recent increase in inequality should not obscure the more enduring, fundamental inequality—between owners and employees—that is one of the defining features of capitalism. Viewed in longer historical perspective, the current levels of inequality are similar to those experienced during the prior two centuries. In 1860, the richest 1% held 29% of total assets in the country. By 1929 that had climbed to 52%, and then it fell after World War II only to rise rapidly again, starting in the 1970s, back to about 42% today.[33] Even when inequality was at its lowest levels of the last century—in the 1970s—those levels were many times greater than whatever inequality might be justified as a way to encourage effort and initiative. Even then, the richest 1% controlled 23% of the entire country's wealth.[34]

In capitalist firms, disempowerment flows from this relation of exploitation. We are just employees—exchanging our capacity for work and submitting to management direction in exchange for a wage or salary. We are merely means to the enterprise's ends. Our own ends are irrelevant. The relationship between employer and employee is therefore fundamentally instrumental. Companies employ us only to make profits, and we work for them primarily to "pay the rent." Yes, in very small firms, owners are under some pressure to consider the concerns of their employees with whom they work every day. But most of us work for larger firms. Here, ownership is in the hands of nonworking investors, and daily decision-making power is concentrated at the top of a managerial hierarchy. Yes, even in these big firms, managers and employees need to cooperate in their daily work; otherwise nothing much gets done. But the major strategic decisions of the firm are beyond employees' reach. We have no voice in deciding whether factories and stores open or close, create jobs or destroy them. Nor do we have voice in deciding whether we produce socially useful products and services or ones that are harmful, nor whether we build oil-powered cars that poison the air or electric cars that pollute far less, nor whether our workplaces will be oppressive sweatshops or will offer jobs with dignity.

This disempowerment is not due fundamentally to managers' disrespect for employees: it is built into foundations of the capitalist system of private enterprise. In this system, the firm's most fundamental goal is profitability, regardless of top managers' preferences. If the firm has shareholders, it is they who elect the board of directors, and it is this board that selects the top executive, the CEO. This CEO is accountable to the board, and the board is in turn accountable to the shareholders. Neither the CEO nor the board is accountable to employees, customers, or other stakeholders. If too many shareholders feel their financial interests are not being well enough served by the board or the CEO, they can mobilize to replace either or both. Even if the firm is privately held rather than relying on public investors, it is forced to compete the same way, for fear of being driven out of business.

This diagnosis of our disempowerment may seem at odds with the common claim that we live in a "meritocratic" society. Yes, people sometimes rise to leadership roles in the United States because they are more competent, rather than because of inherited advantages. But even where that merit principle applies, it is of little comfort. In a capitalist society, meritocracy is about who gets to join the ruling elite, so it also means that those who do not make it to the top are left disempowered.

GOVERNMENT'S SUBSERVIENCE TO BUSINESS

In any capitalist society, whether government regulation is rigorous or light, whether government taxes and services are extensive or limited, the economic sphere is separated from that of politics. Living in a capitalist society, we have come to take this separation for granted, but we shouldn't, because it has important consequences. Most notably, it assures the subservience of government to business interests.[35]

Government is an essential precondition of capitalist enterprise and competition. It sets and polices the rules of market interaction. It assures some essential services that cannot be supplied profitably by private enterprise. And it assures national defense. But the bulk of economic activity happens outside the realm of direct government control.

This separation, or differentiation, of the economic sphere from the political has important benefits. It leaves a larger scope for individual autonomy. Much of our daily social interaction proceeds on a voluntary basis rather than being dictated by government or constrained by inherited communal institutions. We get to decide whom we work for, what we buy and sell (within our budgets, of course), how to use what we have, and even whether we try to create a new business ourselves. While capitalism does not automatically engender political democracy—indeed, capitalism's economic inequalities tend to undermine political equality, and capitalism's periodic economic recessions tend to revive authoritarian political solutions—this autonomy in the economic sphere encourages independent thought and creates an expectation of voice and participation, even if that expectation is often frustrated.

Counterbalancing these benefits, however, this separation severely restricts government's ability to ensure that the economy is working to meet the needs of people or the planet. When a society is dependent on the private business sector for the bulk of its economic activity, government cannot rise above the tensions that might pit business interests against those other interests. Government is, instead, largely subservient to business. And it is this subservience that explains government's unresponsiveness to us citizens.[36]

Government's role in a capitalist society is basically limited to buttressing the private sector's activity—setting guardrails through regulation and law, compensating for the private sector's deficiencies through public services, and handling national defense. Government rarely displaces private enterprise from activities that might be profitable, and public enterprises rarely compete directly with private enterprises.

A nice example is public Internet services. These have been slowly proliferating because commercial Internet service providers such as Comcast, Verizon, and AT&T charge such exorbitant prices, offer such poor service, and have not found it profitable enough to serve smaller towns and rural districts. Indeed, in the words of one observer, these providers have been so poor at the job that "American internet service is the laughingstock of the developed world."[37] In response to this failure, some 130 communities have developed publicly owned service offering low-cost or free high-quality high-speed service. The reaction of the business community? Fierce opposition. In 20 states, business interests have prevailed to pass legislation that bars, on the flimsiest of grounds, local governments from offering such services. As a result, merely 1–2 million Americans have the benefit of municipal broadband, out of a total Internet user population of about 300 million.[38]

This limitation on public enterprise is constantly policed by the business sector through all the many ways it exerts influence on government, such as lobbying and donations. But it is also self-imposed by politicians and regulators. Yes, constitutionally, we have the legal right to express our political views and to vote. Yes, there are relatively few impediments to exercising those rights in the US compared to many other countries. And yes, these precious rights classify our political system as a democracy. But the basic structure of capitalism ensures the feebleness of government vis-à-vis business interests, and as a result, our democracy is decidedly plutocratic. We live under the golden rule: "He who has the gold, rules."[39] And this is yet another factor that contributes to the growing income and wealth inequality: the personnel in our political and legal system can rarely bring themselves to enact tax laws that would discomfort the powerful and wealthy.

Political scientists have compiled compelling evidence of this subservience of government to business. One study looked at 1,779 instances between 1981 and 2002 in which a national survey of the general public asked a favor/oppose question about a proposed policy change that was voted on in Congress.[40] The study compared the influence on legislation of the views of four groups—the average citizen, the 10% of Americans with the highest income, "mass-based" interest groups, and business-oriented interest groups.[41] The study found that the average citizen's preferences had no discernable influence at all on the policy adopted. The mass-based interest groups had a modest influence. But the business-oriented interest groups' influence was twice as strong as the mass-based groups'. And the wealthy elite's influence was even stronger still. For the 369 out of 1,779 cases in which both business-based and mass-based interest groups took a stand, the efforts of the mass groups had no effect whatsoever, but the business groups' influence was immense.

What accounts for this subservience? In part, it arises because of the prevalence of promarket ideas. Those ideas have enormous support from the private business interests that control most of our mass media. In part, it is because our laws allow businesses to lobby, make campaign contributions, and offer lucrative "revolving-door" job offers.[42] These factors vastly amplify the voice of corporations and wealthy individuals in our political arena. We should also note that when wealthy people and business leaders use their money to influence politics, those expenditures cost them relatively little but can bring them big economic benefits. For working people, by contrast, the money and time needed to get involved in politics represent a much bigger expense.

However, the more fundamental reason for government's subservience lies in the structural characteristics of capitalism. Precisely because the economic sphere is separated from the governmental sphere, government policy in any capitalist society is constrained by government's financial dependence on the private sector. Government action is funded by revenue from the taxation of incomes and wealth generated in the process of private-sector growth. If investors and business executives think that a government action—such as new taxes, new regulations, or the creation of a new government program—will slow the growth of their own profits, we are very likely to see a "capital strike"—a slowdown in private-sector investment—or "capital flight"—a movement of financial assets overseas. And in either of those scenarios, government would lose both its economic resources and its political legitimacy. As a result, in a capitalist society, no government can prevail for long against private-sector interests. And politicians and regulators know it. Our political system is therefore hostage to these private interests.

The risks of capital strike and flight are not merely hypothetical. To cite one example: When President Obama came into office after the financial meltdown of 2008, nonfinancial businesses were holding an astounding $2 trillion in cash and banks held another $1 trillion. Where did all this cash come from? From profits that they were hoarding instead of investing. In part, they were hoarding this cash because it was difficult to find opportunities for profitable investment amid a systemic crisis. But that's not the only reason: ignoring many promising investment opportunities, business leaders hoarded rather than invested—thus enacting a capital strike— as a way of pressuring Congress not to impose more rigorous regulations on the financial sector.[43] The threat of capital flight was framed as a caution that more-stringent bank regulations would encourage banks to move from New York to London, and if the UK authorities joined in the bank regulation effort (which looked possible for a brief moment), there were plenty of other locations to which they could relocate, such as Singapore. In the face of this threat, our political leaders scaled way back projected financial-sector reforms, modest though these proposed reforms were.[44]

To cite a second example: In 1981, François Mitterrand was elected president of France on a platform that aimed at moving France somewhere beyond regulated capitalism, although far short of full-scale socialism. Within days, billions of dollars and francs had left France. Over the subsequent months, international speculators forced France to devalue the franc several times over. And over the subsequent year, productive investment fell to a trickle. Within two years, Mitterrand's government was forced to abandon entirely their modestly socialistic goals and to adopt instead a neoliberal program of austerity.[45] Similar stories can be told about other countries.[46]

So long as the core of the economy is based on capitalist private property, there is no escaping the structural factors that assure government's subservience to business interests. Even if all corporate lobbying, political contributions, and revolving-door arrangements were outlawed, and even if the media were not dominated by capitalist interests, the government of any capitalist society is forced to tailor its policies to support the growth of private-sector profitability. All it takes is for each individual business and investor to pursue their own economic self-interest, in hoarding rather than investing when profit prospects look dim, or in moving their capital to other countries where profit prospects are brighter. Aware of the possible impact of such moves on the health of the economy, legislators' hands are tied. In this way, the interests of the private sector inevitably shape the issues that do and do not get on the legislators' agenda. These interests inevitably influence the legislation that is enacted on the issues that do reach that agenda. And these same interests inevitably shape the way that legislation is implemented.[47]

Not surprisingly, our fellow citizens lose trust in government. To plutocrats, the resulting political disengagement is a blessing rather than a problem. But to anyone who believes in democratic values, all this has become increasingly troublesome, because it deprives us of the ability to use the potential power of government to solve the other crises and challenges we face. We have abundant resources and strong popular support for common-sense solutions to many of our biggest problems—universal healthcare, a minimum wage that is a living wage, government investment in retraining, free childcare, college and technical education, upgrading our physical infrastructure, aggressive international action on climate change, more sharply progressive taxation to pay for all these—but these solutions are blocked by the power of the business sector over government in our capitalist society.

CAPITALIST ENTERPRISE'S NATURAL EXTERNALITIES

The environmental crisis is due not only to the lack of environmental awareness among corporate leaders, government officials, or the public at large. It is due not only to the campaign of disinformation funded by the fossil fuel industry. It is also a reflection of the basic features of capitalism that we have just reviewed, in particular the growth imperative facing individual firms and the subservience of government to that imperative.

In a private-enterprise system, firms ignore the parts of the natural environment they do not own or do not have to pay for. They will only take into consideration such "externalities" if there happens to be some "business case" for doing so, for example, if it turns out that waste can be sold rather than dumped, or if the firm can save money by switching to more energy-efficient lighting or equipment.[48] That leaves too little incentive for the business sector to develop and deploy pro-environmental technologies.

Unlike economic cycles, where recessions eventually create conditions that encourage an upturn, the tendency toward environmental degradation does not necessarily produce any counteracting, attractive investment opportunities. Yes, if it looks like we might run out of coal or oil, the market responds by boosting prices, and this creates economic incentives to develop more efficient extraction techniques or alternative fuels. But no, if too much carbon dioxide is being dumped into the atmosphere, or if coal-mining waste is polluting our rivers, there is no spontaneous market response that would create economic incentives to reverse the resulting degradation.

Environmental degradation is thus a problem that is left for government to solve. And there is an undeniable benefit to such a narrowing of businesses' responsibilities. Businesses have strong incentives to master the details of their own operations; but they are not well placed to develop expertise in the wider environmental impact of those operations. And imagine that a firm's executives decided to spend part of the firm's profits doing things that they thought could benefit the environment at the cost of the firm's future profitability: investors would object that the executives were attempting to solve a problem that they were neither mandated nor competent to address. Conversely, government seems in principle exactly the right agency to develop that expertise and to formulate appropriate environmental protection policies. Government could tax the polluters to deter them, or it could regulate their activity to reduce the pollution.

Unfortunately, however, government's subservience makes it incapable of assuming this responsibility. In a capitalist society, government is reluctant to impose the necessary taxes or regulations on business. While some environmental interventions by government might help boost business-sector profitability—cleaning up a river, for example, can turn the riverfront into a city amenity that attracts private investment—many other interventions that we need so badly—such as the elimination of fossil fuels—represent a massive reduction in profits for wide swaths of industry. Even if such reductions now would avoid far greater losses later this century, those future losses are too far in the future for investors to value, and the business community is therefore ferocious in its opposition to government action.

The net effect is clear. Capitalism is a system that consumes forests, fish, minerals, soil fertility, and fresh water faster than they can be replenished. It burns fossil fuels at a rate that endangers the climate. It discharges pollution and garbage at a rate that endangers our rivers, oceans, and the air we breathe. Capitalism is thus a system that encourages environmental "plunder."[49] This plunder boosts the corporate bottom line and the value of the wealthy elite's stock holdings, while the costs of this environmental destruction fall disproportionately on the poor and minorities, who are left with polluted water and air and with the associated health consequences.[50]

More: given how slow we have been to act since we became aware of the threat of global warming, it is not clear that capitalism as a system can survive. Notwithstanding some very promising technological advances—leading to the rapid reduction in the price of solar energy, for example—it is hard to see how innovation will allow capitalism to adapt in time to the looming environmental challenges. It is increasingly difficult—in truth, impossible—to see how the competitive market process, even aided by government subsidies and regulations, could mobilize the massive, sustained R&D effort that would be required, how it could drive the resulting new technologies into widespread use, how it could get industry to abandon the huge accumulated capital assets thus rendered obsolete, and how it could achieve all this in time to avert the collapse of numerous ecological and social systems.[51]

The Nobel Prize–winning economist Eleanor Ostrom showed that such environmental destruction is not the inevitable result of human nature. She found that many traditional communities have governed very effectively their use of "common pool" natural resources such as open fields or water supplies, which are accessible by everyone but can be degraded by overuse. As Ostrom herself noted, however, such community governance cannot resolve our climate change crisis, because CO_2 emissions recognize no borders, and reducing these emissions represents a challenge that is far too large in scale and too complex, and the relevant actors are too interdependent. We are going to need much more than a village council meeting to resolve our global climate change crisis.[52] And in a capitalist system, government is constitutionally ill-equipped for this challenge.

We may yet be able to avert the worst of the climate change scenarios—it is still possible that popular protests and enlightened self-interest among businesses will push governments around the world to enact the policies we need. But, as I show in what follows, the policies we would need to put into place would take us far beyond anything resembling capitalism.

CAPITALIST ENTERPRISE'S SOCIAL EXTERNALITIES

In parallel with the deepening environmental crisis, capitalism's characteristic features generate an increasingly multifaceted social crisis. Capitalist businesses treat the *social* preconditions of production as externalities they can ignore, just as they ignore its *natural* environmental preconditions.[53]

The damage done to the fabric of society is enormous, and government's subservience makes it incapable of remedying that damage. While unions and other social movements have sometimes been successful in pushing back on some of these destructive tendencies—more successfully than we have been able to do on behalf of the environment—the basic structure of capitalist societies puts us in the role of Sisyphus—pushing a big rock up a hill, only to see it roll back down every time.

Consider the family. Across all the advanced capitalist countries, we see symptoms of what has been called a "crisis of care" in the growing proportion of single-parent households and of children growing up in poverty, in increasing levels of stress due to the inability to find an acceptable work-life balance, and in a growing flow of women from poorer regions of the world to serve as caregivers and domestic workers in the richer regions. This crisis has been under discussion for many years in feminist circles.[54] It has also been a common lament among conservatives. Conservatives, however, have attributed the problem to moral deficiencies rather than tracing it further back to the foundations of our political-economic system.

To see how this crisis flows from the basic features of capitalism, consider the implications of the fact that workers are born, nurtured, and sustained in families, communities, and neighborhoods. Capitalist firms produce the machinery that is used in making steel, but they do not produce the employees who build or run this machinery any more than they produce the water that they use to cool it. The profit imperative pushes firms to exploit both the social preconditions that ensure the availability of workers and the natural preconditions that govern the availability of water and other natural resources—with little regard for the maintenance of these preconditions. Profitability pressure and the competition between profit-driven firms, in combination with these firms' reliance on employed labor, encourage the destruction of business's environment, both social and natural.

Let us unpack how that works to undermine families. Prior to the early 1800s, most production in the United States was by and for the family, and most men and women worked together on the farm and in domestic handicraft production. But starting around then, the development of capitalist industry began creating a historically unprecedented split in society. On one side of this split, there was market-oriented production, which relies on the efforts of wage earners. On the other side, there was the sphere of care and social reproduction, which harnesses the efforts of those who give birth, raise children, assure their schooling, and care for the wage-earners at the end of their workday. For the main part, men were drawn into wage labor, and women were left as caregivers and homemakers—a development that reflected and reinforced existing patriarchal patterns of the domination of men over women.[55] This split was facilitated by the expansion of industry into prepared foodstuffs, clothing, and household tools. In urban settings and even in rural settings, it became more difficult for families to create these products for themselves, which made men's wage income an essential complement to women's work at home. All through the 19th century, the proportion of US women who participated in the wage-earning sector was below 20%, and these were almost all single women working in domestic and personal services and teaching.[56]

As capitalism developed further, a growing proportion of women began working for wages outside the home, and women have been progressively making their way into a broader range of occupations, with higher relative pay and at higher authority levels. These changes accelerated in the 1970s, under the combined pressure of a reenergized women's movement and stalled wage growth for working-class families. (Indeed, starting in the early 1970s, the growth in men's wages slowed, and as a result it was only by pushing more women into the wage-earning labor force that most families could increase their household income.) The rates of participation in the wage-earning labor force and the average pay levels of men and women have been gradually converging since then, even if we still have a long way to go.[57]

Painfully slow as this transition has been, the cumulative result has been dramatic. In particular, marriage is now no longer the economic necessity it once was for many women. Even as late as 1970, 44% of women aged 30–50 had no independent earnings at all. Now that ratio is down to 25%. The median wage for women in this age group rose from (in today's dollars) $19,000 to $30,000 since 1970. Conservatives bemoan the decline of traditional family structures, but we should celebrate these increased opportunities for women to pursue careers outside the home and to be more selective in choosing partners (and whether to stay with them or leave). The disintegration of the social fabric of our communities has some positive aspects—in the disintegration of structures of domination that pervade that fabric.

These positive trends have, however, come with several dark sides, reflecting both the fundamental limits of the capitalist economic structure and the evolving challenges to patriarchal authority. First, in a capitalist economy, as marriage loses its economic imperative for women, traditional gender hierarchies are increasingly seen as obsolete, and many people—mainly men, but some women too—are uncomfortable with this new world. The persistence and emotional intensity of debates about abortion rights and gender identity are fueled by this anxiety.

Second, when at the same time some categories of men are suffering from unemployment (notably among blue-collar occupations), incarceration, and disabilities, fewer of these men are attractive marriage partners for women. As a result, fewer women in disadvantaged communities marry. More children are born into single-parent families. Those single-parent families are poorer. And more children end up in deep poverty. Currently, 30% of single-parent households are under the poverty level, as compared to only 5% of married-family households. Over three-quarters (76%) of these single-parent households are headed by women, and only 16% of these women have cohabiting partners.[58]

Third, the participation of women in the wage-earning labor force makes for a growing number of families with both a need for help in the home and more financial resources to pay for such help. As a result, there are now some 2 million domestic workers in the United States, cleaning people's houses and caring for families. A survey of over 2,000 domestic workers—caregivers for children and elderly, and housecleaners—conducted by the National Domestic Workers Alliance found that 23% were paid below the state minimum wage; 65% reported having no health insurance; 60% paid more than half their income on rent or mortgages; 29% reported having long-term medical problems from their work. Some 11% were "live-in" employees, and of these 25% had responsibilities that prevented them from getting at least five hours of uninterrupted sleep at night during the week prior to being interviewed. In this sample, 35% were not US citizens and 47% of those were undocumented, adding greatly to their vulnerability to exploitation and abuse.[59]

Stepping back from the specifics, it is important to see that the integration of women into the wage-earning labor force need not create an impossible conundrum. Much of this crisis would be resolved if men and women alike had access to good-quality jobs, and if we had a shorter week, publicly funded and high-quality childcare and eldercare, and decent wages and conditions for paid household help. Is that inconceivable? No. In a saner system, we could have used part of the economy's productivity gains to implement such changes progressively. But in a capitalist and sexist society, such ideas run directly into a unified wall of business-sector opposition. There is not enough profit in it.

Beyond the family, capitalist development brings with it an ever-widening array of social tensions and proliferating crises. Racism was part and parcel of capitalism's origins, and just as with sexism, capitalism has profited from it and in the process, exacerbated it. Capitalism's relentless search for profits not only drives the intensification of exploitation within capitalist production and a continual effort to reduce the costs of reproducing workers' capacity to work but also drives the direct expropriation of people and resources through slavery and racialized domination.[60] Slavery played a key role in the development of capitalism in the United States, just as it did in Britain, France, Spain, and Portugal. It was slavery that allowed the United States to dominate the world market for cotton—a key raw material in the Industrial Revolution. In the early 19th century, cotton accounted for fully half of US exports. Those exports catalyzed the emergence of the United States as a world economic power. Slavery in the South—where, by 1860, some 4 million people were enslaved—was essential to the rise of textile manufacturing in New England and to finance in New York.[61] The legacy of slavery's barbarism is compounded by ongoing racial discrimination—in jobs, housing, policing and criminal justice, and everyday social interaction—to rob the African American community of opportunities to accumulate wealth over generations.

Many more-recent immigrants also face discrimination, even though US businesses have drawn them here, eager for their cheap labor, and even though they have been driven to emigrate by the forces unleashed by their home countries' capitalist economies. More generally, as the capitalist system becomes more globally interdependent, economic and environmental crises are bound to force more people into global migrations, and these migrations will bring workers into increasingly tense competition in the labor market and will create increasing pressure on the business-constrained capacities of government in capitalist economies.

Our systems of care for the sick and the elderly are similarly hobbled by the capitalist character of our political economy. On the one hand, some parts of these systems offer lucrative profit opportunities for business. These firms offer services at high prices, but pay their caregivers poorly and leave clients with poor-quality service. On the other hand, the other parts fall to the government, where funding is constantly held captive by business pressures.[62] In the meantime, we have entire industries—snack foods, soft drinks, fast food—dedicated to profiting from unhealthy food, and their spokespeople are indignant when we try to stop them advertising their junk food on TV to our children.[63]

The capitalist roots of the crises in our neighborhoods, cities, and regions are also clear. Regions must compete to attract private business with whatever natural and social advantages they might have, as well as with whatever tax rebates and outright gifts they are willing to surrender. When in 2017 Amazon announced that it was looking for a second city in which to build another headquarters building, the announcement was partly to put pressure on Seattle to scale back its progressive housing policies. And the announcement unleashed a sad rush by desperate city mayors across the country to offer the most massive tax breaks and subsidies.[64] The result of such regional competition is that some regions prosper and others are left to languish. In 2014, people in some counties enjoyed a life expectancy at birth of 87 years, while in others it is just 66 years. And these disparities have been increasing, at least since 1980. Much of this variation is a function of the disparities in socioeconomic conditions and healthcare availability.[65]

Our housing crisis too has roots that go deeper than current neoliberal policy. Private real-estate interests have successfully scaled back public housing, rent controls, and city planning. Without strong government intervention, it is far more profitable to build luxury homes and condos than affordable housing. So, in many of our major cities we have a glut of luxury units and a terrible lack of affordable ones.[66]

And finally, education. Education is increasingly important to the economic future of both individuals and the country, and this leads us to demand ever more from our schools and universities. But in a capitalist society, the business sector resists the imposition of the taxes that would be needed to fund free education for all, or even to fund decent salaries for teachers. Twenty years ago, public-sector teachers earned 1.8% less than other employees with similar education and experience, but by 2015, the gap had widened to 17%. True, teachers had better benefits; but after factoring that in, the gap was still over 11%.[67]

A HIERARCHICAL WORLD ECONOMY

If international relations are more competitive than collaborative, the root cause is the capitalist nature of the dominant economic powers in the world. To be sure, there will always be rivalries between countries, and there will always be political leaders who see advantage in catering to and stoking further those rivalries. But when the global economy is dominated by capitalist businesses and countries, collaboration is always limited by the growth imperative of those businesses and by the resulting rivalry between those powers. And this rivalry cannot be pacified reliably by institutions such as the United Nations.

From the earliest phase of capitalism, growth pressures pushed firms beyond national boundaries, and competition between the biggest firms was already global. As capitalism developed, businesses and their competitive relations became increasingly global in their scope. These firms sought raw materials in poorer and weaker countries, established extraction and production facilities there, and sold products wherever they could. In this process, they allied with local ruling elites. They marshaled diplomatic and military support from their home-country governments to support their goals if those elites tried to assert their independent interests or if rival firms based in other countries challenged them. By 1800, the richest European countries controlled 35% of the world's territory, and by 1914, that had risen to 85%.[68]

This system of imperialist domination was challenged first by the Soviet revolution in 1917, and then after World War II by the emergence of a socialist bloc in Eastern Europe and Communist China and a "non-aligned" bloc scattered across the continents. But outside the socialist bloc, and even after many countries achieved formal independence from their colonial masters, relations between countries remained structured hierarchically by and to the benefit of the dominant capitalist economies. Among these latter, the United States took over from Britain as the "hegemonic" power on the (non-Communist) world stage.[69]

In this hierarchical system, the wealth of "core" countries (United States, Western Europe) was—and still is—augmented by exploitation in poor, "periphery" countries and in middle-income, "semiperiphery" countries in the rest of the world. Some of that wealth trickles down to working people in the core countries, mainly because this system creates a hierarchical international division of labor. The core countries specialize in higher-value-added industries, which typically require more educated employees and pay higher wages, while the periphery countries provide raw materials and labor, and semiperiphery countries specialize in lower-value-added industries employing relatively less-skilled and lower-paid employees.[70]

This hierarchy is not immutable, of course. Capitalist development within the periphery countries has led some to increasing prosperity, even as others languish in terrible poverty. A handful of periphery countries struck gold—in the form of oil—and carved out a special niche for themselves. Some, such as Argentina, India, Brazil, Mexico, and Indonesia, moved from periphery to semiperiphery. As "middle-income" countries, they offer increasingly attractive opportunities for further investment by companies from the core. Some, such as South Korea and Taiwan, might even be considered part of the core now. The overall path of development of the capitalist world economy is one of interdependent and uneven development. Capitalist development constantly creates inequality between as well as within countries.[71]

With the collapse of the USSR and the socialist bloc in Eastern Europe and with the opening of China and Vietnam to capitalist investment, a vast new pool of labor and new markets for investment and sales were opened up to the global firms of the major capitalist economies. The results of this transition have been threefold.

First, global firms have become even larger and more powerful. Of the world's 100 largest entities by total revenues, 69 are now corporations, and only 31 are countries.[72] These firms have great control over whether and where they pay taxes, because they are largely free to set prices however they like for their internal trade between subsidiaries in different countries, and because they can park their profits in tax havens.[73] They export their environmentally and socially destructive activities to the periphery countries, where government is weak and people are desperate.[74] Their size gives them enormous influence in those host countries. They still deploy their home-country government's resources to support them through political, economic, and military means.[75]

Second, there has been a profound disruption of the US and western European economies. Working people in the less-advanced sectors of these core countries find themselves in competition with workers in these new entrants to the semiperiphery. Since capital has been set free to move between countries but workers' movements are still far more constrained, multinational corporations with facilities in different countries can use the threat of relocation to drive down wages in each of them. And when workers do manage to move to more affluent regions, tensions arise as domestic labor market competition intensifies. In a capitalist system, workers find themselves damned either way, with closed or open borders. And in the absence of a powerful international movement seeking global justice and equity, the emergence of populist, authoritarian, and xenophobic right-wing movements in the core is the predictable consequence.

Third, the United States' hegemonic position in the world economy is being challenged by a rising China. And now that there is no socialist bloc vying for influence in the developing world, the United States, China, Europe, and perhaps Russia are in a four-way competition for influence. The world is even less stable than during the Cold War period, because there is no hegemonic power that can keep this rivalry in check. We are arguably even closer to nuclear Armageddon than ever before.[76]

These underlying tensions explain why it is so frustratingly difficult to reach international agreements on critical issues like climate change, war, migration, nuclear proliferation, and so forth. And why the United States is such an impediment to overcoming those tensions.

Capitalism, of course, is not responsible for every problem we see around us. But the basic features of capitalism—the conflict between a tiny minority who own society's productive resources as their private property and the large majority who must work for those owners in exchange for a wage, the profit and growth imperative driving these owners, and the subservience of government to their interests—create conditions that intensify and render intractable many of our problems, even if they do not directly cause all of them.

CHAPTER 3
A Growing Tension

The features of capitalism we have just reviewed in turn create one further distinctive feature of capitalism: the continual expansion of the web of interdependencies among economic activities. Driven by capitalism's relentless search for profits, growth, productivity, and markets, interdependencies multiply within firms as these firms expand and encompass wider spans of activities, and interdependencies multiply between and beyond firms as they expand their base of suppliers, customers, and government support.

On the one hand, this growing interdependence explains how capitalism has been so successful in increasing productivity and in raising the living standards of many. On the other hand, as capitalism matures, this same trend exacerbates the failures associated with the other features of capitalism. These failures tend to worsen over time as interdependencies multiply. We therefore see an ever-growing tension between an increasingly interdependent system of production and the maintenance of the capitalist private-enterprise system of independent, competing firms.

Let's take those two aspects in turn.

GROWING INTERDEPENDENCE OF PRODUCTION

Capitalism is a system characterized by unprecedented rates of productivity growth—far faster than in any earlier form of society.[1] Production for profit pushes firms constantly to search for lower-cost components, more productive equipment, new product ideas, new customers, and new markets. Employing wage-labor, firms are always seeking new sources of cheap labor and new ways of reducing labor costs. Government supports these efforts through its laws, regulations, foreign policy, and even the use of state violence. And firms are discouraged from taking responsibility for their environmental or social externalities.

The result of these combined pressures is a continually expanding network of interdependent economic activities. This interdependence enables any one center of activity to benefit from productivity- and profit-enhancing innovations generated by other centers. The expansion of this interdependence takes several forms. Firms manage a wider span of activities internally. Firms also buy from a wider range of suppliers and sell to a wider range of customers. They rely on knowledge coming from a wider array of sources. And they rely on an expanding, shared social and material infrastructure. While earlier economic systems developed networks of trade, sometimes spanning continents, capitalism brings a dramatic acceleration in the expansion of these interdependencies. As a result, productivity grows at a historically unprecedented rate.[2]

We can think of this growing interdependence as progressively "socializing" society's productive capabilities. Socialization in this sense refers to the extent to which producers, rather than developing and operating in isolation, absorb and leverage the capabilities of other producers and of other parts of the broader society, benefiting from their know-how and their technologies. Producers' capabilities are augmented when they leverage these other resources in the form of more sophisticated materials, components, equipment, skills, and shared infrastructure. As capitalism develops over the longer term, the sphere of productive activity is increasingly socialized in this sense.[3]

To make this idea more concrete, compare the typical enterprise of early capitalism—say, in the early 19th century in the United States—with its counterpart today.[4] Back then, alongside a few large-scale plantations and banks, the typical enterprise was a small farm or, less often, a workshop or store, in a sparsely populated rural region or small town. If it employed any workers outside the family, they came from the local area. Economically, these enterprises were largely self-reliant. People often grew their own food, built their own buildings, and made their own clothes and tools. If they needed specialized tools or materials (say, horseshoes or fabric) they bought them from local storeowners, who in turn either produced them themselves or brought them in from a nearby city. Producers sold their products to local customers, or perhaps to a storeowner who sold them on their behalf, or occasionally to a wholesale merchant who might resell them in other towns. Recall that in America of the early 1800s, the only practical way to travel and trade across long distances was by sea and river. A few roads connected major cities, but even on these roads travel was difficult and slow. Yes, in the big cities, the span of interdependence, including via global trade, was much greater; but in 1800 fully 94% of Americans lived in rural rather than urban areas, and in 1850 that ratio was still 85%, and in 1890, still 60%.

All these people—owners, workers, suppliers, customers—relied on know-how that was for the main part local and traditional. What they needed to know for their work they learned from their parents or on the job. Few of them had been to school, and if they had, their learning was very rudimentary.[5] Many had learned to read, but most had read only the Bible. Enslaved African Americans were forbidden to read or learn to read. Outside some of the ruling elite, the most intellectually sophisticated among them were the craftsmen: although just a tiny minority of the workforce, craftsmen often brought with them an impressive stock of craft know-how learned through apprenticeships.

Now contrast that scene with a typical enterprise of our own times. The average size of firms and their establishments (plants, offices, stores) has increased enormously, bringing a much wider span of interdependent activities under direct management control. As we saw earlier, over half the labor force now works in firms with more than 500 employees, and this growth in size reflects the intertwined effects of monopoly and economies of scale. On the one hand, firms grow in search of monopoly power—the ability to sell products at an unusually high price or buy inputs at an unusually low price because competitors have been squeezed out. And on the other, they grow because when they bring interdependent activities under unified management control, they can organize work more efficiently.[6]

Socialization in an indirect form—via market ties with suppliers and customers—has progressed too. The typical firm today uses tools and raw materials that embody productivity-enhancing innovations from dozens if not hundreds of suppliers all around the world, and each of these in turn uses inputs from many suppliers that are even more geographically dispersed. The firm probably has customers across the United States and indeed on other continents, and firms often capture innovative ideas from these customers.

Where once travel and communications were slow and expensive, now the firm is linked internally (across its various departments, factories, stores, and offices) and externally (with suppliers and customers) by dense networks of land, air, sea, telephone, and Internet connections.[7] Take even a medium-sized firm such as Patagonia, which sells products in thousands of stores across the globe. It sources finished goods from 81 factories in 14 countries, including Vietnam (18 factories), Sri Lanka (17 factories), and

China (11 factories) and countries to our south (20 factories). And each of these factories in turn has many suppliers for materials and equipment. While this "globalization" has had terrible consequences for many American factory workers, it has also meant real productivity advances that have reduced costs for American consumers and created jobs for many people in poorer countries.

Over this period, socialization progressed not only through the broadening extent of ties within and between firms, and not only through the growing reliance on shared knowledge resources, but also through firms' growing reliance on the shared social and material infrastructure, most of which is provided by government.[8] This shows up in at least three ways.

First, contemporary enterprises are highly interdependent in their common reliance on a vast pool of shared scientific and technological knowledge. This pool of knowledge is continually expanding, enriched by university and corporate research, both domestic and international. The US government funds nearly 60% of all basic research, and is increasingly involved in downstream, applied research too.[9] As compared to 50, or 100, let alone 200 years ago, the role of government in advancing knowledge has grown massively.

Second, enterprises are increasingly reliant on the transmission of society's accumulated knowledge by our system of primary, secondary, and tertiary education. In 1850, less than half the 5- to 19-year-olds in the United States were enrolled in school, including less than 5% of African Americans in that age group.[10] That proportion rose steadily to over 90% today, with nearly identical proportions for all races by about 1980. The proportion of Americans who finished high school was of course much lower in the mid-19th century, and it was still under 7% in 1900, but it rose steadily, to around 88% today.

To be sure, not all this expansion of education is motivated by industry's need for more educated employees. Education is also a way of legitimating the intergenerational persistence of class differences and of disciplining young people and habituating them to the kind of bureaucratic control they will experience in the workplace.[11] However, and notwithstanding commonly heard concerns about jobs in our economy being dumbed down, in reality the long-term trend in industry has been, and continues to be, toward ever-higher requirements of both analytical and social skills, and this fuels the growing demand by industry for a more educated workforce.[12]

And third, industry is increasingly interdependent in its reliance on shared, government-sponsored infrastructure in the form of roads, rail, telecommunications, water and sewage systems, fire departments, pensions, healthcare, industry, and community assistance, not to mention the legal system and the military. Total government expenditures (federal, state, and local combined) have risen rather steadily, from about 7% of gross domestic product in 1900 to about 37% today. While there have been efforts to roll back government's share of economic activity, these have rarely succeeded, except during brief periods when dramatic wartime expansions of government (and more recently, the expansion of government to deal with the financial crisis of 2008) were scaled back at the crisis's end. The neoliberal push toward deregulation and shrinking government was less a matter of scaling back government and more one of privatizing the provision of government services.[13]

In sum: where once economic activity was primarily a local, private affair, conducted by relatively isolated, small enterprises dispersed across largely disconnected locales and each operating rather independently, today each enterprise leverages a vast array of societal resources—in the form of sophisticated materials and technologies, scientific and engineering knowledge, educated workers, and social and material infrastructures—and in this way it is embedded in a growing web of interdependencies within and across regions. In this sense, production has been progressively socialized.

Indeed, this transformation has even reshaped the family farm, which is now much more productive (even if also more environmentally destructive). Farms today rely on immense technological and scientific resources. They sell to global firms like Cargill. They use chemicals and seed provided by firms like Monsanto. They rely on equipment from huge firms like Agco. They are financed by loans from banks. They are supported by subsidies from the federal Department of Agriculture and other government agencies.[14]

When you stop to consider this massive transformation of our economy, it becomes hard to keep a straight face when people say that our economy is based on "private" enterprise.[15]

SOCIALIZED PRODUCTION VERSUS PRIVATE PROPERTY

And yet, if the substance of economic activity has become increasingly socialized, property rights over society's main economic resources have indeed remained essentially private. On the one hand, production activity has become increasingly interdependent, but on the other hand, the resources on which that activity depends—the material and equipment that are needed to make the goods and services that we need to live—are still private property. Private individuals—investors and the CEOs they appoint—hold both the right to buy and sell these productive assets ("ownership" rights) and the right to decide how those assets can be used ("control" rights). These private enterprises are in competition with each other for profits and growth, even as their interdependence deepens.

The growing discrepancy between socialized production and private property exacerbates the problems inherent in each of the other features of the capitalist system. Let's take each of those features in turn and see how that interaction works.

Consider, first, production for profit and the resulting economic irrationality in the form of economic boom-and-bust cycles. So long as firms were small and markets were local—so long, that is, as the socialization of production was limited—economic cycles were largely limited to these local markets. But with the growing interdependence of production across a wider geographic scale, economic downturns now swallow up whole nations and indeed vast spans of the global economy.[16] Financial crises too are increasingly global—as we saw in the 2008 financial crisis, which originated in the United States and spread rapidly to many other countries, devastating many European and other economies. It becomes increasingly irrational and costly to rely on the blind, unplanned, emergent, market process to coordinate production networks that are so far-flung and so tightly interdependent.

As we saw earlier, production for profit also drives a tendency toward concentration, and the associated risks and costs of monopoly grow as socialization progresses. Socialization explains why bigger firms are often more efficient than their smaller competitors; but in a system of production for profit, these larger firms also use their market power monopolistically, in ways that exacerbate inequality and waste. When a few firms dominate an industry, they have the power to drive wages down and prices and profits up.[17] Firms maintain higher levels of excess capacity to deter potential competitors from entering their industry.[18]

The risks of monopoly are further exacerbated by socialization because the latter drives technological advances that afford not only economies of scale but also "network economies." Network economies appear where the value of an asset grows as more people use it.[19] Think of Facebook, and how its value to users grows as more other people use it. And think of how this network effect also attracts more advertisers. No wonder Facebook captures 70% of all online advertising dollars. Or think of how much more effective Google search becomes as more people use and their search results feed the search algorithm, and of how, like Facebook, advertisers too ride this network effect. Network economies can grow much more rapidly than scale economies, and as a result, the digital-based industries are often extraordinarily concentrated . . . and the technology giants wield enormous, and largely unchecked, monopoly power.[20]

Consider, second, how socialization exacerbates the workplace disempowerment that results from wage employment. The socialization of production translates into an increasing average number of employees per enterprise. Under unified ownership, these organizations orchestrate vast networks of activity under their roofs, and they fine-tune the interdependence of these activities to ensure greater economic effectiveness. But control here is in the hands of top managers—leaving employees disempowered, as mere hired hands. It's hardly surprising then that the larger is the company, the less "engaged" are its employees. Some 59% of the employees working in companies with less than 25 employees are not engaged or are actively disengaged at work, but in companies with over 1,000 employees that figure rises to 70%.[21] In a society that proclaims its allegiance to the democratic principle that people should have a voice in the decisions that influence them, our disempowerment at work is increasingly dysfunctional and frustrating—a progressively deepening crisis.

Disempowerment is intensified by socialization via a second mechanism too—rising education levels. As we saw, the socialization of production is also reflected in progressively higher education levels, bringing more people into contact with the wider world of science, technology, literature, etc. As industry develops, manual effort is replaced by mechanical and automated systems. Employees' tasks tend to shift from the direct manipulation of raw materials to the control of machines. This shift usually (although not always) requires employees with more education. But more-educated employees doing more-complex work are even more alienated by the autocratic authority of workplace decision-making. So it is not surprising that levels of disengagement are even higher among college graduates than among employees with only a high-school diploma or less.[22]

Consider, third, the unresponsiveness of government that flows from government's subservience to the private business sector. On the one hand, the socialization of production calls for greater government investment in assuring the private sector's social and physical infrastructure. Government is drawn into more extensive investment in education, transportation and communications infrastructure, R&D, and so forth. But business-dominated government is reluctant to invest where there is no likely benefit to the profitability of the private sector. And the business sector itself is fragmented by competitive rivalries. As a result, even public investments that promise huge private-sector payoffs are delayed, curtailed, or killed.[23] Evidence for this charge would include government's limited investment in basic R&D even in areas where we know there would be huge payoffs, the dilapidated and perilous state of our bridges and highways, and the shortfalls in funding education and healthcare. With the socialization of production, we need a government that is more expansive and more effective, but with a private-enterprise economy, we get only the government that businesses see, with their nearsighted vision, as helping their own profitability.

Consider, too, the environmental unsustainability that flows from the private-enterprise system's disregard for its natural preconditions. Socialization accelerates economic growth, but when profit-driven industry produces more, it also produces more environmental havoc. And in a system based on private enterprise, government is constrained by its subservience to business interests, and is thus incapable of responding adequately to this havoc. Evidence here includes the refusal to act in the face of climate change, and the inability of regulators to slow the growth of toxic waste in agriculture, mining, industry, and electronics.

Consider the impact of socialization on social disintegration and the position of women. The socialization of production has progressively expanded to include much of what used to be household production of food and clothing. Partly because of this, and partly reflecting the other factors we discussed earlier, women have been drawn in greater numbers into wage employment. But in a capitalist private-enterprise system, this socialization of production leaves women and families with increasingly difficult work–life tensions. Or consider our cities and regions. The socialization of production also draws cities and regions into denser interdependence, but in a private-enterprise economic system, the effect is to put them in competition with each other to attract industry and investment. The losers in that competition are left with decaying communities and inadequate government support.

And finally, consider the impact of socialization on international relations. As socialization progresses and transcends national barriers, production, investment, and sales become more global. Big corporations in the core countries mobilize global supply chains, encompassing countries such as Bangladesh and China. We might hope that growing economic interdependence would tend to pacify international relations. But under capitalist conditions, this economic globalization takes an imperialist form, with economic power concentrated in the hands of a small number of global behemoths, who exert ever greater power over national governments. And the globalization of economic competition between firms and their home governments aggravates rather than reduces international tensions and global inequality. Even if our national government were tempted to undertake antitrust actions to break up these monopolistic companies so as to restore competitive conditions in the US economy, such antitrust actions would weaken the position of US-based monopolists in this international competition. This helps explain why we still have banks that are "too big to fail": the Obama administration was deterred from any antitrust action to break them up because such a breakup would have weakened their position in competition with foreign banks.

We saw earlier how the basic features of the capitalist economic system contribute to each of the six crises we face. We have now also seen how these features also drive the progressive socialization of production and how this socialization has two effects in turn. On the one hand, socialization underpins capitalism's remarkable technological innovation and productivity growth—which hold the promise of abundance and material comfort. But on the other, socialization also aggravates the failures of capitalism—intensifying its crises and depriving us of the opportunity to enjoy these fruits of socialized production. To deal with these crises and to unlock this potential, we must resolve the growing tension between increasingly socialized production and the persistence of private enterprise.

CHAPTER 4

The Promise and Limits of Reform

We need to adapt the system of ownership and control of society's productive resources to support the growing interdependence of production and ensure that the fruits of this interdependence benefit everyone rather than just an elite. To do that, we need to find a way to ensure that enterprises are guided by social and environmental considerations rather than by private profit. We need in this sense to "socialize" property, so that enterprises' decisions reflect the priorities of the broader society, not only their own private profitability priorities.

Efforts to socialize property are already visible in a profusion of social innovations all around us. As the science fiction writer William Gibson once noted, "The future is already here—it's just not evenly distributed."[1] Notice, for example, the local neighborhood food co-op that makes its priority healthy food and congenial work relations rather than profits. Notice the growing interest in "B corporations" whose charters explicitly aim to "balance purpose and profit."[2] Notice the city-level planning efforts to provide affordable housing, against the profit-driven real-estate industry interests. Notice the national movement to pull health insurance out of the private sector. Notice the various NGOs that provide philanthropic alternatives to the market. And notice the "open source" projects, such as Wikipedia, that create powerful new tools through entirely voluntary effort without any profit incentive. All these testify to a growing awareness that a system based on profit-driven accumulation of private wealth is failing us and that we need somehow to ensure that our productive resources are used to support the well-being of people and the planet rather than only profits.

While we should celebrate these social innovation efforts, it is not clear whether the reforms they propose offer robust solutions to the six big crises. Let us assess the potential of each of the four main clusters of ideas underlying these efforts—I will call them ethical capitalism, regulated capitalism, social democracy, and techno-utopianism.

These reform models are distinguished by their commitment to maintaining the private-enterprise system while broadening the firm's goals to incorporate the needs of a broader range of stakeholders and/or strengthening the role of government. Like the more radical, democratic-socialist model we will discuss later, these reform models would bring social and environmental priorities to bear on enterprise decision-making. But such reforms would only partly socialize the control of enterprises, and I will argue that because of this constraint they are destined to fall far short as solutions to our intensifying crises.

ETHICAL CAPITALISM?

Ethical capitalism is a model where the values and conscience of consumers, investors, and executives would lead firms to prioritize the needs of people and of the planet over short-term profits. As a strategy for getting us to a better world, it differs from other strategies in focusing on the business sector itself as a force for good. In a period when many of us are frustrated by the unresponsiveness of government, it is not surprising that people turn to business to solve our problems.

The ethical-capitalism model comes in two main variants. First, ethical capitalism might take the form of firms that become more committed externally to social and environmental goals. This idea appears in the media under such labels as "corporate social responsibility," "conscious capitalism," or "shared value."[3] Companies such as Unilever and Patagonia are often mentioned as examples, for their efforts to support organic agriculture, sustainable seafood, and environmental and social stewardship in palm-oil plantations. Second, such corporations might commit internally to a "high-road strategy" in relation to their employees, where they invest in employees' training and give them more voice opportunities. Here, companies such as Southwest Airlines and Costco are often mentioned as examples, for their better-than-market wages and benefits and more participative management approaches.[4]

Ethical capitalism offers an attractive cluster of ideas. We should celebrate the fact that many of our fellow citizens are pushing firms to act more responsibly, and that some far-sighted business leaders see the wisdom of accepting such responsibility. Surely, it would alleviate many of capitalism's failures if more firms took this path. And later, I will argue that socialists have much to learn from the innovative management systems some of these companies have deployed. Moreover, we have a lot of evidence that taking this path can sometimes help a business's competitiveness. And we have even more evidence that many firms can act more ethically than they currently do without hurting their profitability.[5]

On the other hand, however, this model faces major hurdles if we rely on it to resolve our biggest crises. One concern is simply that when some firms take responsibility for the impact of their negative externalities— for the harms their actions could cause to the lives of their employees, to the wider community, or to natural environment—they are likely to incur extra costs, and when they do so, they make themselves vulnerable to being undercut by less-responsible competitors. While creative thinking can sometimes help firms identify ways to mitigate these externalities without incurring higher costs, and while it is wonderful to see firms encouraged to pursue those "win-win" opportunities, there is simply no good reason to imagine that the massive environmental and social problems we face can be addressed seriously if we rely only on such win-win steps.[6] That would presuppose that the whole idea of externalities is just an optical illusion.[7]

Proponents of the ethical-capitalism model respond to this concern about higher costs by directing our attention to the potential for higher revenues. They argue that more socially and environmentally conscious stakeholders—consumers, employees, investors, executives—would be willing to pay a little extra for the products and services of more responsible companies. Patagonia, for example, attracts many customers who want to support its environmental and social commitments, and who are willing as a result to pay a little more for their products.[8] Proponents of ethical capitalism believe that the gains in market share garnered by these leading firms will force their competitors to follow suit.

The sad reality, however, is that, on average, becoming more ethical does nothing for a firm's profitability. While some case studies suggest that ethical behavior "pays," in many cases the causality is the other way around: if a firm happens to be highly profitable, it is in a better financial position to fund environmental or social initiatives. And while some studies of broader samples of firms show positive financial returns to ethical behavior, the more systematic research tells us that neither internal nor external social or environmental responsibility leads *on average* to better financial performance. Given that finding, the force of market competition is too feeble to force the mass of less-ethical firms to switch to a more ethical path.

And in that case, the ethical-capitalism model loses credibility as a path to overcoming the failures of capitalism.[9]

Let us take the firm's various stakeholders one at a time and see how far their pressure could drive firms to adopt more ethical policies. Consider, first, customers. Are consumers willing and able to pay more for products that are responsibly sourced or produced? Many consumers certainly *say* that they care about firms' social and environmental records, but far fewer actually *choose* the more responsible product when there is a cheaper, less responsible alternative available. Most people are just not interested in the practices of the firms making the products they buy.[10] Yes, more-ethical firms can charge a bit more and still keep their appeal to more-ethical consumers. And yes, as issues of social and environmental sustainability become more salient to consumers, we should expect that a greater number of ethical firms will step forward. But when these firms step forward, the less ethical ones are in an even stronger competitive position to attract those consumers who care less about ethics and more about price. If some firms, perhaps a growing number of them, move in an ethical direction, this will be counterbalanced by the consolidation of the market position of the less ethically driven firms.

Now consider employees. Could ethical firms achieve some competitive advantage by being more responsible in the way they treat their employees, and thereby drive their competitors to behave more responsibly? To be sure, firms that offer better pay and working conditions can attract better employees, and those employees have an incentive to work more diligently to keep those good jobs. That is why for many years, even if not so much these days, you often heard managers say, "High wages make for high profits." But the question we must address is rather different if we have in mind the major crises we face today: it is whether an ethical firm can avoid layoffs when there is a serious economy-wide recession. The answer is simple: if the financial viability of the enterprise is threatened, the firm will have no choice but to lay off employees. To do otherwise would not only limit the firm's competitiveness once the economy revives, but would also constitute a breach of the managers' fiduciary duty to its investors.

True, more-ethical firms have policies that aim to limit such layoffs, and some might be willing to absorb (modest) financial costs to meet that commitment. And many firms pay for "out-placement" services to help laid-off employees find other jobs. However, in an economy-wide recession, especially one that lasts longer, these measures are far too weak to protect employees from the risks of unemployment. In recent years, many firms have tried to buffer their "core" employees by relying on temporary, contract workers to absorb the ups and downs of the business cycle. While this helps the core employees, it leaves the growing mass of temporary employees in an even more precarious situation.

There is one version of ethical capitalism that might overcome this challenge, at least in part: this is the more radical version that advocates a shift from capitalist firms—owned by investors and staffed by employees—to worker-owned cooperatives—where the workers are the co-owners.[11] Such cooperatives certainly give workers real influence within the enterprise, and thereby address the crisis of disempowerment. Their boards of directors are not elected by outside investors but by workers themselves. Whereas capitalist firms respond to weaker sales by laying off workers, cooperatives typically respond by reducing the number of hours worked per week and the corresponding pay. As a result, cooperatives have fewer layoffs. On the other hand, however, for those same reasons, they typically pay lower wages and their wage levels are more volatile.[12] Moreover, they grow more slowly, because their members are cautious about adding new members and because they cannot leverage outside investors. It is hardly surprising then, that whatever benefits worker cooperatives might offer, these advantages are not enough to drive the diffusion of the cooperative model across industry in an economy that remains basically capitalist.[13]

What about the impact on employee recruitment of the firm's external social and environmental conduct? Do ethical firms do better in attracting better, more motivated employees? While there are clearly some people who care enough about this aspect of their employer's policies, we have no evidence that these people are numerous enough or that they can afford to be selective enough in their choice of jobs to drive change in firms' social and environmental practices. The effect of labor market pressures on firms' social and environmental performance seems to be just as weak as the effect of product market pressures.[14]

What about investors? Can pressure from ethical investors and from socially responsible investment (SRI) funds that cater to these investors push firms in a better direction? Yes, a growing number of investors care about social and environmental performance of the firms in their portfolio. [15] But why do they care? Almost invariably, it's because they anticipate stronger government regulation—not because they want to "do the right thing."[16] There is simply no evidence that, absent this "regulatory risk" factor, investors are shifting their priorities. So, this argument hinges on the likelihood of regulation, which takes us out of the ethical-capitalism model and into the regulated capitalism model we will discuss later.

Moreover, competition between these SRI funds leads them to focus on financial returns and avoid any socially or environmentally motivated investments that are likely to yield less profit than the overall market. They are eager to show their clients that they can "do well by doing good," because these funds too are in profit-driven competition to grow their SRI market share. It's not surprising then that many of these funds base their choice of target firms on how well they perform *compared to* other firms in the same industry, and that as a result over 90% of the *Fortune* 500 companies—including the big oil companies—show up in one or more of these SRI funds.

The ethical-capitalism model cannot progress far if it cannot eliminate competition from less ethical firms. The only way to do that is for government regulation to block the "low road" by setting a higher floor for social and environmental standards. So, even though many proponents of the ethical-capitalism model have little faith in government regulation, it seems that the model cannot get far without it.[17]

REGULATED CAPITALISM?

There is another, more fundamental reason why government intervention is essential. Even an economy composed entirely of ethical firms (or worker cooperatives) cannot deal with the systemic nature of the most serious of capitalism's crises. We cannot expect firms to go into the red just to help fight unemployment. We cannot expect oil, gas, and coal companies to put themselves out of business in the name of environmental responsibility. Responding effectively to such systemic crises requires government intervention.

There is little doubt that stronger regulation would help us advance on numerous dimensions.[18] A higher minimum wage, monetary and tax policy aimed at full employment, stronger and more systemic enforcement of antitrust, environmental, and antidiscrimination regulations, etc.—it is not hard to see how government policy changes such as these could make real, tangible improvements in the quality of our lives and the effectiveness of our economy.

But it is important to see the limitations of this model for resolving our bigger challenges. When it comes to the six crises, it would be wishful thinking to imagine we could get enough business-sector support for stronger government action. Let us look at some examples.

Consider, first, the prospects for getting business-sector support for eliminating the unemployment caused by our irrational economic system. There is probably no way a market-based capitalist economy can avoid economic cycles; but arguably these cycles—and the waves of unemployment they cause—could be considerably shortened by aggressive government action in the form of stimulus spending.[19] The famous economist John Maynard Keynes demonstrated how it works. Any unemployed worker would be offered a decent paying job in the public sector. There is a long list of social and environmental needs they could be employed to address; but even if they produced nothing of value, the wages that the government paid them would be almost entirely spent on goods and services produced by the private sector. Seeing this new demand, private-sector businesses would be prompted to reemploy more workers, and public-sector employment could then be cut back again. Government expenditures on this temporary job creation would be financed by borrowing—borrowing funds that would otherwise, in a recession period, have remained idle in any case. And the subsequent growth in incomes would be taxed to pay off the debt incurred by the government borrowing in the downturn.

One might imagine that the "enlightened self-interest" of business leaders should lead them to support such Keynesian policies. After all, business suffers too in these business-cycle downturns, as profits contract and the stock market falls. But in reality, while business leaders might wring their hands about the suffering of the unemployed, they are overwhelmingly opposed to a policy of full employment.[20]

There are several reasons for this, but the most fundamental is simply that unemployment has a beneficial effect for business, albeit one that is hard to mention in polite society: it acts as a disciplinary device over employees. The most basic factor driving the economy into a downswing is poor profit prospects, and a sure way for a company to improve profits rapidly is to cut wages and push employees to work harder and longer. Higher unemployment holds down wages, and saps employees' willingness to resist autocratic managers.

If regulated capitalism does not seem capable of dealing with economic crises and their attendant unemployment, could it do any better with the crisis of disempowerment? Yes, an organized political effort could conceivably lead to new legislation facilitating union recognition, enforcing better workplace standards, improving unemployment coverage, and funding retraining schemes. But no, it is hard to see how even such legislation could successfully challenge the control of top executives over business decisions, let alone dislodge investors from their privileged place in setting corporate objectives.

Could regulation forestall the deepening environmental crisis? Again, it is hard to see how. Confronting climate change would require regulations that are stringent enough to force radical changes in the conduct of some of the world's biggest and most powerful companies—perhaps even putting them out of business. That would include not only the oil and gas and coal companies such as Chevron and ExxonMobil and Peabody Coal but also the companies whose products run on oil—companies such as General Motors, Boeing, United Airlines, and FedEx. And further afield, there are other, vast swaths of industry whose products and processes contribute to climate change, and which therefore must be radically and rapidly transformed—in agriculture, cement, mining, forest products, fishing, water systems, many consumer products—and here too we will need to confront huge and powerful companies.[21] Could our legislators and regulators succeed in this battle? It is difficult to see how, so long as we have a private enterprise, capitalist economy.

As for our multifaceted social crisis, stronger government regulation would surely be enormously helpful. Consider how much progress we could make if government enforced stronger antidiscrimination measures and higher safety standards in workplaces, and mandated that firms provided more maternity and family leave, longer annual vacations, and bigger contributions to unemployment insurance. But now consider the reaction to such regulations that we are sure to encounter from the business sector. Opposition would be ferocious to the accompanying higher tax rates and to the encroachments on the prerogatives of the private sector.

Finally, in the international arena, can we imagine our government playing a more constructive role? Not realistically—at least, not where there are economic interests at stake. It is wishful thinking to imagine that our government could embrace international collaboration if that collaboration required that the government act against the profit interests of any substantial segment of US business. The case of climate change is altogether too obvious. Arms sales is a second case: our arms industry is huge, and the United States is by far the biggest exporter of arms in the world, so efforts to limit the arms trade, even where the trade is with terribly oppressive governments, have consistently failed.[22] Our government is an enthusiastic booster of the international sale not only of big-ticket items reserved for the military but also of small arms that fuel violence by nonstate actors. Intellectual property is a third arena of contention: developing countries cannot afford the exorbitant prices demanded by US pharmaceutical companies, so many have chosen to ignore those patents, particularly where they are dealing with health emergencies like HIV. The US government has consistently supported the pharmaceutical industry interests in threatening sanctions against such countries.[23]

Despite the similarity between the labels, social democracy and democratic socialism are very different models. Where democratic socialism aims to replace private enterprise with public ownership, social democracy leaves the core of the economy in the hands of private investors and relies on government to mitigate the various problems that might follow from that by stronger regulations and by more extensive government investment in social welfare. Some social-democratic countries—notably Sweden and Norway—embody a "corporatist" model in which government, industry federations, and centralized union confederations cooperate in shaping national and industry-level policies, while within firms, unions and management cooperate in "codetermination" structures. The successes of the Nordic social democracies—Sweden, Denmark, Norway, Finland, Iceland— stand as testimony to the possible benefits of such a powerful government role and of such cooperation between government, business, and labor.[24]

After nearly 40 years of neoliberal capitalism, it is hardly surprising that many progressives look to the Nordic social democracies for inspiration. This model combines ethical- and regulated-capitalism models with strong environmental regulation, with expansive state-sponsored welfare provisions covering healthcare, maternity and paternity leave, childcare, and training, and with institutionalized forms of labor-management cooperation. Over the past couple of decades, these countries have retreated considerably from that model and turned toward neoliberal capitalism, and more recently their hospitality toward refugees has provoked the emergence of an ethnonationalist populist backlash; nevertheless, the model remains an attractive one. These countries have been far better able than the United States to assure a decent standard of living for working people.[25]

However, one fundamental constraint limits the value of social democracy as a model for dealing with the six major crises we face. In this model, progress is limited to those steps that do not harm the profitability of the private-enterprise business sector. While there are surely many progressive changes that are possible within this constraint, many changes that we need to overcome these crises are not.[26]

First, the social democratic model leaves the country at the mercy of the instability of the capitalist core of the economy.[27] The Nordic governments' efforts to stimulate growth in the face of recent recessions led them to roll back egalitarian policies. These countries have not been able to avoid long periods of extraordinarily high rates of youth unemployment—far higher than in the United States. Families spend ever-greater shares of their income on a continually accelerating housing bubble. Household debt has soared since the 1990s, to levels far above even those in the United States, and far beyond anything sustainable.

Second, employees in the Nordic social democracies achieve only limited empowerment within enterprises. Yes, employees have the right to elect some representatives to the firm's governing boards—a great advance over the neoliberal capitalism model here in the United States. But these representatives are decidedly junior partners. Their power is not on a par with that of investors and employers. Employers are still agents of financial investors, and when push comes to shove, it is these financial interests that prevail. The core of the economy remains in private hands, and as a result, society's wealth remains very concentrated. The richest 10% in Norway control 50% of that nation's wealth; in Sweden, 67%; and Denmark, 69%. These ratios are all lower than the 75% we see in the United States, but they belie social democracy's claim to egalitarianism and worker empowerment.[28]

Third, responding to the environmental crisis is going to require steps that hurt the profitability of many private enterprises—too many to expect the private sector to acquiesce willingly. Environmentally, the Nordic countries (apart from Denmark) have a smaller per-person "environmental footprint" than the United States, but no smaller than other advanced economies that are not particularly social democratic, such as France, Italy, and the United Kingdom.[29] While their records in reducing CO_2 emissions are better than the United States', that is far too low a bar.

In their international relations, the Nordic social democracies have been inspiring in some dimensions. Most notably, Sweden has made feminism and gender equity a key consideration in their foreign relations.[30] But it is a policy that does not cost Sweden much. In contrast, curtailing its huge arms exports business would put the government in opposition with a powerful industry led by such firms as Saab and Bofors.[31] Sweden is the third-largest arms exporter per capita, after Israel and Russia, and continues to sell arms to Saudi Arabia, even during the atrocious Yemen war.[32]

Or consider Norway's declared support for international efforts to fight climate change. Notwithstanding these pronouncements and some very positive policy initiatives, Norway's economy remains largely dependent on oil and gas exports—it is the world's 15th-largest producer and the fifth-largest on a per capita basis—and is aggressively developing new oil fields in the North and Barents Seas. The country's own greenhouse gas emissions are low, but if we include the emissions that Norway exports with its petroleum sales, it turns out to be the seventh-largest emitter in the world.[33]

BETTING ON TECHNOLOGY?

The dramatic effects of the ongoing digital transformation have prompted many progressives to see this technological revolution as the harbinger of positive social change. It certainly represents a striking further development in the socialization of production, facilitating more effective management of interdependencies between and within firms, generating huge gains in efficiency and a cornucopia of new products and services.

Moreover, this digital technology revolution seems remarkably in tune with the needs of our time. Four opportunities seem particularly exciting. Digital technology might allow us to move from a system based on huge hierarchical corporations to networks of smaller firms and workers' cooperatives. It supports peer production networks that might replace intellectual property monopolies. It could allow us to reduce work time dramatically. And it could greatly enrich democratic deliberation and voting. This is a striking contrast with the last great technological revolution, which yielded the mass-production assembly line—hardly an inspiring image of a better future!

What, then, will it take to redeem this promise? Capitalism is such a dynamic system, so open to technological innovation, that competitive pressure will surely lead firms to adopt and deploy these new technologies. But will this competitive process realize those opportunities and transform society in a direction more consistent with the needs of people and the planet? That is the hope offered by a variety of techno-utopian perspectives.[34]

I think this hope is misplaced. Let's review the four main opportunity areas in turn. In each case, we will see exciting opportunities to leverage this technological revolution for a better world, but we will also see how the basic features of the capitalist system stand in the way of realizing these benefits. The basic tension between the progressive opportunities created by the socialization of production and the limitations imposed by the capitalist private-enterprise system has never been as profound as it stands today in the context of this latest technological revolution.

First, some see the new technologies driving a shift from large-scale, centralized corporations to small-scale, local production.[35] They highlight two main trends. The first is the development of low-cost digital production technologies such as 3D printing and computer-controlled machining tools. These technologies reduce economies of scale and scope in production. With older, predigital technologies, a larger volume of production allowed the factory, warehouse, or office to invest in more-specialized equipment and employees, and to spread overhead costs over a larger volume of output, and thus reduce per-unit costs. With the new technologies, at least in some industries, firms can now produce one or ten units of a product at close to the same per-unit cost as 10,000 units, and indeed produce many variants of a product at a similar per-unit cost as the same total volume of a single variant.

New digital technologies reduce not only production costs but also communications costs. Think of the Internet and the associated technologies such as cloud computing, social media, and mobile telephones. These technologies reduce the cost of interfirm coordination. And this should enable networks of small, specialized firms to compete more successfully with big, vertically integrated firms. Using older, predigital technologies, it was cumbersome and expensive for a firm to work with a supplier to refine iteratively the design of a component, because that involved sending engineers back and forth. It was often easier for the firm to produce such customized components for themselves. By contrast, with new digital technologies, digital prototypes can be shared between supplier and customer on their computer screens and tested in computer simulations. The cost of coordination is far lower.

That new communications technologies allow firms to expand their networks is indubitable. This is part of the socialization process, facilitated by and in turn facilitating technological advance. However, a trend to smaller firms seems unlikely to materialize, for the simple reason that these same production and communication technologies also enable large corporations to increase the efficiency and flexibility of their internal operations.[36]

But let's assume we do see this trend toward smaller firms. How would such a transformation affect us? On the one hand, as its proponents argue, such a shift might help mitigate our crisis of disempowerment. An economy composed of smaller firms and flexible networks might indeed be more responsive to the needs of employees and local communities. Moreover, with lower capital requirements, it would be easier to set these firms up as worker cooperatives.

On the other hand, this shift alone can offer little relief from the other five crises. The problem is simple: the sources of these other crises lie beyond the individual firm, in the broader structure of a capitalist political economy. An economy of small flexible networks would still be characterized by myopic capitalist competition between those firms and networks. So we would still suffer the economic irrationality of recurring recessions and wasteful production. Government would still be constrained by the need to protect the profitability of this newly configured private-enterprise sector. The profit pressures on these small firms would lead them, just as it leads big corporations today, to degrade the environmental, social, and international preconditions of our well-being.[37]

The digital revolution also challenges property rights, by making such rights more difficult to enforce. Take an example. The original introduction of sound-recording technologies revolutionized the music industry by making it possible to sell many more records than concert-hall seats. And more recently, the digitizing of music and distribution via the Internet has reduced the cost of duplicating those recordings to virtually zero. And indeed, original music itself can be produced by electronic synthesizers and by electronically sampling existing recordings.[38] At the same time, this technology has made it more difficult to enforce intellectual property rights.

Seizing on these features of digital technology, proponents of "open source" argue that they portend a new era of "peer production." Access to digital content can be made free and open to all, as can participation in elaborating this content and access to the resulting output. Open-source software (Linux) now runs most of the servers supporting the Internet. It is peer-produced—mainly through uncompensated contributions by developers, each working on aspects of the system that they feel need improvement. Wikipedia is an inspiring example of the power of open-source peer production.

These examples are inspiring, showing how much voluntary cooperation can achieve, without the coercive pressure of bosses or market competition. Peer production provides one model of how we could overcome workplace disempowerment and reliance on production for profit.

It is less clear, however, that many of society's needs can be met this way. First, most of this peer production is in fields where not much equipment is needed beyond basic computers and access to the Internet. It is not clear how this model generalizes to industries that need substantial capital investment. Second, peer production projects are all characterized by a high degree of "modularity," in which the components are quite independent of each other (as in Wikipedia's individual entries) or where their interdependence is managed by easy-to-enforce interface standards (such as those required to add a new module to the Linux system). But much of what we rely on every day is not modular in this sense. That is why, for example, the vast majority of houses are still built one at a time, by craftsmen who tailor each subsystem (say, the electrical wiring and lighting or the plumbing) to the others (the physical layout of the house and the spatial configuration of other subsystems). Moreover, even if this modular form could be generalized, we would still need a radical transformation of our social system to ensure that the contributors to these peer production projects earned what they needed to live on.[39]

The third domain affected by the digital revolution is employment. The acceleration of the new digital production technologies—the most commonly mentioned in this context are robotics and artificial intelligence—could mean that in the not-so-distant future our economy will simply not need so many workers. If we could use these technologies to reduce the burden of work, that would go a long way to resolving some aspects of the crises of economic irrationality and of workplace disempowerment. But how do we get there?

We have reasons to be skeptical of the forecast that this technological revolution will generate a massive wave of unemployment.[40] Yes, capitalism has always generated unemployment, but major crises of unemployment have had only little to do with technology changes. (In part, that's because growing unemployment reduces consumer demand, which in turn makes further investment in automation unprofitable.) Nevertheless, it is possible that this technological revolution is different from earlier ones, and that we face the prospect of massive and permanent unemployment: what then should be our response?

Some have proposed a "universal basic income" to protect people against the negative effects of this disruption and to open up new opportunities for self-development. The appeal of this concept is clear. If the income level were set high enough, it would greatly mitigate the economic insecurity of working people. It would set a high floor for wages and help rectify the power imbalance between employers and employees. And it would allow more people to engage in creative or caring activities that are currently not rewarded in the marketplace. Moreover, the underlying assumption is reasonable: at least in the advanced economies, we have surely reached a level of productivity that should allow us to guarantee everyone a decent standard of living, regardless of their employment status.[41]

Three problems, however, confront this scenario. First, it is difficult to see how to assure the financing required to assure people of anything more than poverty-level income. And the higher the income level, the more people would leave wage employment to take it, making its financing less and less feasible as the scheme got closer and closer to its goal.

Second, if the average workweek needed to meet our needs was, say, 20 hours, it would not make sense to have half the population working 40 hours while the other half did not have to work at all. If indeed the digital revolution proves to reduce dramatically (rather than incrementally) labor requirements for a wide (rather than narrow) swath of the economy, then the more logical thing to do—and a far more inspiring goal—would be to use this as an opportunity to reorganize work and to reduce work hours and maintain pay levels for everyone.[42]

And third, it is hard to see how universal basic income would prove to be a galvanizing idea when there is such a vast range of needs that currently go unmet—environmental remediation, renewal of dilapidated infrastructure, care of our children, our sick, and our elderly, just to name a few. These needs are unmet for the simple reason that private enterprise has not found a way to make their satisfaction profitable enough. While some of these needs might be met through the voluntary activity of those benefiting from the basic income, many others would not. The most straightforward answer to mass unemployment would not be to offer universal basic income to those who can no longer find waged work, but rather to create publicly funded programs to put people to work meeting these societal needs. A federal jobs guarantee would be a first step.[43] And we have already seen that the implementation of such a guarantee would necessitate a far more radical change in our political-economic system.

Democracy is the fourth main domain affected by the digital revolution. The ease of communication afforded by the Internet enables us to imagine how democratic governance could be enhanced by more frequent citizen consultation and voting, by wider debate, and by more systematic information dissemination—much more than is allowed by our traditional cycle of elections and predigital media. These are exciting prospects. But it is difficult to see how they can materialize—or more precisely, how they can materialize in a form that strengthens rather than undermines democracy—absent a fundamental societal transformation.

This review of the main models of reformed capitalism leads to a strong conclusion: they all offer useful ideas that would take us forward from the prevailing neoliberal model, but none of them can resolve our six main crises. We cannot hope to overcome these crises and unleash the benefits of advanced technology so long as the core of our economy is composed of capitalist firms driven by profit. Indeed, the tension between the progressive socialization of production and the maintenance of private enterprise ensures that these crises are destined to deepen. We need to replace market competition with a process that allows us to decide together, democratically, on what and how we produce. Democratic socialism is the name we give to this process.

CHAPTER 5

Managing Our Economy, Democratically and Effectively

G iven the degree of socialization of production we have already achieved, we can resolve the crises we face and assure the progress we need only if we socialize to a comparable extent the control of our society's productive resources. To put it differently, we need to ensure that we use our resources to meet society's needs rather than meeting only private enterprises' need for profitability. That is the fundamental goal of democratic socialism.

In a democratic-socialist system, we would decide together on our economic, environmental, and social goals, and we would manage our resources strategically to pursue those goals. Instead of leaving it to individual firms and market competition, we would decide democratically on the volume and mix of products society would produce; the technologies we use to create those products; the level and types of investment going to the various enterprises, industries, regions, and R&D initiatives; economy-wide working hours and pay levels; and the economic, environmental, and social criteria that we use to assess government programs, enterprise performance, and investment proposals.

If we are to overcome our crises of workplace disempowerment and government unresponsiveness, this economy-wide strategic management process must be democratic. But it must also be effective in overcoming the other crises we face. At the most general level, for our system to be effective, it must meet three further challenges. It must support innovation: we face crises whose solutions will require innovative contributions from the many, not only from a select few. It must be efficient: it would be foolish to assume that in a democratic-socialist society material scarcity would simply disappear or that efficiency would no longer matter. And finally, it must ensure that people are sufficiently motivated to contribute to those innovation and efficiency goals. Even in utopia, we cannot assume humans are angels.

How could democratic socialism meet these challenges of democracy, innovation, efficiency, and motivation? Answering this question calls for a difficult balance of realism and imagination. On the one hand, our picture of this system would not be realistic if it ignored the basic laws of physics or psychology, nor if it implied a degradation in people's quality of life.

On the other hand, to draw such a picture requires us to imagine a world we have never experienced—and that is difficult. Living in ancient Greece, where the economy was based on slave labor, the philosopher Aristotle—one of the greatest minds of his era or indeed any other—was convinced that political democracy with a universal right to vote could never succeed.[1] Yet most of us today are committed to that model, even if we accept that its implementation is never perfect. The analysis of the earlier chapters has led us to the conclusion that the democratic principle must be extended from the political realm to the economic. But we have grown up in a capitalist world, so it is as difficult for us to imagine a viable economic democracy as it was for Aristotle to imagine a viable political democracy.

In the paragraphs that follow, I offer a preliminary sketch, extrapolating from the practice of strategic management in some of our biggest corporations. I argue that in their internal workings, each of these corporations is like a small economy, and that within some of them we find a miniature working model of a surprisingly democratic and effective way of controlling that economy. To enable the principles underlying this model to take root at the enterprise level and to deploy these principles at the scale of the whole economy, we will need to match the new system of *control* with a new system of *ownership*, and I will sketch the resulting democratic-socialist system in the following chapter. First, however, let us try to imagine what democratic and effective control over our economy would look like.

MANAGING THE WHOLE ECONOMY

To bring democracy to the control of individual enterprises, we need to put each of them under a governing board composed of representatives of employees and other external stakeholders. If the board represented this spectrum of interests rather than only the interests of capitalist investors as boards do today, it could orient the enterprise to serve people and planet, not only profits.

If, however, we are going to democratize the economic sphere, it is not enough to democratize the governing boards of individual enterprises. Two further steps will be needed.

First, management *within* these enterprises must also be democratized, replacing the autocratic, top-down control that is characteristic of capitalist firms. This democratization might be easier if today's massive (capitalist) enterprises are broken down into smaller (cooperative) ones. And, as we saw in the earlier chapter, perhaps the new digital technologies will help us move in that direction. However, we would not want to forego all the efficiency benefits of economies of scale and scope. So we will need to find a way to ensure the democratic quality of management even in large-scale enterprises.

Second, we will need to assert democratic control not only over activities *within* enterprises, but also over the interdependencies *between* enterprises. The earlier chapters showed that given the extensive socialization of production we have already achieved, there are several critical, systemic interdependencies that cannot be managed effectively through a decentralized process, no matter how decisions are made within each of the participating enterprises. Even the combination of democratized enterprise boards and democratized internal management will not eliminate cyclical unemployment, nor equip us to ensure sufficiently rapid and radical CO_2 emissions reductions, nor allow us to address our various social crises and international challenges. These broader, more systemic interdependencies must be managed centrally—by a process that aligns the local enterprise-level choices with needs we define democratically at the higher levels of the region, industry, and nation.

This is a difficult point for many progressives, because it implies a significant degree of centralization in our decision-making. We are accustomed to seeing centralization as a tool of domination and exploitation, so it may be difficult to imagine how it can be a tool for enhancing democracy. Nevertheless, unless we equip ourselves with higher levels of governance that can challenge local enterprises whose actions would detract from society's overall well-being, and unless these higher levels can undertake investments on behalf of us all, there is no way we can overcome the economic, environmental, social, or international crises that confront us.

Here, we bump up against the limits of our imagination. It is not obvious how we could assure the democratic quality of centralized decision-making on such a vast scale. It is even less obvious how we could ensure that such a system was effective in dealing with the other three challenges—let alone more effective than one based on private enterprise, with all its limitations. How could innovation be sustained without the benefit of the capitalist market system's decentralized entrepreneurship? How could efficiency be maintained in such a system, without the benefit of external competitive pressure or managerial command authority? And how could such a system hope to maintain people's motivation when they are torn between simultaneous calls to subordinate themselves to the efficiency needs of the collectivity and calls for individualistic, divergent thinking to support innovation?

LEARNING FROM CAPITALIST ENTERPRISES

If we are looking for answers to these questions, I propose that we start by examining some of our largest business firms. Yes, this is not an obvious place to look, but three factors make these firms' experience a valuable source of lessons for democratic socialism.

First, the largest of these enterprises are massive—the size of quite a few nations. Reflecting the progressive socialization of production, the scale and complexity of some of these firms are truly astounding. Walmart has 11,700 retail outlets around the world, employs 2.3 million people, and sells 4 million products coming from over 100,000 suppliers. Amazon has over 740 distribution facilities across the globe, and a total of nearly 2 billion items are shipped from these warehouses each year to approximately 300 million customers.

Second, the activity within many of these firms—that is, the activity that takes place between the supply of inputs and sale of outputs—is coordinated mainly by strategic management rather than by capitalist market-type competition between subunits.[2] That is, their subunits do not pursue their own profitability in competition with other subunits. Instead, they work toward common objectives and harmonize their plans for doing so. If they charge other subunits for materials and services they provide, they do so at prices that reflect the overarching goals of the corporation rather than the independent profit goals of the transacting subunits. The firm's management system aims to minimize negative externalities in their interunit interactions—such as when one unit's plan to withdraw from a new market would undermine the competitive position of another unit—and to maximize positive externalities—such as when one unit has developed a new technology that could be shared with others.[3]

The third reason for studying these large firms is that each of these firms confronts internally, in the microcosm of their own organization, the same four challenges as we will confront in our socialist management of the entire economy. And in their efforts to meet these challenges, some of these firms, in particular those that follow what I called earlier the high-road approach, have developed organizational principles that we could use at that larger scale: I call them *Collaborative Strategizing, Collaborative Innovating, Collaborative Learning*, and *Collaborative Working*.[4] The emphasis is on collaboration—working together to define both our goals and what we need to do to meet these goals.[5]

Of course, in even the most advanced high-road firms, such collaboration is limited and often undermined by the persistent profit and growth imperative, the pressure of capitalist competition, and the power of employers over employees. However, if we were to democratize the governance of these enterprises, collaboration could be made more systematic within each workplace. And in a democratic-socialist society, these principles could be scaled up to help us manage democratically and effectively our economic activity at the regional, industry, and national scales too.

Before describing each of these principles, we should pause to note that it should not be so surprising that our vision of democratic socialism be informed by the management practices of capitalist firms. If socialism is going to be an advance over capitalism, it is in part because socialism can build on capitalism's accomplishments. Among these accomplishments, the socialization of production is perhaps the greatest. This socialization has yielded not only dramatic progress in technology but also powerful new techniques for the strategic management of huge, complex enterprises. The techniques that firms have developed to manage these internal interdependencies are a precious legacy. Critics surely have a point when they argue that these techniques—just like technologies—are currently designed and used to buttress capitalist exploitation and domination. But it stands to reason that democratic socialism can nevertheless derive much benefit from the principles that underlie these techniques and technologies, adapting them to the new society's needs.[6]

COLLABORATIVE STRATEGIZING

If we are to manage our enterprises, regions, industries, and the overall national economy to overcome the six crises, we will need a process that allows us to identify our common goals, develop plans and allocate resources for achieving them, and revise those plans and goals over time in light of our successes and shortcomings.[7] Big capitalist firms do this internally through their strategic management process. In many of these firms, strategic management is a very autocratic top-down process—quite the opposite of democratic. High-road firms, however, have developed a different approach to strategic management, one that is much closer in spirit to our democratic-socialist aspirations, even if in practice they do not take it far enough.

The high-road strategy aims to engage the entire workforce in finding creative solutions to business problems. In their strategic management process, these firms therefore try to empower lower-level managers and front-line employees. And in doing so, they have confronted, in microcosm, the same democracy challenge we would face in our democratic-socialist efforts to manage the whole economy. That challenge can be stated simply: centralized decision-making seems antithetical to the autonomy that many people see as essential to real empowerment.

The key to meeting this challenge, these high-road firms have found, is participation. Where activities are interdependent, empowerment depends not on autonomy but on participation. After all, autonomy is only a negative form of empowerment: it represents freedom *from* coercive constraint. It is an important form of empowerment, to be sure, but we must also consider the positive form—freedom *to* realize one's potential.[8] Autonomy does not represent much empowerment if our individual autonomy impedes us from working together to capitalize on opportunities that require collaboration.

Effective strategic management in a large, complex organization requires centralization, but centralization can create empowerment (in the form of freedom-to) when it is combined with participation. Centralization is about whether you are autonomous in your decisions or you are subject to system-wide policies that apply to everyone. Participation is about how much voice you have in setting these system-wide policies. Centralization is the opposite of autonomy and freedom-from; but a centralized structure can be more democratic or less so, depending on how participative it is.[9] Of course, participation in the form of *direct* democracy may not be possible in the governance of very large organizations or societies; but participation in the form of *representative* democracy can operate at any scale.[10]

The combination of centralization and participation may seem paradoxical. Centralization is often assumed to be the opposite of participation. Indeed, in capitalist firms and societies, it usually is. Decision-making authority is most often centralized in the hands of powerful elites, and this centralization serves as a weapon against subordinates—and a weapon against their participation—because the economic interests of those in power are so often antithetical to the interests of those below them. In capitalist firms, executives typically centralize decision-making in their own hands and restrict both the range and intensity of employee participation. For many progressives, the idea of centralization has been tainted by this history.

High-road firms try to escape this legacy and institutionalize participative centralization in their strategic management process by using the principle I call Collaborative Strategizing. Under this principle, a wide range of people in the firm have a voice in shaping the organization's goals and in deciding how best to reach them.

These firms' success in implementing this principle is limited by the persistence of the basic capitalist structure of the intrafirm employment relation and interfirm market competition. As a result of these factors, participation rarely extends all the way down the organization's authority hierarchy to front-line employees. It rarely extends far up into the critical strategic issues facing the firm. It rarely extends far across peer subunits. And it rarely gives much real influence to those who are consulted. The experience of such disappointingly limited programs has also tainted the idea of participation.

Notwithstanding these limitations, we can find instructive efforts at Collaborative Strategizing in many high-road firms.[11] Let us examine some of them and consider how the principle could be strengthened within enterprises and extended to democratic economy-wide strategic management.

To take the centralization dimension first, we should note the extraordinary success of many large firms in integrating all the information needed for strategic management. Modern systems of "enterprise resource planning" and "sales and operations planning" integrate essentially all the data that a modern enterprise needs for its strategizing—everything from the financial and accounting data to engineering data on products and processes, demand and sales forecasts, project management tools, personnel records, and interconnections with customers and suppliers.[12] More advanced versions even incorporate "knowledge repositories" and allow employees to identify rapidly the most knowledgeable experts on any issue. Such systems break down the walls between the organizational fiefdoms that are so common in larger firms, and thus lay an essential foundation for centralized decision-making. The effectiveness of these systems is all the more impressive when we recall that it was not so many years ago that one of the popular arguments against socialism was that the modern economy was too complex, and that no central agency would be able to capture or collate all the relevant information in a timely manner, especially given that much of this information was in physical quantities and engineering specifications rather than financial in nature.[13]

Second, we should note the development of techniques for ensuring the effective harmonization of subunit goals. Large corporations have for many decades relied on a cascade process for translating top-level strategic goals into subunit goals and into the corresponding allocation of resources down through the various layers of the organization. If the top level decides, for example, that the firm should enter a new geographical market, the next level down responds with a plan for how to structure that initiative and how much it will cost, and further down again that plan is in turn translated into assignments of specific teams and specific budgets. This cascading process often integrates the identification of goals and budgets for the coming period with the assessment by the higher-level units of lower-level units' performance in the last period. This downward cascade, moreover, is not restricted to financial aspects of performance. Similar cascading processes have been developed for new product planning. In the "Quality Function Deployment" process, for example, features that are valued by customers are translated into detailed engineering requirements and then into design tasks for specific employee teams.

The development of this vast apparatus of centralized strategic management has been married in many high-road firms with equally impressive efforts to expand bottom-up participation. In these high-road firms' cascade process, the higher-level goals are offered as "proposals" for review by the lower-levels—not as commands. At each step in the process, the lower level is encouraged to push back if the goals proposed by the higher levels are overly ambitious because they ignore local constraints, or if they are insufficiently ambitious because they do not capitalize on local opportunities and capabilities. These firms also encourage horizontal participation, by creating forums where people from different parts of the organization as well as from several vertical layers of authority work together to assess past performance and develop strategic goals and budgets.

Kaiser Permanente (Kaiser, or KP, for short) is one organization that offers an interesting image of Collaborative Strategizing in action. The scale of activities brought under Kaiser's common strategy is impressive. Kaiser is the largest healthcare provider and one of the largest healthcare insurance companies in the United States. In 2017, it had nearly 12 million health-plan members, about 208,000 employees, 21,000 physicians, 54,000 nurses, 39 hospitals, and 680 medical offices. Kaiser is unusual in its scope as well as scale, bringing the participating doctors, hospitals, and insurance activities under a single unified strategy. This results in enormous savings in administrative costs. It has also led to much better preventive care than is possible in the decentralized structures that predominate in most of the US healthcare system, where insurance companies battle healthcare providers, hospitals compete for physicians, and physicians in independent practices compete with each other.[14]

Collaborative Strategizing was institutionalized in various ways at Kaiser. One key component was what Kaiser called their "Value Compass." The Value Compass contributed to Kaiser's centralization by specifying a system-wide commitment to four key strategic goals, represented visually as four points on a compass: best quality, best service, most affordable, and best place to work.[15] On each of these four dimensions, specific goals were cascaded down from headquarters to regions and from there to all the facilities and to all the departments within each facility. At each level, "dashboards" tracked progress on all four dimensions relative to goals and relative to external, best-in-class performers. This information was widely shared, and its interpretation and action implications were widely debated. Performance on each dimension was woven into leaders' evaluation and incentive plans, and was the basis for bonuses for front-line, unionized employees. Operational leaders were held accountable for progress toward these goals. Each dimension of performance was considered important in itself, not merely as a tool for improving financial performance.[16]

Kaiser is impressive not only for its centralization but also for its level of participation. This participation reflected Kaiser's long, storied history as a high-road enterprise.[17] Unions have been an essential part of Kaiser Permanente going back to its founding in 1945. Today, about 80% of Kaiser's nonphysician, nonmanagerial employees are unionized, including nurses, technicians, clerical employees, social workers, food and janitorial service staff, optometrists, and IT personnel. In 1997, a coalition of most of the unions at Kaiser, led by the Service Employees International Union, signed a historic agreement launching a labor–management partnership that is unique in its scale, ambition, and durability.[18] That partnership gave institutional robustness to an exceptional level of participation. And due in no small measure to the success of this partnership arrangement, Kaiser performed near the top of the rankings of healthcare delivery organizations on almost all measures of clinical quality, innovation, efficiency, and patient satisfaction.[19] Anonymous surveys of employees showed high morale as well as widespread support for the partnership process and its outcomes. These outcomes included wage and benefit gains as well as growth in union membership.[20]

The participation dimension of Collaborative Strategizing was institutionalized in several ways at Kaiser. First, across the various layers of management involved in the cascading planning process, lower levels were encouraged to communicate upward their concerns and innovative solutions. In some cases, top-level goals for improving clinical results were seen by regional units as too aggressive, and when these units pushed back, the goals were moderated. In other cases, local units saw opportunities for cost reductions that were not visible to headquarters, and when they brought forward those opportunities, headquarters revised their goals accordingly.

Second, participation was unusually strong not only vertically but also horizontally, across departments. One key technique for achieving this was the "matrix" authority structure, in which managers from different departments shared authority and responsibility for activities that required cross-department collaboration. Matrix management has a bad reputation across much US industry. More autocratic organizations typically reject it because it requires managers to share authority and responsibility. For this sharing to work effectively, these managers need to feel committed to some shared higher-level goals, but autocratic leaders rely on command authority and have little patience with efforts to cultivate subordinates' concern for such higher-level goals. Kaiser, by contrast, valued the horizontal participation that the matrix structure affords, and so persisted in creating conditions for its successful deployment, in particular through coaching and financial incentives.[21]

Third, participation reached both far up into strategic issues and far down into the organization. The top-level goals of the Value Compass were not dictated by top management; instead, they were jointly defined through intensive dialogue within and between all three components of Kaiser (health plan, hospitals, physician groups) and the union coalition.[22] As a result of this participation, the organization's top-level strategic goals were not to satisfy bond-holders or increase market share, but instead were ones that mattered to employees just as much as to management and doctors. Nor were they, from the employees' point of view, simply about ensuring the organization's financial success so as to preserve their jobs and wages. These goals were values-based, not merely instrumental.[23]

In parallel with the unusually participative structures within the management hierarchy, KP had a system of joint labor/management forums, at the national, regional, facility, and department levels. This joint governance structure undoubtedly added organizational overhead in the form of more meetings, but it also helped ensure that the strategic decisions made at higher levels were seen as legitimate by employees and union representatives at lower levels. It gave employees confidence that these decisions were oriented toward their shared interests rather than toward management's separate interests.

This legitimacy enabled Kaiser to undertake several changes that otherwise would have generated major conflict. Some of these changes involved big staff reductions in clerical departments whose tasks were being auto-mated by the shift to electronic health records (an arena in which Kaiser was a world leader). These reductions were handled without conflict thanks to advance joint planning and the partnership's commitment to retraining and redeploying workers whose jobs had disappeared.[24]

Kaiser is far from alone in its efforts to democratize the strategic management process. Indeed, pressured by intense competition and accelerating change in their business and technology environments, a small but growing number of firms have gone even further, opting for what has been called an "open strategy" model based on crowd-sourcing. This model typically invites employees, and often external stakeholders too, to join Internet-enabled company-wide dialogues on key strategic issues.[25]

Collaborative Strategizing has proven effective at Kaiser and at various scales in other firms. That should give us confidence that in a democratic-socialist system, this principle could be deployed to ensure even wider and deeper participation in the strategizing efforts of enterprises under democratized governance.

Moreover, given its effectiveness at the massive scale of KP, it is not diffi-cult to imagine how the key elements of Collaborative Strategizing could be scaled up to guide strategic management at the even-wider scale of the re-gion, industry, and nation. The key elements are not intrinsically limited to the scale of a single enterprise. These elements are all scalable—democratic determination of top-level goals (paralleling the Value Compass), a cascading process for translating these downward to lower levels while en-couraging upward communication of concerns and suggestions from those lower levels, and forums for horizontal (cross-unit) and vertical (cross-level) dialogue in this planning process.

Imagine, for example, how we could use the Collaborative Strategizing principle to guide the country's much-needed rapid transition away from fossil fuels. Nationally, we could organize a debate on how rapid this tran-sition will be, and how to balance and integrate the goal of decarbonizing with our other goals such as raising incomes and providing good jobs. Based on the results of this debate, a democratic "national economic council" could identify areas where the national government needs to drive invest-ment (such as in R&D programs aimed at advancing the key technologies and in shutting down the most-polluting activities). Democratic economic councils (elected or selected from the citizenry by lottery[26]) governing cities, states, and industries would bring forward to the national council proposals for how they might contribute to the transition goals. The na-tional council would push back on lower-level proposals where they were not sufficiently aggressive to reach our national goals and where they were incompatible with each other. The dialogue on how to reach our strategic goals would be not only vertical but also horizontal, bringing together representatives of the national council with those from cities, regions, industries, and community groups, to learn from each other's ideas and develop a shared strategy for the transition.

COLLABORATIVE INNOVATING

To deal with the crises we face and to benefit further from the socialization of production, we will need considerable innovation in our technologies, products, and processes. We have much to learn from capitalist firms about how to manage innovation at a very large scale.

Large capitalist firms leverage the socialization of production and their scale to accelerate innovation. They do that by mobilizing a critical mass of experts in centralized R&D units. On the one hand, this allows firms to save money by avoiding duplicative, parallel research efforts in their operating units. And on the other hand, this allows them to "internalize" the positive externalities of R&D. Instead of relying on a capitalist market process that would lead the R&D unit to charge other units for the development and use of their innovations, the firm funds R&D directly out of "taxes" paid to headquarters by the operating units, and makes the innovation freely available to all those units.[27]

Our democratically managed economy would be similarly well served by creating centralized R&D organizations—not only within enterprises, as we see in capitalism, but also at the region, industry, and national levels. Under democratic guidance, these R&D organizations could be tasked with advancing our shared goals—in contrast with corporate R&D, whose mission is always limited and distorted by its subservience to the profit goal.

But the centralization of innovation—whether in a capitalist or socialist system, and whether at the enterprise level or beyond—encounters a potentially important hurdle: does this centralization not weaken innovative entrepreneurship relative to what we see in a decentralized, capitalist, market system? In the capitalist system, entrepreneurs use their tacit knowledge of local circumstances to identify new business opportunities, and market competition among these entrepreneurs sorts out which of these opportunities are in fact profitable. Proponents of capitalism concede that in this market process, coordination among firms and between firms and consumers may be only approximate. That's because coordination here happens only *ex post* (after the fact), as firms discover whether their entrepreneurial bets have paid off or failed. There is therefore some duplication of effort in parallel projects, and some waste of society's re-sources in that trial-and-error process. However, proponents argue, this process promises more innovation and faster growth than *ex ante* (be-fore the fact) coordination via centralized management, because only local entrepreneurs have enough detailed, firsthand knowledge of local conditions. And entrepreneurs will find it difficult if not impossible to com-municate this knowledge to remote managers at corporate headquarters because it is often tacit and difficult to quantify.[28]

In reality, however, not all innovation comes from dispersed entrepre-neurs discovering opportunities in their local operating environments. On the contrary, once the socialization of production has reached even a modest level, the main locus of innovation shifts from local experimen-tation by artisans to the globalized world of science and engineering. Today, much innovation in industry comes from discoveries in science and technology based on research that is conducted far from daily shop-floor operations.

Nevertheless, the risks of overcentralization are real, and so some firms— notably, those that have adopted a high-road strategy—go further in their innovation management than the establishment of centralized R&D units. They recognize that if innovation activity is reserved for a select few spe-cialized personnel, this means forgoing the opportunity to tap the innova-tive ideas of the much larger mass of its employees. They also recognize that when centralized R&D staff develop their innovative ideas in isolation, their innovation efforts are likely to be handicapped by their ignorance about the contexts in which their innovations would be deployed. For example, they may not be aware of the biggest obstacles facing the operational units and may as a result not be directing their efforts at the most fruitful targets. And they may come up with innovative designs that are too difficult to implement.

Recognizing that they are not forced to choose between centralization and participation, high-road firms rely on the principle I call Collaborative Innovating, which encourages innovation in *both* centralized R&D staffs *and* local operating units, working *both* separately *and* jointly. Under the Collaborative Innovating principle, these firms create systems that stimu-late, capture, sift through, and rapidly deploy innovative ideas coming from both central and local units, and create opportunities for staff and line per-sonnel to collaborate in identifying research goals and in undertaking in-novation projects.

If this idea of Collaborative Innovating seems implausible, it is partly because the underlying combination of centralization and participation is unusual, and partly because we are so accustomed to seeing low-road cap-italist firms, eager to save on labor costs, segregate "creative" work (like in

R&D) from "routine" work (in their operations units). Indeed, Collaborative Innovating is costly. It requires training for people at the lower levels, so they can take part effectively in the organization's innovation efforts. And it requires maintaining effective channels of communication between higher and lower levels in the organization and between R&D and operating units. Low-road firms shy away from the associated costs. But high-road firms treat these costs as investments, and trust that they will pay off over the longer term in higher rates of innovation.

Kaiser Permanente also offers an illustration of this collaborative approach to innovation. Innovation efforts at Kaiser were a mix of top-down and bottom-up. In top-down mode, centralized R&D staff units came up with new products, services, and work processes, and brought them to the local, operational, line units. Kaiser worked hard to make this top-down process participative. The staff experts did not work in isolation, but instead joined forces with people in the line units to identify opportunities, design solutions, and develop appropriate implementation plans.[29]

For example: among several central R&D units, Kaiser had created one called the Innovation Consultancy that worked with front-line personnel and patients to identify problem areas and redesign work systems to enhance healthcare delivery. One of their projects, launched in 2007, focused on improving the handoff of information between nurses at the shift change. Nurses are often harried, and this handoff was laborious, so it often failed to communicate key elements—endangering patients' health in the process. Working with front-line nurses and patients, the team developed a new way of managing this task, where the exchange happened at the patient's bedside rather than at the central nursing station. One key advantage: patients were encouraged to participate, to make sure that no critical information was overlooked. The team also developed a new software tool for capturing key elements of the handoff in a standard format. And the innovative handoff procedure was then shared with all KP's hospitals. We should note too that this Innovation Consultancy then went on to create an "Innovation Learning Network" of 16 like-minded healthcare organizations that researched common problems and shared the resulting innovations.[30]

The bottom-up path of innovation was driven mainly through unit-based teams (UBTs). Employees in every department across the entire Kaiser organization were organized into UBTs—over 3,500 of them—operating under management and union co-leadership. In these UBTs, union and nonunion staff, management, and physicians cooperated both in managing their daily work and in innovation efforts aimed at locally relevant Value Compass priorities.[31] Where the department was small enough, all the staff worked together in the UBT, usually meeting weekly to discuss innovation projects. Where the department was larger, the UBT was staffed by volunteer employee representatives. (Proposals developed by such representative UBTs were regularly discussed with the other department members, who were also involved in running experiments designed to test those proposals.) UBT "fairs" allowed teams to share successful innovations widely across departments.

Working in these UBTs, managers and physicians were challenged to give up their hierarchical, status-based authority and to work collaboratively with nurses, technicians, janitors, and clerical personnel.[32] And these front-line personnel were drawn into more creative activity aimed at generating and testing innovative ideas. The projects typically focused on improving service or clinical quality, on reducing costs without impairing quality, employee engagement, staffing, and workplace or patient safety. Some of the UBTs included patients in projects aiming to find ways to improve the patient experience.

Other high-road organizations have developed more technology-enabled approaches to Collaborative Innovating. One of the most impressive was at IBM. IBM employs some 366,000 employees, and IBM Research—the world's largest corporate R&D organization—employs over 3,000 researchers scattered across six countries. It leads the world in patenting. When the CEO, Sam Palmisano, toured the labs in 2006, he was excited by the technologies he saw, but frustrated by how few of them had been translated into useful products and services. A few years earlier, IBM had developed a process for engaging organization-wide discussion about its direction and values; they called it a "jam," evoking jazz improvisation. IBM's leaders decided to deploy this jam process to engage their entire workforce in a collective brainstorming effort aimed at identifying new uses to which these technologies could be put. The "innovation jam" took place over two three-day phases in 2006. It brought together some 150,000 participants—mostly IBM employees and managers, but also some suppliers, customers, and university researchers.[33]

The jam was a massively parallel online conversation, divided into several discussion forums, supported by many interlinked bulletin boards and web pages. Over 46,000 ideas surfaced for how to deploy the new technologies that were under discussion. Senior executives and researchers sifted through the first round to focus on 31 of the most promising, and then a second round of the jam aimed to turn these into business proposals. The result was a corporate commitment of about $100 million to funding for 10 new businesses.[34]

Collaborative Innovating has proven effective at Kaiser and IBM, and that should give us confidence that it could be deployed more widely in a democratically managed economy. It is not difficult to see how it could be introduced in any enterprise under democratized governance. Education, training, and work-time opportunities could be provided to help a wide range of people participate effectively to address the innovation challenges we face.

Moreover, the proven success at the massive scale of Kaiser and IBM gives us confidence that the Collaborative Innovating principle could be scaled up even further to ensure rapid and targeted innovation at the region, industry, and national levels. Its key elements are not limited by scale. All this can be done at any scale: investment in both centralized R&D and local innovation activity; projects that bring together R&D staff and front-line personnel; investments in the requisite training, support, and incentives; overarching goals to orient these innovation efforts. Indeed, we already have some key elements of such a national structure for the health-care industry in the National Institutes of Health and for the defense base in the Defense Advanced Research Projects Agency, and these models could be adapted for other industries.[35]

To make this idea more concrete, let us see how we could deploy the Collaborative Innovating principle to support the rapid decarbonization transition discussed in the previous section. We need massive investments in R&D to advance technology for solar energy, wind power, energy storage, and so forth. The national economic council would deploy federal funds to create several national R&D programs aimed at the critical technologies we need. University labs would be invited to submit proposals to participate and receive funding. We would also want to stimulate local innovation hubs dedicated to developing ways to reduce our energy consumption, for example through home and commercial building insulation and through wider and cheaper public transportation options. The national and local innovation efforts would be in dialogue and would team up on projects. And horizontally, the local innovation hubs would collaborate, meeting regularly and exchanging information continuously on their various efforts. In a democratically managed economy, the centrifugal effects of interfirm competition would disappear, and research collaborations between enterprises would become far easier to form and sustain. As citizens and workers, we would be encouraged not only to implement the resulting technologies but also to develop our own innovative ideas for energy conservation and generation. Investments in science and technology education could help foster "citizen science" initiatives in this arena too, as our entire society mobilized under the Collaborative Innovating principle to meet the massive challenge of a rapid and just energy transition.[36]

COLLABORATIVE LEARNING

Our democratic-socialist economy will need to be efficient. Notwithstanding great advances in automation, most work today is a matter of routine, repetitive operations rather than creative tasks. Over the coming century, automation may well eliminate many of these jobs, but that transformation is not happening quickly.[37] Our management of the economy must therefore ensure that we are efficient in the performance of these routine activities. As workers, we might prefer to take it easy on the job, but as consumers—even socialist consumers—we will be resentful if other workers are inefficient. This means that efficiency—as distinct from creativity and innovation—will remain a major challenge far out into any foreseeable future, including under socialism.

What can we learn about how to address this challenge from capitalist management practices? The answer is hardly obvious. It is true that capitalist firms often achieve high levels of efficiency, but the path to achieving that efficiency is often ugly. In smaller firms, it often relies on coercive pressure and threats. In larger firms, where many people perform similar tasks, management assigns staff experts to identify the most efficient procedures for each of those tasks (or more precisely, to identify what the experts *think* are the most efficient procedures). The experts then codify those procedures into work standards and communicate the standards to line managers, who in turn order employees to follow them.[38] Managers can use pay incentives and threats of firing to pressure employees to conform to these standards. Managers can replace employees with automated systems when these systems are cheap enough. Managers can replace expensive and skilled employees with less expensive and less skilled ones. And competition forces firms out of business if they are too inefficient compared to their peers.

Will, then, our democratically managed economy also need to rely on "efficiency experts" dictating standards and procedures to workers? Surely not! This top-down approach would aggravate rather than alleviate our current crisis of workplace disempowerment.

The lessons of high-road capitalist firms are particularly interesting in this regard. High-road firms recognize that standardization is the key to efficiency, but also that the conventional top-down approach to standardization has drawbacks. The staff experts often do not know enough about real operating conditions to come up with standards that can be implemented efficiently in practice. And even if their standards are good ones in principle, imposing them on front-line employees creates alienation and resistance, especially when they intensify and accelerate work.

High-road firms avoid those drawbacks and increase their efficiency even further by mobilizing rank-and-file employees in the standardization effort itself. Using a principle that I call Collaborative Learning, these firms train and mobilize employees to study their own work processes and find ways to improve their efficiency. Under the Collaborative Learning principle, staff experts support front-line employees in this standardization effort, rather than imposing their own ideas of best practice. High-road firms guarantee that no one will be laid off as a consequence of employee-driven efficiency improvements—these firms commit to retraining any employees whose jobs are made redundant by employee suggestions. They train employees in ergonomics, so that they recognize job designs with too much stress. And they often share the resulting productivity gains with their employees in the form of bonuses or higher wages.

Under those high-road conditions, employees often cooperate in defining, implementing, and refining work practices. The resulting standardization is experienced by employees as enabling rather than coercive. So long as line managers maintain an appropriately participative and respectful approach in daily operations, the standards will be used as best-practice templates that inform and enable front-line activity—enhancing freedom-to rather than coercive control-over. Standardization here becomes a way of collaboratively learning how best to get work done, and as a way of accelerating the process of learning how to do things even better.[39]

If this Collaborative Learning principle seems implausible, it is because we are accustomed to thinking of standardization in the context of low-road firms, where the interests of employees and managers are so often so starkly opposed. Standardization is used there as a weapon against employees. And there, as a result, employees feel an urgent need for freedom-from—freedom from coercive supervisors and from oppressive standards. In this context, we find very plausible the theories of work motivation that tell us that standardization saps the intrinsic satisfaction of work, and that standardization is therefore intrinsically demotivating and alienating.[40] Standardization is indeed demotivating and alienating when it is imposed by managers on employees from the top down, and when its goal is the profitability of the firm at the cost of employees' well-being.

By contrast, in high-road firms, managers see employees' engagement as a source of competitive advantage, and employees can join with management in efforts to improve efficiency to their mutual advantage. Since these are still capitalist firms, the Collaborative Learning principle is often short-circuited in practice. Managers often get impatient for business results and use their authority to harass employees to accelerate the pace or to ignore safety considerations. But the underlying principle is one we could adopt.

Collaborative Learning was a prominent feature of one automobile company I have studied—New United Motor Manufacturing, Inc. (NUMMI). NUMMI was a unionized auto assembly plant in Fremont, California, jointly owned by General Motors and Toyota, but operating under Toyota's day-to-day control. NUMMI followed a high-road policy until the plant shut down in 2010.[41] The company inherited its facility and almost its entire workforce (but none of its managers) from GM. GM had shut their Fremont plant in 1982 because it was one of the worst-performing plants in the entire GM system in terms of quality, productivity, and work stoppages. With much the same workforce and the same United Automobile Union Local 2244 leaders, but now operating under Toyota management, NUMMI reached world-class levels of productivity and quality within two or three years of opening.

This astonishing turnaround was a result of the rigorous implementation of the Toyota Production System, combined with a high-road partnership with the union. The collective bargaining agreement opened many facets of company operation to influence by the union and gave workers a no-layoff guarantee.[42]

A key part of the Toyota system was its "standardized work" policy. Whereas at GM work standards were determined by Work Methods staff engineers and were a frequent source of contention, at NUMMI standardization was the task of front-line workers themselves. Toyota taught workers how to use a stopwatch and how to analyze and compare alternative work methods. The goal was to maximize work efficiency and production quality while maintaining worker health and safety. And indeed, assembly-line employees typically worked some 57 seconds out of each 60-second cycle—as compared to about 35 seconds at GM. Yet because they had so carefully choreographed their gestures and the placement of parts and tools, workers found the new pace less burdensome. To quote one assembly-line worker I interviewed at NUMMI:

"At GM-Fremont [. . .] we'd work really fast to build up a stock cushion so we could take a break for a few minutes to smoke a cigarette or chat with a buddy. That kind of 'hurry up and wait' game made work really tiring. There was material and finished parts all over the damn place and half of it was defective anyway. [At NUMMI] being consistently busy without being hassled like that and without being overworked takes a lot of the pain out of the job. You work harder at NUMMI, but I swear it, you go home at the end of the day feeling less tired—and feeling a hell of a lot better about yourself!"[43]

Workers were encouraged to identify improvement (in Japanese: *kaizen*) opportunities, and both supervisors and staff engineers were tasked with following up on those suggestions. Suggestions were rewarded with only very modest payments, yet over 80% of blue-collar workers contributed at least one suggestion per year. On average each worker contributed over three suggestions per year, and more than 85% of them were accepted and implemented.

Workers embraced this standardization. In the words of one of them, comparing the way work methods and standards were set at the old GM-Fremont plant and at NUMMI:

"The GM system relied on authority. People with rank—the managers—ruled regardless of their competence or the validity of what they were saying. It was basically a military hierarchy. At NUMMI, rank doesn't mean a damn thing—standardized work means that we all work out the objectively best way to do the job, and everyone does it that way. I might make some minor adjustments because of my height, for example, but I follow the procedure we've laid out because it makes sense. [. . .] Management has delegated responsibility to the people who do the work and that gives workers a sense of pride in their jobs."

NUMMI's Collaborative Learning efforts were expensive. Training for workers was far more extensive than at comparable GM plants. Engineers were dispatched to follow up on workers' suggestions. Considerable time and attention were needed to manage all this *kaizen* activity. But NUMMI saw these costs as investments that paid off handsomely not only in improved labor relations but in continuously improving efficiency and quality.

Kaiser offers another illustration of how the Collaborative Learning principle can be institutionalized. Take Kaiser's use of clinical guidelines.[44] Clinical guidelines specify step-by-step instructions for clinical diagnosis and treatment—somewhat like Toyota's standardized work. While many medical professional associations develop guidelines and publicize them to their members, these associations have no way to exert pressure on physicians to adopt them. Insurance companies also develop guidelines— ones that maximize their own profits—and, in contrast with the professional associations, they impose their guidelines on physicians by refusing to pay for services that do not comply. Physicians deeply resent being forced in this way to practice profit-driven "cookbook medicine."

In contrast with both the associations and the insurance companies, Kaiser brought physicians together with their peers and with other clinical and nonclinical personnel to define guidelines that offer the best quality and most affordable care. And Kaiser created a management system that effectively encouraged physicians to adopt these guidelines without abrogating their professional discretion. The guidelines were regularly updated, after soliciting practitioners' and patients' concerns and suggestions. As a result, guidelines were not resisted but embraced as useful roadmaps. And they proved very effective in eliminating unwarranted variation in treatment, which helped reduce costs while simultaneously improving clinical quality.[45]

This enabling form of standardization was also used by Kaiser's UBTs to improve the efficiency of their departments' work processes. Unit-based team members—physicians, managers, nurses, clerical and janitorial staff, etc.—worked together to analyze each step of their work processes, then to develop and test process-improvement ideas, so they could develop high-quality, standardized work processes. Display boards were installed in many units to make visible the standardized workflow, its status, and the progress of improvement projects. Staff experts codified UBT innovations to facilitate their diffusion across the regions.

Standardization also brought efficiency to the UBTs' improvement activities themselves. The UBTs relied on standardized "plan-do-study-act" cycle to improve the efficiency and effectiveness of their improvement efforts. They conducted regular "daily huddles"—short (usually about five minutes) stand-up meetings of the whole department team at the start of their shift, led by either the labor or management UBT co-leaders, aimed at both reviewing the day's operational schedule and any "tests of change" the team was pursuing in improving its own procedures.[46]

Kaiser's Collaborative Learning effort did not come cheap. Kaiser invested a lot of time and effort in both its guidelines effort and in training front-line personnel in the techniques of process improvement. The UBTs often also needed coaching to ensure they were working effectively together. And front-line personnel needed time away from their regular tasks, both for training and for the UBT meetings. But the investment paid off handsomely, in higher quality, more efficient work processes, and more engaged personnel.

Now consider a third illustration, this one in the field of software development. Like medical diagnosis and treatment, software development is a field of relatively nonroutine work, where you might expect standardization to be counterproductive. But you would be wrong. Indeed, software development has gone further than medicine by developing an industry-wide approach to standardization. Software development thus offers further lessons for how democratic management of the economy can assure efficiency.

The origins of this industry-wide effort lie in the extraordinarily high proportion of large-scale software systems that either fail entirely or are delivered late, over budget, and with poor quality.[47] Frustrated by this "chaos" in software development, in 1984, the US Department of Defense funded the Software Engineering Institute (SEI) based at Carnegie Mellon University to create a model of a more reliable software development process.[48] The SEI mobilized nearly 1,000 "external reviewers" from across the software industry in this effort, and the result was released in 1991 as the Capability Maturity Model (CMM). The CMM was inspired by Total Quality Management principles very similar to Toyota's, emphasizing the power of standardization as a learning mechanism. It defines five, progressively more "mature" forms of the software development process, where higher maturity means a broader reach of standardization. Level 1 represents an ad hoc approach. Level 2 represents the standardized management of individual projects. At Level 3, standard processes are defined and used for the organization's entire portfolio of projects. Levels 4 pushes standardization even further, specifying mechanisms for quantifying the development process. Level 5 specifies standards for assuring the continuous improvement of that process.[49]

The CMM itself does not specify the content of the standards that the organization should use; instead, it functions as a framework for assessing the level of maturity of the company's own standards. Firms invite certified assessment teams to evaluate their process maturity level. They advertise high levels of maturity to reassure customers of their reliability. And some customers set a minimum maturity level for the companies they hire for software consulting and services.

The CMM (broadened as of 2000 to include a broader range of functions, and therefore renamed CMM-Integration, or CMMI) quickly spread far beyond the defense world and became one of the most popular means for improving the efficiency and quality of large-scale software development. Evidence is strong that achieving higher levels of CMM process maturity does indeed improve quality, cost, and timeliness—without impairing the innovativeness of the resulting software. An early report on the extraordinary efficiency achieved at the highest levels of CMM maturity described the work of the team of 260 developers who wrote the software that controlled the space shuttle: "[T]he last three versions of the program—each 420,000 lines long—had just one error each. The last 11 versions of this software had a total of 17 errors. Commercial programs of equivalent complexity would have 5,000 errors."[50]

Early efforts to bring standardization to software adopted a coercive, top-down approach. Predictably, this provoked revolts among software developers and failed entirely. Over time, however, most software organizations turned to a high-road approach of Collaborative Learning and worked with their developers to specify software development standards.

The Computer Science Corporation's (CSC) Government Services division was one of these high-road firms.[51] When I studied it, before it merged with a unit of HP, CSC was one of the largest professional software services firms in the world. In the divisions that had embraced the CMM, the level of standardization was astonishing, and these standards had been drafted with extensive participation of the developers themselves. Separate "work instructions" covered such tasks as high-level design, each of two types of low-level design and two types of code reviews, testing, change-request implementation, change-request resolution, and root-cause analysis. Each instruction was detailed—several pages long, often specifying forms to be filled in and showing flowcharts to describe the sequence of steps involved. In the past, the binders describing these processes took up some eight feet of shelf space. Now, this documentation was online, and workflow procedures were increasingly built into automated collaboration systems. A standing committee of developers and managers—the Software Engineering Process Group—encouraged developers to bring forward suggestions for changes to the standards. And developers were regularly involved in process improvement projects aimed at reviewing and refining existing standards and developing new ones.

Because each software development project is different, often in critically important ways, these instructions could indeed stifle innovation if they were applied blindly. But instead of abandoning standardization, CSC's standard process included an initial phase—the "tailoring cycle"— during which the project leader would consult with the developers to identify which standards they needed to use on this project, which were irrelevant, and which needed to be adapted to the specific challenges of the project.

The role of staff experts was very different in this Collaborative Learning model than in the top-down models, as it was based on participation rather than coercive control. Take, for example, the role of Quality Assurance (QA). In the past, QA was often remote from the daily work of developers, arriving on the scene at the end of the work cycle to audit the output. Relations between these staff experts and developers were notoriously antagonistic. Now, explained one of the QA staff people,

"The [standardized] process forces people out of their functional or module silos and into structured communication across those boundaries. QA for example gets a defined place in our reviews and our process improvement cycle. But QA is not a policeman! QA is there to help the project—help you identify the processes you need, tailor existing ones to your needs, learn that process, and do a check to see if you're using it. If I find a problem, it's my job to help the project work out how to address it and how I can help."

Using this Collaborative Learning approach, CSC's standardization was seen by developers as a tool that helped rather than hindered creativity. The standards helped clarify their goals and provided valuable, best-practice guidance for accomplishing them. Developers liked it: turnover among developers was far below the average for this industry. And the performance results for CSC were impressive. In the most "mature" units, operating at CMM Level 5, costs for comparably large and complex projects were cut by 60% over 10 years, error rates were reduced by 90%, and the accuracy of projected schedules and budgets was doubled.

Collaborative Learning has proven effective at driving efficiency in enterprises as different as Toyota, Kaiser, and CSC. That should give us confidence that enterprises under democratic governance could implement it in any industry. Moreover, given the massive size of these enterprises, we should be confident that this principle could also inform efforts to improve efficiency at region, industry, and national levels. Education, training, and work-time opportunities could be provided to enable a wide range of people to participate effectively in process improvement activities. Experts could help spread frameworks such as the CMMI across enterprises, and they could codify the best practices that emerge from the application of these frameworks to facilitate the diffusion of those practices.

Let's imagine how the Collaborative Learning principle could be applied in a democratically managed economy to improve the efficiency of our healthcare delivery system and reduce the atrocious number of avoidable medical errors. The target seems a worthy one: the inefficiency of our healthcare system is notorious, and avoidable hospital medical errors are now the third leading cause of death, numbering some 700 per day.[52] Imagine now that our national economic council mobilized all the medical associations, nursing associations, healthcare unions, and patient advocacy groups to develop a system for defining clinical guidelines for all the medical conditions where the volume of cases was sufficient.[53] Imagine too that in every healthcare delivery organization, teams were mobilized, such as at Kaiser, to review these guidelines, adapt them for their local needs, review their implementation and effects, and pass along results of those reviews to higher-level councils so the guidelines could be refined over time. We could in this way reduce the hugely inequitable variation in the type and quality of treatment that patients receive depending on their location, income, insurance, and race, while at the same time improving the overall quality of care and reducing costs. The same kind of industry-wide effort could be organized in every industry, unleashing a wave of efficiency-improvement effort that would revolutionize our economy.

COLLABORATIVE WORKING

Socialism has long been associated with collectivism. Indeed, an effective democratic-socialist economy will require the widespread acceptance that what's best for the whole enterprise and for the whole society should weigh substantially in our individual preferences. But many worry that this collectivistic ethos would undermine the individualism that has proven so potent under capitalism in motivating effort, creativity, and innovation.[54]

Individualism is an important historical accomplishment of capitalism. In precapitalist societies, most individuals' aspirations were constrained by collective traditions and inherited status. In freeing people from these constraints, capitalism unleashed the power of individualistic, divergent thinking and action, which are wellsprings of creativity, innovation, and economic development.[55]

A democratically managed economy therefore needs both collectivistic and individualistic motives—and that seems to pose a dilemma.

Large capitalist enterprises have confronted this dilemma in microcosm. On the one hand, they need a collectivistic ethos to encourage conformance with centralized policies and standardized procedures. On the other hand, they need individualism to fuel creativity and innovation.

Low-road firms resolve this dilemma by segregating routine tasks and creative tasks. In the units focusing on routine tasks—such as assembly-line work or most of the support activities in a hospital or professional-services firm—their employees are expected to adopt a conformist orientation. And in the units focusing on more creative tasks—such as medical diagnosis and treatment, software development, or R&D—their employees are allowed, indeed often encouraged, to adopt a more individualistic orientation.

We have seen both the advantages and drawbacks of this segregation in low-road firms. Such specialization promises to reduce costs, insofar as the firm needs fewer people for the creative tasks. But it is less effective, for several reasons. Communication and collaboration between the two groups are impaired. The people doing the creative work have considerable autonomy but little interest in using it to improve their efficiency. The people doing the routine work have less autonomy and just as little interest in improving efficiency. Nor do they have capacity or incentive to contribute to innovation. And absent opportunities to contribute their ideas, employees are likely to find such routine work alienating.

And we have seen too that high-road firms aim to overcome this dilemma by developing employees who are committed both to implementing the agreed-on plan *and* to contributing novel ideas in the development of that plan—to performing their routine tasks efficiently *and* to contributing creative ideas for improving their performance. But this implies that people somehow combine collectivistic and individualistic motivational impulses. Is that really possible? If so, what do organizations do to encourage that synthesis?[56]

Some high-road firms have made considerable progress in meeting this challenge by nurturing an ethos of *interdependence*—creating a basis of motivation that goes beyond both *independence*, where self-worth is based on individual accomplishments, and *dependence*, where self-worth is based on the approval of the people around you. Here, what is most valued is the contribution of individuals and teams to the goals of the broader organization. Where creativity requires individualistic, divergent thinking, this will not be experienced as being in conflict with enduring collectivistic commitments to those goals. Where routine work requires an embrace of collectively decided standards, this collectivism will not be experienced as being in conflict with the individualistic creativity required for identifying improvement opportunities and for developing innovations that contributed to those goals.

If this synthesis of individualism and collectivism in an ethos of interdependence seems so implausible, it is because in any capitalist society there is a real tension, a real trade-off, between concern for oneself (individualism) and concern for other people (collectivism). In a society in which success is a matter of competition—between firms as between people in the labor market—striving for one's own success often comes at the expense of caring for others.[57] In the workplace, the goals of the firm—especially the low-road firm—are often in conflict with those of employees, so collectivistic commitment to those goals is for suckers. Conversely, in spaces where caring for each other is legitimate—at the family dinner table, and in the employees' lunch room—individualism often seems like an unaffordable luxury, and collectivistic mutual support seems far more important to survival in the turbulent world created by market irrationality and coercive management.[58] Individualism thus often appears as a form of alienation—as possessive, competitive, antisocial—and collectivism appears as a form of dependence—suppressing individual aspirations and creativity.

High-road firms try to overcome this dilemma and to synthesize an ethic of interdependence by institutionalizing a principle I call Collaborative Working. Collaborative Working relies on four main levers. First, it requires the articulation of collective goals that are meaningful to employees. When the executives leading high-road firms proclaim that satisfying shareholders is a lower priority than meeting customers' needs, we are entitled to be skeptical; but we also need to understand why they are driven to say it. The reason is simple: if employees are going to work together to contribute creatively to the firm's success, it is because they see that success as meaningful to them personally. Delivering great shareholder returns is typically not. And concern about keeping your job yields only very modest discretionary effort.[59]

Second, Collaborative Working relies on ongoing, reasoned discussion about how these collective goals relate to everyday work decisions. Making those connections requires dedicated time and structured discussion forums. It is in the context of such forums that real deliberation can happen, where participants are called on to defend their point of view not in terms of their individual self-interest but in terms of everyone's well-being. We cannot assume people are angels, but when someone voices their point of view in such deliberative settings, it brings out their "better angels."[60]

Third, Collaborative Working relies on evaluation and pay systems that reinforce this combination of individualism and collectivism, by recognizing both individual and collective contributions to the organization's shared goals. While evaluation and pay systems cannot by themselves do much to inculcate an ethos of interdependence, they can support it rather than undermine it. And that support is important, because poorly aligned evaluation and pay systems rapidly corrode any sense of interdependence. Systems that recognize only individual performance can powerfully undermine commitment to shared goals. And systems that reward everyone equally, regardless of their contribution to the organization's success, can discourage individual effort.

Finally, Collaborative Working relies on a distinctive set of skills. Without the skills needed to turn interdependent motivation into effective interdependent action, employees cannot sustain that ethos. High-road firms therefore invest in the development of "T-shaped" skills among their personnel. The vertical bar of the T represents the depth of individual specialization, and the horizontal bar on the top of the T represents the breadth of complementary technical, managerial, and social skills needed to collaborate effectively with other specialties.[61]

The four enterprises we have discussed all offer interesting images of Collaborative Working. Kaiser illustrates most compellingly the motivational effect of defining collective goals in a way that is meaningful to employees. As we noted earlier, the top-level goals of the Value Compass—best quality, best service, most affordable, and best place to work—were defined through dialogue with the union coalition. They were goals that employees, physicians, and managers all found personally meaningful. They could all identify with them and internalize them as their own.

The interdependent ethos of Collaborative Working was particularly striking among Kaiser physicians. The medical profession has a deeply ingrained occupational culture that prizes the autonomy and independence of the individual physician. Kaiser pushed hard to get beyond this individualism. As we have seen, Kaiser physicians' work was structured by clinical guidelines, and they were actively engaged in developing these guidelines. Kaiser also organized regular discussions among physicians about their cost and quality performance and how it could be improved. In medical department meetings, each physician saw a chart showing his or her own performance ranked against their peers in the department. The department members would discuss the variation among them—how frequently and why each followed or ignored the guidelines, and the outcomes from those different cases.

Similarly, medications were standardized in the form of a drug formulary. A committee of physicians, nurses, and pharmacists assessed the available generic and brand name drugs to identify those that offered the greatest clinical benefit for the lowest cost. Doctors could prescribe anything on that list that they thought the patient needed. They could also prescribe drugs that were not on the list, but if they did so often, they would receive a call from a colleague asking for a peer-to-peer discussion about their choices.

Here is the view of one physician I interviewed talking about his experience in a part of the organization that had recently pushed hard to strengthen this ethos of interdependence:

"The group here tended to practice as though they were individual practitioners and were just renting office space. They would meet in interdisciplinary teams, but these didn't really function as clinical teams so much as social outlets. These are the people that you ventilate with about the difficult patient that you saw; these are the people that you go out to lunch with, that kind of thing. But there was no clinical interdependency in those teams. We're shifting towards a situation where people actually work together—more of them talk about *our* patients, not *my* patients, and more consider what's good for the clinic, not just for their own practice."

Of course, this mix of individualism and collectivism was not experienced so positively always and everywhere. In some cases, doctors felt that challenges to their individual judgment were driven by Kaiser's bottom-line concerns and risked sacrificing the patient's health interests. And in some medical centers, a more traditional ethos prevailed. But the average level of physician engagement in these collaborative discussions was high, as was physicians' average level of work satisfaction.

If the main hurdle to interdependent motivation among the physicians was their individualism, in contrast, among Kaiser's nonprofessional staff the main hurdle was ensuring that everyone felt free to speak up. Speaking up, as it was institutionalized at Kaiser, was a matter of exercising *individual* agency to improve the team's *collective* performance. The UBTs and huddles both relied on and cultivated this sense of interdependence. An internal KP document explained:

> Putting in place mechanisms that encourage employees to speak up is another way to foster open communication around errors and performance improvement. Such systems also provide a forum where people learn how to express themselves clearly and non-emotionally—and help to reconnect them with the value and purpose of their work.[62]

Kaiser buttressed Collaborative Working with its evaluation and reward systems. Physicians new to Kaiser went through a three-year probationary period during which they were regularly evaluated not only on their individual technical competence but also on their collegial relations with other physicians, the respect they showed for other staff and patients, and their willingness to contribute ideas and effort to improving the organization's performance. After the probationary period, physicians continued to be evaluated regularly on these dimensions. And any physicians who took on supervisory responsibilities was the object of regular "360 degree" reviews, where subordinates, peers, and superiors all contributed their evaluation. Kaiser physicians were salaried—and therefore under no financial pressure to rush patient visits or order expensive tests or treatments. Their annual bonus was based entirely on patient satisfaction and clinical outcomes, not on the cost implications of the physician's decisions nor on their "utilization" rates. Any cost savings the medical group made (relative to the targeted overall annual cost-per-patient) were reinvested in medical equipment and programs.[63]

Kaiser was also impressive in its commitment to equipping staff—managers, doctors, nurses, and other employees—with the T-shaped skills needed for Collaborative Working. Apart from the normal opportunities to deepen their technical skills and strengthen the T's vertical bar, physicians were challenged to strengthen and extend their T's horizontal bar by building skills in management, business, and leadership competencies. All Kaiser staff categories—down to shop stewards and rank-and-file employees—were drawn into a wide range of training programs that aimed to build horizontal-bar skills in areas such as problem-solving, leading meetings, analyzing work processes, identifying improvement opportunities, team leadership, collective-bargaining contract management, and dealing with conflicting views and divergent interests, as well as understanding the business side of Kaiser and the economics of healthcare. A comprehensive curriculum had been developed and a training budget was created to support these skill-development programs.

At NUMMI, the development of interdependent motivation required, first, a redefinition of the enterprise's goals toward ones that were meaningful to workers—ones that engaged their sense of pride and purpose. The strategic priority was on quality rather than cost, on the Toyota principle that improving quality was the surest way to lower costs. Toyota made customers' detailed quality ratings visible to workers on each segment of the assembly line. That way, workers could see the impact of their work on customers and could pinpoint activities that needed improvement. And management committed to listening to everyone's ideas on how to improve quality. Where GM managers at Fremont had put great weight on maximizing the time that the assembly line was running, Toyota encouraged workers to stop the line when they saw a quality problem. If they noticed a problem, workers were instructed to pull a cord (in Japanese: the *andon* cord) or press a button to alert their (unionized) team leader, and if together they could not resolve the problem within 60 seconds, the line stopped and the team convened to work on it, bringing in managers and engineers as needed.

In their daily activity, workers were in teams of four to six people under a team leader, and they rotated tasks during the shift. Developing and revising standardized work sheets, too, was done in teams. Workers in each team needed to come to consensus on the methods they would all follow and to reach agreement with the corresponding team on the other shift.

With more meaningful goals, Toyota could encourage an evolution for workers away from the defensive collectivism that had been so powerful at the old GM-Fremont plant. That old collectivism was expressed in strong worker solidarity and numerous strikes against abusive supervision. At NUMMI, collective identification with other workers remained strong, but it was now combined with an individualistic eagerness to contribute creative ideas. One assembly-line worker, a veteran of the GM days, expressed it this way:

> "Here, we're not autonomous because we're all tied together really tightly [by the assembly line]. But it's not like we're just getting squeezed to work harder, because it's us, the workers, that are making the whole thing work—we're the ones that make the standardized work and the kaizen suggestions. We run the plant—and if it's not running right, we stop it."

Other workers saw the scope of their interdependence extending even further, reflecting Toyota's efforts to tap the creativity of both employees and suppliers:

> "In 23 years working for GM, I never met with a supplier. I never even knew their names except for the names on the boxes. Now, we're working with suppliers to improve our products. Workers sit down with our engineers and managers and the suppliers' people and we analyze defects and develop improvement proposals. We even do that with equipment vendors. Stuff like that really gives us a better perspective on how our jobs relate to the whole process. We're not just drilling holes and slamming nuts onto bolts anymore. Now we have a say in how the product should be made."

For some workers, interdependence became an internalized norm that shaped their attitudes and behavior beyond the workplace:

> "I wish you could talk to the guys' wives about the changes they've seen. I was a typical macho horse's ass when I worked at GM. When I got home, I'd get a beer, put my feet up and wait for dinner to be served. I'd figure, 'I've done my eight [hour shift], so just leave me alone.' Now, I'm part of a team at work, and I take that attitude home with me, rather than dump my work frustrations all over my family. I'm much more of a partner around the house. I help wash the dishes and do the shopping and stuff. My job here is to care, and I spend eight hours a day doing that job, so it's kind of natural that I take it home with me."

IBM offers an example of an orchestrated, highly participative discussion of values as a path toward an ethos of interdependence. IBM's Innovation Jam was, as I noted earlier, modeled on an earlier cycle of jams, of which the first pair, in 2003–2004, focused explicitly on values and culture.[64] In that case, during the first three-day cycle, nearly 4,000 employees participated with over 9,000 posts, while another 60–65,000 followed the conversation without posting. The second cycle, focused on how to inculcate these values, drew over 13,000 active participants and over 35,000 posts. The discussions were "free-wheeling, comprehensive, often passionate, often conflictual, involving all levels of the company from top to bottom, across occupational groups and geographies." [65] The jams did not lead to a formal vote, but they did influence the formal values statement that was adopted after the first Jam and that set the basis for the second cycle in 2004 that focused on translating those values into operating policies.

A key focus of debate during the first cycle of the values jam was whether the values of the "old IBM"—"Respect for the individual; the best customer service; the pursuit of excellence"—fit the new business context facing IBM. In practice, the old IBM culture emphasized a collectivistic loyalty to one's boss and to the company (symbolized by the ubiquitous IBM uniform of blue-suit-white-shirt-and-dark-tie), which balanced uneasily with an individualistic understanding of ethics, integrity, and technical excellence. As one employee put it:

> "IBM was known for a simple credo. . . . As long as you work hard and do a good job, the company would take care of you." [66]

The new IBM needed an interdependent ethos that would encourage people to collaborate with customers to understand their needs and to collaborate with IBM staff across its various units to develop solutions for those client needs. The jam brought out clearly the need for a more robust, interdependent motivational foundation that would support "nimbleness and responsiveness . . . improve cross-boundary coordination around customer solutions."[67] To help effect this shift, IBM followed up with significant changes to training, to compensation, and to business processes such as how to price bids so that they reflected IBM's overall interests rather than just the local business unit's. In the words of one Japanese engineer who participated:

> "For a team to success [sic], team members need the interdependent spirit instead of dependence and independence. We should help each other and respect each other. I suggest we set up a system to reward the person who has a propensity to helping other persons."[68]

And indeed, subsequent jams have addressed rewards and performance management in this spirit.[69]

At CSC, developers were acutely aware of the shift in values and motivation that the CMM discipline required. Most strikingly, developers were not resentful of the considerable documentation burden they shouldered in this more disciplined process—where documentation is one of the loudest complaints of developers in less mature organizations.[70] Documenting the code they produced was now seen as a natural part of the developer's job, since that job was interdependent with others for whom the documentation would be essential. As one developer explained it:

> "I think that our process—and even the paperwork part of it—is basically a good thing. My documentation is going to help the next person working on this code, either for testing or maintenance. And vice versa when I'm on the receiving end."

Another developer used a sports analogy to convey this new spirit of interdependence:

> "A more mature process means you go from freedom to do things your own way to being critiqued. It means going from chaos to structure. It's a bit like streetball versus NBA basketball. Streetball is roughhousing, showing off. You play for yourself rather than the team, and you do it for the love of the game. In professional basketball, you're part of a team, and you practice a lot together, doing drills and playing practice games. You aren't doing it just for yourself or even just for your team: there are other people involved [. . .]. You have to take responsibility for other people—your teammates—and for mentoring other players coming up."

To manage our economy democratically and effectively will require a form of work motivation that synthesizes individualism and collectivism in an ethos of interdependence. The Collaborative Working principle we see in action at companies like Kaiser, NUMMI, IBM, and CSC has proven effective in cultivating just this kind of motivation. Here too it is not difficult to see how all the key elements could be used even more systematically in democratically governed enterprises, industries, regions, and at the national scale.

First, when our enterprises and government at all levels are oriented toward goals that speak directly to people's real needs—rather than to goals such as shareholder wealth or GDP growth or the stock market indexes—we can expect these goals to elicit stronger commitment.

Second, the generalization of democratic deliberation as the means of setting these goals and deciding how to pursue them would encourage the diffusion of this ethos of interdependence. To democratize the functioning of our enterprises means drawing everyone into regular deliberations about the goals of their work team, their department, and their enterprise as a whole. To make our political system and our economic management system genuinely democratic requires, similarly, that citizens engage in regular deliberation in their neighborhoods, cities, regions, and nationally. At the larger scales, workers' and citizens' involvement might only be indirect, either by elected or randomly selected representatives; in a genuinely democratic system, their representatives would be in regular dialogue with those they represent, seeking direction from the rank-and-file, which implies further collective deliberation.

Third, under democratic management of the economy, we could generalize the use of evaluation and pay systems that support interdependent motivation by recognizing both collective achievements and individual contribution to those achievements.

And finally, we could create economy-wide education and training policies that ensure opportunities for everyone both to deepen their chosen specialization (the vertical bar of the T) and to broaden the social and technical competencies (the horizontal bar on the top of the T) that they need to collaborate effectively with other specialists.

These policies would institutionalize the principle of Collaborative Working and take us far toward the diffusion of an ethos of interdependence and its widespread internalization. And they would help ensure that our economic management meets the challenges of democracy, innovation, efficiency, *and* motivation.

FROM HIGH-ROAD CAPITALISM TO DEMOCRATIC SOCIALISM

Under capitalist conditions such as we see them in low-road firms, the four organizational principles we have just reviewed appear impossible—internally contradictory, paradoxical, oxymorons. The common thread running through our discussion of these principles was that this apparent impossibility is due to the fundamentally undemocratic power asymmetry built into the private-property foundations of capitalism—an asymmetry that is on full display in today's low-road firms.

When capitalist enterprises pursue private profits to the detriment of the welfare of people and the planet; when such firms' governance structures give managers the authority and incentive to hire and fire workers to attain those goals; and when workers are in competition with each other on labor markets—then, under those conditions, centralization precludes participation, and as a result Collaborative Strategizing seems utopian. Under those conditions, innovation is top-down and reserved for an elite, while most employees are confined to routine work, and Collaborative Innovating too seems utopian. Under those conditions, standardization takes a coercive form, and it also seems wildly utopian to imagine that we could rely on Collaborative Learning to ensure that the most efficient standards guide everyone's work. And under those conditions, individualism precludes concern for others and vice versa, and if we try to combine them we get at best just a little bit of each rather than a full dose, so Collaborative Working too seems utopian.

If the high-road firms described in this chapter were able to go as far as they did in implementing these principles, it is because—and to the extent that—they managed to moderate these power asymmetries.

First, their massive size gave each control over a vast array of activities that were thereby shielded from the centrifugal effects of market competition. Kaiser benefited from the fact that the Permanente Medical Groups brought together some 21,000 physicians—in contrast with many other parts of the healthcare industry where physicians operate as independent small businesses competing with each other for patients and profits. Kaiser also benefited from the close collaboration between the hospital system, the insurance system, and the medical group—in contrast with many other parts of the healthcare industry where these entities are constituted as independent firms, each pursues their competing financial goals, and where they interact only at arms' length. And Kaiser was also shielded to some extent by the not-for-profit status of its health-plan and hospital components. NUMMI, owned jointly by Toyota and GM, was buffered from the corrosive effects of competition by its enormous parents. IBM and CSC were huge in their own right. Collaborative Strategizing, Innovation, and Learning were stimulated by efforts to derive performance advantages from such massive scale.

And second, internally, these firms' commitment to a high-road approach moderated the centrifugal effects of the capitalist employment relation. In high-road firms, employees have an unusual degree of influence in setting policy and standards. In some cases, this reflected the strength of unions (SEIU and the union coalition at Kaiser, UAW at NUMMI). In other cases, it reflected the strong labor-market position of highly professionalized staff (physicians at Kaiser, software developers at CSC, professional consultants at IBM). All four organizational principles were powerfully stimulated by the unusual amount of power enjoyed by employees in such settings.

On the other hand, however, none of these businesses could escape the constraints imposed by the capitalist character of the firm and its context. As a result, in every case the implementation of the four principles was limited. These limitations revealed themselves in various ways depending on the circumstances.

Centralization was only somewhat participative, and Collaborative Strategizing was therefore limited. At Kaiser, while front-line personnel could influence higher-level policy through their union leaders, these leaders' influence was limited and they were excluded entirely from some policy discussions. At NUMMI, workers had no input at all into the broader strategic choices of the company. Most fundamentally, Collaborative Strategizing was limited to the single firm, and it was therefore impotent in the face of the vagaries of the market. As a result of these vagaries, NUMMI was eventually shut down, and CSC was merged into another firm.

Collaborative Innovating was limited by the short-term cost pressures ever-present in capitalist enterprise. IBM conducted innovation jams; but these were time-bound initiatives, after which staff returned to work roles that were only a little less segregated. At Kaiser, UBT innovation efforts were often stymied by supervisors who were under short-term performance pressure and were therefore reluctant to allow front-line employees to leave the unit to participate in the necessary training. At NUMMI, workers had no real voice in vehicle design: proposals for even minor design changes aiming to facilitate the assembly process were routinely ignored.

Collaborative Learning was often undermined, as managers came under performance pressure and some began using standards as a weapon to "drive" performance. Physicians at Kaiser and developers at CSC sometimes felt that guidelines got in the way of professional judgment. As one middle manager at CSC expressed it:

> "One key challenge [in pursuing process improvement] is maintaining buy-in at the top. Our top corporate management is under constant pressure from the stock market. The market is constantly looking at margins [. . .] That doesn't leave much room for expenditures associated with process improvement— especially when these take two or three years to show any payoff."

Workers at NUMMI suffered from repetitive strain injuries when managers ignored their complaints that some of the standards did not capture accurately the ergonomic load they bore.[71] Accountable to people above them and not to those below them, middle managers under performance pressure find it difficult to resist the coercive use of their authority.

Finally, Collaborative Working was often undermined by parochial loyalties and competitive individualism. Middle managers were often fearful of looking bad in the eyes of their bosses, and sometimes demanded conformist loyalty from subordinates. If employees felt alienated by bad experiences with abusive managers, they often adopted an individualistic, "what's in it for me" attitude.

My claim is therefore not that these high-road firms embody perfectly the new organizational principles that we need for our democratically managed economy. It is rather that the new principles are visible here, even if we have to squint a little to see them because the principles are in tension with the more conventional capitalist pattern of autocratic centralization, top-down innovation, coercive standardization, and competitive individualism.

I also contend that the success, albeit limited, of these principles on such a large scale as we see in these firms should give us confidence that under socialist conditions they can be deployed even more widely and more systematically to ensure that our management of the economy will be both democratic and effective. If we can assert democratic control over decision-making in enterprises and over interdependencies at the region, industry, and national levels, what now seems utopian will become feasible and indeed normal. These contradictory-sounding principles will become both possible and necessary. Possible, because we will have abolished the power of capital over labor and of competition over cooperation. And necessary, because we will need these principles to meet the challenges facing our management of the economy as concerns democracy, innovation, efficiency, and motivation.

Of course, these management principles are just that—principles. A democratic-socialist society will need to give them substance by giving them a specific institutional form—in laws, regulations, organizations, norms—and finding the right institutional form will require much experimentation. However, we cannot proceed far down that experimentation path before we encounter a key hurdle: the new organizational principles cannot preside over a democratically managed economy so long as the ownership of our productive resources remains private.

CHAPTER 6

A Democratic-Socialist Society

To overcome the six big crises we face—economic irrationality, workplace disempowerment, unresponsive government, ecological unsustainability, social disintegration, and international conflict—and to capitalize on the potential of advanced technologies—to assure material comfort for all, human dignity, and opportunities for individual and collective development—we must develop a democratic strategic management process that encompasses the country's entire economy. We have four organizational principles that give us guidance on what this process might look like. But to implement these principles, we need to be able to override the veto currently exercised by private enterprise against measures that would hurt business profits. If the ownership of society's productive resources remains private, our efforts to control democratically how we use them will be contested, curtailed, and eventually defeated.[1]

The democratic-socialist model offers a radical resolution of this dilemma—radical, as in going to the root of the problem, and radical, as in requiring a qualitative change. We must replace private enterprise with publicly owned enterprise. Both aspects of property—control and ownership—will then be socialized to a degree compatible with the socialization of production. And this in turn would yield an economy that works for us—for the 99%.[2]

What will such a democratic-socialist society look like? I will try to answer this question in three steps. First, I will briefly survey various places where we see something like democratic socialism at work today at the local scale. Second, I will take us back to a period in US history in which the control of industry was socialized to a significant extent on a nationwide scale, although only for a brief period of emergency—the World War II economic mobilization. And finally, I will build on these sketches to describe in more detail how the six crises could be overcome if the socialization of property were generalized across the economy and our democratic strategic management of the economy were able to blossom.

IMAGES FROM AROUND US

At the margins and in the interstices of the US economy today, we find many examples of what is possible if the veto power of private property is weakened. They give us a glimpse of what a democratically managed economy will look like.[3]

Consider first cooperatives. Cooperative ownership structures help overcome our disempowerment as employees. Some 40% of Americans are already members of some kind of cooperative, even if few take up the opportunity to participate in their governance. We have a long history of agricultural cooperatives that help bring farm products to market. Cooperative credit unions hold assets of about $1 trillion on behalf of over 95 million Americans. Many of us are members of consumer cooperatives such as Recreational Equipment, Inc. (better known as REI).[4]

The most impressive worker cooperative is not in the United States but headquartered in the Basque region of Spain. There the Mondragon confederation brings together over 80,000 workers in some 120 cooperatives—factories producing consumer and capital goods, construction enterprises, a bank, several R&D centers, a social security system, several schools and technical institutes, and retail stores across Spain. While these Mondragon cooperatives compete with capitalist firms on product markets, they operate internally on a democratic basis, and they cooperate rather than compete with each other. As in other worker cooperatives, if sales are slow, they reduce working hours and wages rather than lay people off. If a cooperative needs to downsize or fails entirely, Mondragon's size allows it to find alternative jobs in other enterprises under their umbrella.[5] Pay differentials are decided democratically, and the top managers of any of the enterprises earn no more than eight times the lowest paid cooperative member—as compared with the United States today, where the average CEO in the biggest corporations receives about 300 times the pay of the typical American worker.[6] Mondragon's planning process reflects the Collaborative Strategizing principle, with stronger vertical participation than in capitalist firms, even high-road ones.[7] The United Steelworkers union has launched a program with the support of Mondragon to establish Mondragon-type worker cooperatives in the United States and Canada. This program has begun yielding results, for example in the Cincinnati Union Cooperative Initiative.[8]

We also have some experiments where cooperatives enjoy support from public or quasi-public agencies in their local communities. Take, for example, the Evergreen Cooperatives in Cleveland.[9] Evergreen is currently a family of three worker cooperatives—a laundry service, a solar energy business, and an urban garden—that aim to provide living-wage, socially useful employment to people in low-income neighborhoods. They are supported by a consortium composed of the Cleveland city government; the Cleveland Foundation, which provides some seed funding; the Democracy Collaborative, which provides consulting and training; and three large nonprofits that rely primarily on government funds and act as anchor institutions (Cleveland Clinic, University Hospitals, and Case Western Reserve University). The anchor institutions channel some of their purchases to these cooperatives. The laundry service, for example, services the Cleveland Clinic and Hospitals. Such initiatives provide a pathway for progressive change in our local communities, even in the absence of change in the wider, national political economy. Similar initiatives have emerged in some other cities in the United States.[10] A growing number of cities are using their authority to pull together the relevant industry and community stakeholders to develop strategic plans for economic development and for a just ecological transition.

Another promising line of development aims to make government itself less subservient to business and more focused on serving people and the planet. In the United States, about 15% of the population gets its electrical power from municipally owned utilities. Notwithstanding business opposition, we have over 500 cities that provide some kind of public Internet service. In some areas, cities build and operate their own hotels. One-fifth of our hospitals are owned by public agencies. Some 19 states offer financial support for worker-owned firms. North Dakota has a state bank that supports local business. These all represent, to varying degrees and with varying success, efforts to bring democratic control to bear on our economic sphere.

In the public sector, we have seen many innovations aiming to give citizens more opportunities to participate in government policy-setting. These innovations appear under labels like "deliberative democracy," "empowered participatory governance," and "collaborative governance."[11] Such innovations help us imagine a way past unresponsive government.

If government today is so unresponsive, it is not only because of its sub-servience to the business sector but also because decision-making power is taken out of the hands of citizens and given to a few professional representatives and bureaucrats. As citizens, we have little opportunity to participate in debating and influencing the choices that these experts make. Those experts fall under the influence of the most powerful actors in society—often from the business sector. In contrast, these innovative programs encourage legislators and regulators to engage citizens and stakeholders in determining local goals, to work collaboratively with peer localities to learn from each other, and to work collaboratively too with higher-level, central administrative units. Such participatory governance schemes have been implemented in a growing number of cities in the United States and in countries around the world, in arenas like municipal budgeting, school governance, policing, and environmental planning.[12]

We also have a vast ecology of nonprofits that provide important services, and some of them provide valuable lessons for democratic socialism. The latest wave of social innovation in the nonprofit world is the open-source movement, which has given rise to services such as Wikipedia and software systems such as Linux. Here, ideas, software code, blueprints, and other material are made freely available. When people turn their back on private intellectual property and contribute their ideas freely this way, others can more easily build on and improve those ideas, and the rate of innovation accelerates. Supported by the development of the Internet—itself originally an open-source project—we have seen the development of open-source communities in software and hardware design, medicine, educational material, citizen science, and many other sectors. Democratic and participative governance structures have emerged to assure the coordination of many of these communities.[13]

As prefigurative precursors of a new, socialist system, these innovations are inspiring. Their limitations, however, are instructive too. In many cases, these enterprises and agencies lack strong democratic accountability, either by design or through lack of member and citizen involvement. More fundamentally, it is difficult to see how they could be scaled up to deal with the wider dimensions of the six major crises we face. Clearly some broader institutional framework would be needed to give these local- and community-level institutions coherence, support, and direction. And just as clearly, in this new framework, the power of the for-profit business sector over our economy and polity will need to be curtailed radically if these innovations are going to shift from the margins to the core of the economy.

About a century ago, the United States saw numerous cities come under the control of socialist mayors, who attempted to build publicly owned alternatives to capitalist enterprise.[14] At the height of this movement, in 1911, there were 74 self-declared socialist mayors across the United States. Their efforts at "municipal socialism" successfully socialized the supply of ice, water, electricity, gas, railways, scales, docks, cemeteries, and harbor pilot, towing, and dredging services, among others. These measures were highly popular with the electorate. But the movement was stifled and corralled into harmless enclaves by the combined effects of political opposition from the business sector, conservatives in the courts, and dependence of the cities on state-level approval for financing initiatives. Eventually, all that was left of these efforts was a tangled mess of thousands of overlapping "quasi-governmental" agencies, delivering commodified services (where users pay per use) rather than functioning as public infrastructure, lacking in democratic accountability, and subtracting rather than adding to the momentum for wider social change. This history should serve as a caution to the many progressives today who propose to build alternatives upward from the local level.[15]

Many American progressives also look back fondly at the New Deal as a model we can build on for a better future. However, the New Deal suffered from the limitations intrinsic to the regulated and social-democratic reform models. The New Deal left private enterprise in control of the core of the economy. Government's efforts to deal with the Great Depression were confined to actions that would help and not impair the private sector's profitability. Government programs such as the Works Progress Administration alleviated working people's suffering, but they employed people in public-works projects—not in activities that the private sector claimed as its own terrain. With the support of the private-sector business interests, the courts and conservatives in government constantly neutralized Roosevelt's more radical proposals. Federal government deficits were never allowed to exceed 3% of national economic output. Not surprisingly, recovery from the Depression was slow and halting.

If we are looking for a model that affords more hope of dealing with the six crises we face today, we may have more to learn from the mobilization of the US economy to fight World War II. Indeed, some environmental activists have called for us to adopt this mobilization as a model for responding to the emerging climate crisis.[16]

During World War II, some 12 million American men and women were mobilized in the military, 17 million new civilian jobs were created at home, and the production of ships, aircraft, munitions, and other military material accelerated at an astonishing rate. The mobilization rapidly brought unemployment down from a prewar level of around 18% to under 2%, and income inequality plummeted, as high incomes were taxed and low incomes boosted. Real wages increased over the war years, and the quality of housing improved. Notwithstanding resistance from the business sector, government encouraged families to plant gardens at home. Some 20 million "Victory Gardens" were planted, supplying nearly 40% of America's vegetables during the war. Not only was the mobilization successful, but unemployment, poverty, and infant and maternal mortality rates plummeted, and the status of women and minorities improved dramatically, with the exception of the deplorable internment of Japanese Americans.[17]

The success of the mobilization was the result of the government's strategic management of the economy. It was not a result of spontaneous market coordination, nor of industrialists' patriotism. Indeed, many business leaders resisted converting to military production, fearful of losing market share to competitors who did not convert. As a result, the drive to conversion was led by public officials, and most companies responded only reluctantly, under duress.[18]

The federal government's strategic management of the economy encompassed the bulk of private-sector production for both military and civilian uses, as well as a greatly expanded public sector. Government banned or restricted activities that did not contribute to the war effort, such as the production of civilian refrigerators, vacuum cleaners, phonographs, and washing machines. Government agencies also determined production quantity targets, prices, rents, and wages across most of the economy. Huge military departments designed and produced weapons and materiel. When government agencies contracted out military production to the private sector, they often specified designs and set prices and profit margins for the contractors. Government officials often selected subprime suppliers and provided components directly, rather than let prime contractors make their own sourcing decisions. The federal government developed and deployed a massive skill-development program ("Training Within Industry") to prepare over 1.6 million workers and foremen for their new tasks.

By the end of the war, government expenditures accounted for almost 50% of the economy's total output, as compared to just 18% in 1940. Government exercised considerable management control over much of the civilian sector, controlling prices and wages to avoid inflation (successfully), and rationing scarce consumer goods such as gas and oil, coffee, butter, tires, shoes, meat, cheese, and sugar, ensuring everyone received a fair share. The government imposed a progressive tax on all income, and taxed particularly aggressively any business profits it judged excessive. Government reserved (and not infrequently, exercised) the right to reset prices retroactively where officials believed private contractors' profits were too high. Private financing of investment in plant and equipment continued during the war (totaling some $6.9 billion over the 1940–1943 period), but this private-sector investment was dwarfed by the government's investments (totaling $13.7 billion over that same period). Some of this investment created "government-owned, government-operated" facilities, most notably in many shipyards. Most of it was "government-owned, contractor-operated," but even in these facilities, government officials tightly controlled operations.

Although an emergency such as the war might have been expected to lead to a more authoritarian form of government, democratic participation expanded rather than contracted in both the workplace and the political sphere. The urgency of the war effort gave workers a powerful lever with which to assert influence over both firm-level and government-level policy (even though that same urgency was sometimes used as a lever against workers, for example, in breaking unauthorized strikes). Senior labor union leaders such as Sidney Hillman, head of the Amalgamated Clothing Workers of America and a key actor in the founding of the Congress of Industrial Organizations, played prominent roles in the war planning effort. As a result, the War Labor Board institutionalized many long-standing union demands for union security, grievance arbitration, seniority, vacation pay, sick leave, and night-shift supplements, forcing these measures onto a broad swath of recalcitrant businesses. Union membership grew from 9 million in 1940 to nearly 15 million in 1945.[19] But there were limits to this democratization. The War Production Board tried to create "joint labor-management committees" to improve manufacturing efficiency at both the plant and the industry levels, but business opposition stalled the program.[20]

Ownership over society's productive resources remained largely private, but control was largely socialized. The success of the mobilization therefore relied to a considerable extent on the private sector's cooperation, but there was little doubt that government would impose its will if that cooperation was not forthcoming. The point was driven home by several dozen plant seizures by government, among them leading producers of military aircraft, warships, telecommunications equipment, and coal, as well as oil companies, railroads, and even one of the largest retailers, Montgomery Ward. Admittedly, about half those seizures were motivated by workers' unauthorized strikes, but the other half were directed at misbehavior by corporate leaders—incompetence, corruption, or refusal to abide by labor regulations. It was not uncommon for these seizures (and for the far greater number of seizure threats) to be prompted by workers' appeals to government.

Government's economy-wide strategic management worked—and that worried the business sector. Business associations organized an advertising campaign that portrayed industrialists rather than government or labor as the heroes of the mobilization story. The campaign relied on all the usual antigovernment stereotypes of excessive paperwork and bureaucratic incompetence. It was massively funded by business leaders, reflecting the deep anxiety felt by many in the private sector that the success of the government-planned mobilization would bolster support for a further expansion of government's role in the economy after the war's end. In December 1943, General Motors' chairman Alfred Sloan addressed the annual meeting of the National Association of Manufacturers, posing a rhetorical question: "Is it not as essential to win the peace, in an economic sense, as it is to win the war, in a military sense?" To ensure this peacetime victory, he said, it was essential that business leaders create jobs for returning veterans. Indeed, many people at the time feared a return of Depression conditions when these veterans reentered the labor market and government war expenditures shrank. If jobs did not materialize in the private sector, government would create jobs for them in an expanded public sector, just as it had begun to do during the Depression—and that would be to lose the peace. It would mean, in Sloan's words, "the socialization of enterprise," and that was simply unacceptable.[21]

To many observers at the time, the United States at war's end could only tip forward into more comprehensive socialist planning or tip back to capitalism.[22] The stakes were indeed high. As it turned out, the proponents of a stronger role for government in the US peacetime economy were divided, red-baited, and outmaneuvered. America's experiment with a democratically managed economy was rapidly shut down.

The patriotic feelings aroused during World War II created a sense of shared and urgent purpose that surely helped the mobilization effort succeed. Today, in thinking about our future, we cannot assume the same degree of shared purpose as we saw under wartime conditions. On the other hand, enterprises in a democratic-socialist system will have goals that speak directly to our needs, and we should not underestimate how much a change in the form of economy and society might change everyday expectations and motivation.

Let us therefore see how such a democratic-socialist system could overcome the crises we face today, taking each crisis in turn.[23]

First, a socialist transformation will aim to end our crisis of economic irrationality. The main means of coordinating the economic activity of regions, industries, and the overall economy will no longer be the capitalist market but instead democratic strategic management. This will require that we establish public ownership over society's main productive resources. Only then can we ensure that production, investment, financing, innovation, and foreign trade are consistent with our democratic priorities, rather than capitalist profit and growth imperatives.

A socialist economy of this kind will experience none of the economic and financial instability characteristic of the capitalist system. Investment and job creation will no longer be unreliable results of private businesses' decisions based on their individual profit expectations. They will instead be decided democratically, based on society's needs. The democratic-socialist model will deepen, expand, and democratize something like the World War II economic mobilization.

Ownership: Beyond Private Enterprise

By putting society's main productive resources under public ownership, we will turn the core of our economy into one giant enterprise. Many of today's competing firms will be transformed into subunits of that enterprise. This will allow us to manage strategically these subunits and their interdependencies, much as top executives in a big corporation manage the operations of their firm's subunits—but democratically, applying the Collaborative Strategizing principle on an expanded scale.

To do this, we will need to socialize the ownership of society's productive resources—equipment, buildings, land, technological know-how. That means taking from private individuals the right to buy and sell those resources and vesting those rights in the community, whether at the municipal, regional, or national level. To be clear: socialism has no interest in abolishing private ownership of personal resources. Your after-tax income from work will be yours to spend as you wish, and your phone will be yours to keep or to trade.

We should expect enormous opposition to this socialization of property from the current private owners. To compensate the current owners—including all working people whose savings had been tied up in stocks, bonds, and land—the government will issue long-term annuities.

The socialization of property will take a variety of forms, offering differing degrees of socialization. We can visualize the main forms as three concentric rings in the structure of the socialist economy.

The first, innermost ring will offer the most complete socialization, in the form of direct public ownership and government control. Ownership might be at the national, regional, or municipal level. Enterprises in the industries that matter most for our well-being—because of their economies of scale or their impact on the rest of the economy—will be in this ring. This ring will include some entire industries, such as banking and finance, telecommunications, public transportation, healthcare, pharmaceuticals, energy, automobile, steel, aluminum, and the defense industrial base. It will include the Internet and all land. It will include specific companies that have grown to the point where they have systemic effects, such as retail giants like Walmart and Amazon, and agricultural distribution giants like Cargill. It will include traditional utilities such as water, sewage, protective services, etc. And it goes without saying that the ownership of formerly public agencies that have been partly privatized under the prevailing neo-liberal policies, such as prisons and schools, will return to the public sector. After several decades of experience, it is too obvious that contracting with private enterprise to provide public services and "public-private partnerships" cannot deliver what we, the public, need, and instead leads to crony capitalism.

The second, or middle, ring will be composed of what we might call "social-ized cooperatives"—cooperatives whose governing boards include not only the workers of the enterprise (as in a traditional worker cooperative) but also other stakeholders such as customers, local community, and local gov-ernment. These cooperatives will become part of the "socialist core" of the economy along with the first-ring enterprises if they agree to work within the framework of the national economic council's strategy process (which will set economic as well as social and environmental goals) in exchange for the benefits that brings them (which we will discuss shortly). Like the first-ring enterprises, they will not own their equipment, buildings, or land, but rent them from the government. And as part of the socialist core, the prices they pay for their material and human resources and the prices they earn for their products will be set by higher-level economic councils. These prices will aim to internalize all the relevant externalities, and will there-fore reflect each resource's full economic, social, and environmental costs.

However, compared to the enterprises in the first ring, these cooperatives in the second ring will enjoy more control over what they produce and how. Each enterprise will negotiate economic, social, and environmental goals with the councils, but they will retain more autonomy in planning how to reach those goals and the compensation of the enterprise's personnel will be based in part on how well they meet those goals. They will alert the relevant industry and regional economic councils of any change in investment or production plans, so that these plans can be coordinated with those of other affected enterprises.

The third, outer ring will be composed of a much smaller private sector, made up of small-scale and family enterprises, as well as cooperative enterprises that choose to remain outside the national economic strategy process. Their workers will participate as citizens in the economic strategy process that sets top-level priorities, but the enterprises themselves will not participate in the socialist core's process of working out how best to achieve those priorities. The enterprise's income will be based directly on its success finding buyers for its products, rather than being budgeted by the higher-level councils as a function of its contribution to society. They will be financed by banks (now public) or by retained savings.

The socialization of property in this third ring will be thus limited and indirect. These enterprises' profits will remain private, but control will be socialized in several ways. Government regulations will protect these enterprises' workers and local communities. These enterprises will rely on products sourced from the socialist core, whose variety and prices will reflect our collective strategic priorities. They will employ people who will have the option of high-quality employment conditions in the socialist core. And any external financing of these enterprises will come from banks, which, being now publicly owned, will use our democratically determined strategic criteria to make credit-allocation decisions.

Overall, the economy will be dominated by the first and second rings—the socialist core. Some people fear that this will lead to vast government monopolies, and that these will be even less efficient and less responsive to customers and communities than corporate monopolies are today. Three factors should allay those concerns.

First, we already have extensive experience with publicly owned enterprises under public control. And even with their current limitations, such enterprises are just as economically efficient on average as privately owned firms.[24]

Second, where economies of scale do not make doing so uneconomical, we can establish several competing enterprises. We will encourage these enterprises to compete on quality and service by setting a common price for their services. (If we allowed competition on price, we would be creating a powerful incentive to squeeze labor, and that would be contrary to our goals.)

And finally, we will improve the oversight and accountability of the core enterprises relative to what we see in the public sector today. Currently, the agencies that are supposed to provide this oversight are severely handicapped by government's subservience to business interests. These agencies' budgets have been starved. Roadblocks have been created to make it difficult for them to attract high-quality staff. Revolving doors have undermined their integrity. Under democratic socialism, those impediments will be swept away.

We should recognize, however, that complaints about inefficiency and unresponsiveness will be to some extent inevitable—and can be a healthy sign. Under capitalist conditions, prices and wages are formed through the blind process of market competition. If I think a firm's product is too expensive or its quality is poor, or if the firm offers me a wage that is too low, all I can do is look for another firm that can make me a better offer. There is no one to blame if I do not find a better alternative. And there is no one to blame if the entire industry is selling their products at too high a price or offering products of shoddy quality or paying low wages—that's just "what the market is telling us." Under socialism, these issues will become objects of democratic deliberation, and as a result, criticisms of poor performance inevitably will be far more common. And these criticisms will be positive signs that we are taking control over our economic destiny rather than remaining victims of the market process.[25]

Let us try to imagine what this socialist core would look like. Take first the auto industry. We already had a brief period when we had de facto government ownership of two of the biggest auto companies, GM and Chrysler, in the wake of the 2008 crisis. But the Obama administration used this period to force workers to accept pay cuts, to restore the firms to profitability, and hand them back to the private investors. Instead, we could have nationalized them and kept them in the public sector. In the socialist model, they will become public enterprises, operating under the authority of an elected national transportation industry council. They will have advisory boards that include elected representatives of workers, suppliers, and customers. And, as part of the socialist core, these enterprises will be tasked to become leaders in all-electric cars and public-transportation systems.

Second, consider banking. In the immediate aftermath of the 2008 crisis, it would have been quite possible to nationalize the entire US banking system.[26] Our banks were able to function only because the government bailed them out. In the socialist model, we would take them over entirely. Sweden did this very successfully in the wake of a financial crisis in 1992. But the Swedish government (in good social-democratic style) reprivatized them as soon as their balance-sheets were cleaned up. Instead, we will keep them under public ownership, restructure them along rational lines, and fold them into the new socialist core. This new public banking system will direct public investment funds to enterprises across the economy as a function of their potential contribution to our democratically determined strategic goals.

Imagine now that our largest retailers—Walmart, Costco, Kroger, Amazon, McDonald's—become socialist enterprises, accountable to us citizens. These enterprises will be tasked by our elected regional and national economic councils to offer a wide selection of responsibly sourced consumer goods and foods. They will be staffed by well-trained and decently paid personnel. These workers will elect (or select at random) representatives to their advisory boards, who, along with representatives of consumers, suppliers, and local government, will ensure that the enterprise is meeting the economic, social, and environmental goals set through the strategic economic management process.

And imagine too that we nationalize land. Current occupants will not be expelled unless some public purpose dictated a change; but they will begin paying rent to the government, not to private landlords—if they pay any rent at all. No rent will be due unless the property has some locational advantage, for example, for housing in more-desirable locations and for more-fertile agricultural land. There will be no profit in building and selling or renting out new housing: housing construction will become a government mission. Public housing will become the norm. Local councils, bringing together residents and local government, will manage these housing complexes, and higher-level councils will ensure their financing is adequate to meet our housing needs.

Strategic Management of the Economy: Beyond Market Myopia

As we discussed earlier, during the World War II mobilization, the US government planned output and investment for much of the economy. In a democratic-socialist society, with the key sectors of the economy under public ownership, we will generalize and democratize a similar strategic management process.

We will organize periodic deliberations and voting in councils at every level to set our economic, environmental, and social goals and our plans for reaching them. These councils will give voice to citizens in their neighborhoods, cities, and regions, and to workers in their work-teams, enterprises, and industries. The national economic council would synthesize their input. Decision-making will be as decentralized as possible, and as centralized as necessary. Decisions will be made at the lowest level at which all the parties affected can come together to deliberate and decide, to ensure that the strategic-management process benefits as much as possible from local knowledge. Where the affected parties are spread over the entire economy—such as in industries with massive economies of scale, with widespread effects on upstream suppliers and downstream customers, or with serious effects on our natural or social environment—decision-making will be more centralized. Whether the decision-making is more centralized or more local, we will need to be vigilant in assuring its participatory, democratic quality.

Based on the input from these lower-level councils, the democratic national economic council will decide our society's main economic goals for the coming period, based on input from citizens and from enterprises in the socialist core. These goals will cover things such as weekly and annual working hours; the volume and type of basic needs that will be met through free distribution; the other consumer needs for which payment will be required; the amount of investment that will be directed to the various branches of economic and social activity; the balance of economic, social, and environmental criteria that the economic councils and banks will use in assessing enterprise performance and investment proposals; and the investment dedicated to reducing inequalities between regions and groups.[27]

In the past, critics of socialist planning have argued that the complexity of the modern economy is so great—with so many millions of products—that it would be computationally impossible to develop such production and investment plans in sufficient detail and in a timely way.[28] The critics argued that the market economy is far superior at ensuring a balance of supply and demand for all these products, because the market relies on price information rather than physical quantities and because it decentralizes decision-making to individual firms and consumers. However, modern computers make calculations of compatible production and investment plans across an entire economy entirely feasible, so we no longer need the capitalist market process to reach this result.

We should pause briefly to underline the contrast between this strategic management process and the process of competition in the capitalist market system. In the capitalist system, prices emerge after the fact. Firms bring products to market with a price tag attached; but since they do not know competitors' plans, they often find they need to adjust that price down or up to respond to their competitors' actions. Competition threatens with bankruptcy those firms whose costs and prices proved to have been too high and threatens those firms' workers with unemployment. In the socialist strategic-management system, prices will reflect our shared strategic goals. They will incorporate the costs of various externalities—such as pollution—and our concern for the more-distant future—by taxing carbon emissions for example. Under capitalism, strategic management is confined to the individual firm and is therefore subordinate to the market. Under socialism, the market will be subordinate to our economic strategy and will be a means of implementing it. Such strategic management does not preclude competition between enterprises. A well-managed socialist system will encourage enterprises to compete to offer more-attractive products and services, and it will leave customers free to express their preferences among them in the marketplace.

It will be important for the effectiveness of this strategic management process that enterprises communicate to the economic councils an accurate estimate of their capabilities, and that they work diligently to meet their mutually agreed-upon goals—neither understating these estimates to make it easy for them to achieve their targets, thereby creating gluts, nor overstating them to acquire more resources, thereby creating shortages.[29]

To this end, we will have three tools, which we can use in combination. First, transparency. Since workers as well as external stakeholders such as suppliers, customers, and economic councils will have full access to all the relevant information about the enterprise, and since the strategic management process brings them all into dialogue, information will surface, and biases will be revealed and rectified more rapidly.

Financial incentives are a second tool. We will offer workers a collective bonus that rewards them if their enterprise achieves high output but also penalizes them if their output is either below or above the target. This will help ensure that the economic councils are receiving good information from the enterprises about their capabilities.

A third tool is competition. We will avoid monopoly situations where there is only one supplier for a given product. Distributing supply contracts across multiple enterprises and/or empowering enterprises to choose their suppliers will give the enterprises and the economic councils comparative performance data. Financial incentives combined with symbolic recognition will spur the laggard enterprises and reward the high performers. Industry forums will help the laggards learn from the leaders.

Finance: Beyond Profitability

Today, a handful of banks control our entire banking sector. Instead of breaking up these big banks and trusting that capitalistic market competition will yield a healthy credit system, we will socialize their ownership and control. The entire apparatus of the stock and bond market will disappear, and along with it the speculative casino capitalism we see around us today.

The banking sector will be divided into consumer banks and industrial banks—both under public control. The consumer banks will operate like savings and loans associations, paying interest on savings and charging interest on consumer loans. The industrial banks will fund the rebuilding of the economy, relying on criteria developed in the strategic management process at regional, industry, and national levels. These industrial banks will replace the financial markets as the source of investment capital. They will become vehicles for channeling credit to enterprises in the second and third rings of the economy. The industrial banks will fund investment based on a combination of economic, social, and environmental criteria and on the economic councils' strategic goals.

Production: Beyond Growth at All Costs

Work in a democratic-socialist system will be reorganized to make it more intrinsically satisfying, with less narrow specialization and more opportunities for skill development and promotion. And hopefully, many people will find satisfaction in contributing to the common good. Nevertheless, for many other people, perhaps even most, work will still be something done out of necessity rather than desire. So, free time—time for family and social interaction, time to cultivate interests and talents—will be treated as a precious form of social wealth.

Under capitalism, the work-time needed to assure a decent standard of living has only been reduced as a result of arduous political struggles by working people against business interests. Under democratic socialism, we will aim to give more meaning to work, but will also aim for a quite different work–life balance.[30] In a socialist society, we will shorten the work week, expand annual paid vacation, as well as paid medical and family leave.

This reduction will be achieved mainly by eliminating wasteful production. The opportunity is enormous—and not only because our socialist society will also greatly reduce military expenditures.

We will eliminate capitalism's wasteful overhead. Indeed, while critics of the socialist model are quick to raise concerns about the bureaucratic overhead costs involved in centralized planning, they forget the time our society wastes in the work of private healthcare insurance intermediaries, advertisers trying to make us buy more, stockbrokers and investment bankers, and lawyers and courts dealing with commercial conflicts. Almost all these activities will be unnecessary in a socialist system.

Beyond these wasteful overhead costs, under capitalism we also incur massive unnecessary production costs. Consider, for example, all the effort spent in auto production and repair that the country will avoid when we simplify the range of car designs and standardize components across car models—*and* when we invest in a comprehensive, free, public transportation system. Consider, too, all the environmental benefits of such a reorientation.

Through our democratic economic management, we will eliminate a vast number of useless jobs. And we will share the resulting wealth and work by reducing working hours. The best current estimates suggest we will be able to maintain our current level of material prosperity if everyone works an average of about 20 hours a week.[31]

Innovation: Beyond Venture Capitalism

A socialist economy will create far more opportunities for creative entrepreneurship than capitalism affords. The reduction in weekly work hours will free up time for entrepreneurial activity for many more people who might be interested. Moreover, instead of relying on venture capitalists, entrepreneurs in a socialist economy will have funding from the public industrial banks and the enterprises within which they currently work. Whereas venture capitalists invest only where they see a good chance of multiplying the value of their investment by a factor of at least 10 over three to five years, our public industrial banks will be less greedy, and they will base their investment on the proposal's impact on the long-term well-being of people and the planet.[32]

Some of this entrepreneurial activity will happen in pockets within the first- and second-ring enterprises—today, we call such activity "intrapreneurship." In a socialist system, opportunities for such creative action will be expanded.[33] And some of it will happen in the third-ring enterprises. This third ring will thus be a place for experimentation by new enterprises operating on the margins of the national strategic management process. If these innovative enterprises prove successful and grow big enough, their founders and workers will have an easy "exit strategy" by attracting a takeover by one of the first- or second-ring enterprises.

Whereas in a capitalist system this entrepreneurship process is associated with the personal enrichment of the founders and their venture capitalist investors, in a socialist society, entrepreneurs will be rewarded with modest monetary rewards but ample social recognition. Critics of socialism sometimes argue that economic development depends crucially on the creativity of the few, and that without the prospects of huge financial rewards, huge creative breakthroughs will not be forthcoming. But the evidence is strong that creative innovators are motivated much more powerfully by the prospect of serving humanity and by social and professional recognition than by personal wealth.[34]

Beyond bottom-up entrepreneurship, innovation in a dynamic democratic-socialist economy will be guided and stimulated by centrally managed, democratically decided programs of innovation development and deployment. The urgency of such programs is great, given the importance of technology in responding to the environmental crisis. Government "mission-oriented" investments along with the corresponding policy supports for local enterprises will be critical if we want to capitalize on the huge potential of the digital-technology revolution to get us onto a sustainable, green development path.[35]

A dynamic socialist economy will deploy the Collaborative Innovating principle to ensure that centralized, top-down innovation and local, bottom-up innovation worked in concert. The economic councils will fund national-, regional-, and industry-level R&D agencies, taking lessons from the success of the National Institutes of Health and the Defense Advanced Research Projects Agency. The councils will simultaneously encourage enterprises not only to offer the products specified in the strategic planning process but also to explore alternatives that might be of interest to customers. A successful outcome for their entrepreneurial "bet" will yield bonus income to the enterprise's workers, and will also provide information to the economic council and the other enterprises, information that will be folded into the next strategic planning cycle. Insofar as this innovation requires important up-front capital investment, our strategic management process will socialize the costs, the risks, as well as the benefits, of this investment.

Of course, some innovations pose health or environmental risks. We will therefore need specialized agencies to conduct proper review, testing, and oversight. Today, regulatory agencies such as the Food and Drug Administration are hamstrung by the weight of business interests, and as a result, their failures are appallingly common. Socialist regulators will be able to make decisions that better balance the benefits and the risks of innovative new technologies.

The socialization of property will enable us to resolve our crisis of disempowerment in the workplace. No longer will we work as "employees," giving management the right to control our work and its fruits in exchange for a wage or salary. We will work as citizens, empowered to participate in the governance of our workplace (and of the wider economy) as equals.[36] From experience in both high-road businesses and worker cooperatives, we already know much about how such enterprises can be organized to preserve both democratic participation and economic effectiveness. The democratic-socialist model will expand Collaborative Strategizing, Innovating, Learning, and Working at the enterprise level.

Enterprise: Beyond Hired Hands

Legislation will mandate workers' representation on the boards of all enterprises over a certain size, alongside representatives of other stakeholders such as customers and community groups. In the inner ring composed of public-sector enterprises, these boards will be advisory, because their strategies will be so dependent on the relevant government agencies operating under the economic councils. In the second ring, the socialized cooperatives, these boards will have broader autonomy.

Beyond the board, what does democratic management of the enterprise look like? In smaller enterprises, major policy decisions will be made in general assemblies of all the workers, voting as equals. In larger enterprises, exclusive reliance on a general assembly would be too cumbersome to embody our democratic values. Here, at the enterprise level just as in the political sphere, democracy will take both direct and representative forms. And just as in the political arena, we will rotate the representative roles, or assign them randomly, to ensure a healthy diversity of views and avoid the emergence of a privileged social layer of professional representatives. There is much we can learn here from the experience of larger worker cooperatives, such as the Mondragon cooperatives in Spain.[37]

Digital technologies will help us here. Capitalist firms have little interest in subjecting their strategic choices to a vote of their employees. By contrast, in socialist enterprises, digital technologies will facilitate wide discussion and frequent voting by enterprise workers and other external stakeholders. When democratic forums are convened for making decisions about investing in or divesting from specific industries or regions, digital technologies will enable us to calculate almost instantaneously the implications for jobs and well-being—across enterprises, locations, and occupations—and to organize citizen voting between the competing scenarios.

Unions will be a vital part of the democratized governance of the socialist enterprise. Workers will participate directly and via representatives in the enterprise board, but practical experience suggests that problems and opportunities surface much more effectively if there is also a second line of communication between front-line workers and the enterprise leadership.[38]

Beyond these changes in enterprise governance, we will launch a massive campaign to reorganize day-to-day work along more humane lines. Today, for every high-road firm that has moved toward more engaging forms of work organization and that relies on teamwork on the shop floor and front lines, there are many more firms where work is stultifying, leaving workers stuck in narrow and repetitive jobs for years on end, without opportunities to contribute their ideas for improvement, and without opportunities for personal development. In a socialist society, workers in every enterprise— especially those in the socialist core—will be encouraged to rethink the organization of their daily activity along more empowered lines, and to organize skill- and career-development pathways. Collaborative Innovating will become a standard practice across industry and government agencies.

Skeptics doubt that democratic-socialist enterprises would be able to meet let alone surpass the level of efficiency achieved by capitalist enterprises. The Collaborative Learning principle provides an effective response to this concern. Socialist enterprises will be governed democratically. Their boards will be in dialogue with the relevant economic councils in other firms, in their region, and in their industry, and they will deliberate to set the enterprise's goals to meet the needs of workers, communities, and environment, as well as the product preferences and affordability constraints of consumers and of the broader society. The benefits of greater efficiency will not take the form of greater profits for the firms' owners and investors, as they do today. Instead, the benefits will be shared equitably among workers and other stakeholders. Under these new conditions, workers will have both a real interest in helping to find the most efficient way to do their jobs.

As a result, in a socialist economy, standardization will be more extensive and help achieve greater efficiency than is possible under capitalist conditions—and will function without the coercion and alienating effects we see today. Collaborative Learning will be generalized as an organizing principle within enterprises. And at the industry-wide level, economic councils will support cross-enterprise standardization efforts both for products, such as in the case of auto design that we discussed earlier in this chapter, and for processes, such as with the software industry's CMM that we discussed in the prior chapter.

Work and Income: Beyond Insecurity

One of the ultimate goals of a democratic-socialist system will be to guarantee all people a good life, freed from the compulsion to "work for a living." But that goal is as yet remote; in a democratic-socialist society, we must therefore find a way to ensure a fair distribution of work effort even as we seek to enrich work and reduce work time.

On the one hand, we are technologically advanced enough to meet many basic needs for free. No one, whether they work or not, will lack the basics as concerns food, clothing, housing, education, healthcare, mobility, communications, utilities, etc. On the other hand, there are many other goods and services that we will treat as discretionary, and consumers will pay for those out of their earnings.

How then will these earnings be determined? The basic pay levels for different types of jobs will be determined (in the socialist-core sector) by the economic councils. More fine-grained differentiation of pay levels will be decided by enterprise boards. Workers in different categories will need to explain to each other why they think this kind of job is worth more than that kind.

Pay differentials will be much smaller than today. As I explain below, by making education free and paying students a decent stipend, we will socialize the cost of the investment in further education—in contrast with the current system where it is funded by the student and their family—and as a result, much of the capitalist rationale for pay differentials will disappear.

Beyond basic pay, bonuses will be designed to support a socialist ethic of interdependence and contribution to the general good, by rewarding both groups and individuals for that contribution—relying on the Collaborative Working principle. There may be some further evolution of society that brings us to the point where economic incentives for hard work and initiative are no longer needed; but for the foreseeable future, even modest differences in pay will have great benefits, particularly in jobs that offer limited intrinsic interest. Social-psychology research teaches us that even quantitatively small differences in pay can assume large symbolic significance.[39]

How, then, will people be matched to jobs in such a system? Just as within a large capitalist firm today, people will be asked to change jobs when such changes would improve overall economic performance, such as if we need fewer people producing car engines and more producing wind turbines. But in a socialist system, economic performance will be measured in terms of meeting society's needs, rather than improving the capitalist firm's profitability. And the requested job changes might involve moving between enterprises, rather than only within a capitalist firm. Where such requests do not elicit enough volunteers, wage rates will be adjusted to make the job changes more attractive.

OVERCOMING GOVERNMENT UNRESPONSIVENESS

The socialization of property will allow us to eliminate the subservience of government to private-sector business interests and thus to overcome the main reason for government's unresponsiveness. The structural power of the private-enterprise business sector and its ability to threaten a capital strike and capital flight will be eliminated. So too will be the various pathways (lobbying, contributions, revolving doors, etc.) that give business and wealthy interests the power they enjoy in the current political process.

In setting government policies in a democratic-socialist society, we will have real equality as citizens, not just formal-legal equality. Our political system will be transformed, from plutocracy—operating under what we called earlier the "golden rule," that he who has the gold, rules—into a real democracy. We will need new political institutions in which citizens can come together to debate, deliberate, and decide on policy. We will capitalize on the potential of electronic systems to enrich public discussion and to simplify the conduct of popular voting.[40] Expanding the scope of democracy to our economic system, we will need a host of new governing institutions at every level, from the neighborhood to the city, region, and country as a whole, and we will need new mechanisms for ensuring the democratic quality of the decisions made in these institutions.

To guard against the risk of a slide toward oligopoly, we will rely on a range of mechanisms. Freedom of speech and of association will be essential. We will also need safeguards for minority rights. In some domains, we may want some kind of federalism to ensure there is wide support for national policy decisions and that local concerns are not ignored by the majority in making those decisions.

In a democratic-socialist society, we will aim to enable direct forms of democracy wherever feasible and will work just as diligently to ensure the robustness of indirect forms wherever they are necessary. We know a lot today about how representative forms can degenerate and how professional politicians can capture an election system, but we have also learned a lot about how to guard against that risk.[41] Instead of elected representatives, we might rely on the sortition system of ancient Greece, where randomly selected citizens rotate through political functions for short terms.

Another threat to democracy comes from our need for technical expertise. Indeed, experts today often monopolize the conversation and hijack the decision-making process. Our legislative forums, such as the economic councils, will need specialized experts to help provide data and analysis— but we must ensure that these experts are "kept on tap, not on top."[42]

To ensure the democratic quality of government decision-making, we will leverage a considerable body of experience with various forms of deliberative democracy. We are accustomed to a conception of democracy profoundly shaped by our capitalist context, where citizens are assumed to each vote in accordance with their individual material interests. In a deliberative democracy process, before any vote on an issue, we will rely on an organized process for mobilizing expert information, for informing voters, and for orchestrating a process of authentic dialogue. In this dialogue, participants will be challenged, and given an opportunity, to present arguments publicly—arguments that in this context will naturally be framed in terms of the public interest, rather than individual material interest. Such a situation evokes an ethos of interdependence and helps overcome purely individualistic orientations.

Critics of deliberative democracy argue that it is feeble because it will always be undermined by differences in economic and personal resources. But these criticisms, like Aristotle's fears of political democracy, are inflated. Yes, deliberative democracy is indeed likely to fail if we attempt to implement it in a society characterized by capitalism's structural inequalities. But those concerns will be largely obviated in a democratic-socialist society.[43] Yes, sexist and racist attitudes, or personal characteristics such as reluctance to speak in public or closed-mindedness, can undermine the deliberation process. But to imagine that such problems invalidate the whole deliberative scheme is to make the perfect the enemy of the good. These are not fundamental impediments. They are practical problems that we will deal with in a practical way.

Of course, not all decisions in a democratic society can be made in the consensual manner that deliberation aims for. Some issues will leave a minority unhappy. However, that does not make democratic government a fantasy. Even where we are dealing with deeply held and irreconcilable differences in values, there is no reason to think we cannot treat each other respectfully as adversaries, albeit passionate adversaries, rather than enemies to be eradicated.[44]

One distinctive feature of government under democratic socialism should be underscored: it will require far wider and more frequent participation from all of us. As workers, we will be called on to participate in decisions that are currently the preserve of managers. As citizens, we will be called on to participate far more actively in decisions about a host of policy issues that are currently the preserve of professional politicians and bureaucrats. This will mean a lot of meetings, but they will be substantive meetings, where our voices will really count. Capitalism has sucked the life out of democracy. In a socialist society, democracy will become our form of life.

OVERCOMING ENVIRONMENTAL UNSUSTAINABILITY

It is not difficult to identify the requirements for environmental sustainability.[45] Renewable resources such as fish, soil, and groundwater must be used no faster than the rate at which they can be renewed. For example, fish stocks must not be depleted faster than the fish can reproduce. Nonrenewable resources such as minerals and fossil fuels must be used no faster than renewable substitutes for them can be put into place. For example, we should be reinvesting profits from fossil-fuel-powered processes into renewables such as solar or biofuel, and doing so fast enough to ensure that there will be adequate energy available when oil is no longer an option. And pollution and wastes must be emitted no faster than natural systems can absorb them or render them harmless. For example: releasing sewage into a lake or river is not sustainable unless it is at a pace slow enough for aquatic life to absorb the nutrients.

There is no nature-given reason we cannot satisfy these requirements, even with a total world population projected to level out at about 10 billion. Population growth is a challenge, but not an insurmountable constraint. The world economy has been growing at about 3% per year since 1970, and that is about twice as fast as population growth over that period, which averaged about 1.5% per year and is slowing. Yes, we are crossing planetary ecological boundaries. But it is not primarily population growth that is driving this trajectory. It is the prevailing capitalist form of production and consumption. Yes, we must switch from fossil fuels to renewables—this is imperative and urgent.[46] But we are assured by scientists that we can in fact power the entire planet with wind, water, and solar power.[47] Yes, it will take an enormous effort to convert our economy, indeed an effort that would not be profitable for business. But it is feasible.[48]

The basic impediment to achieving environmental sustainability is the capitalist private-property system. Profitability pressures limit the ability of capitalist firms to factor environmental externalities into their decisions, and hamstring governments' efforts to regulate appropriately. As a result, capitalism puts into jeopardy the ecological balance of the planet and thereby threatens our well-being.

To respond to this threat, we need a mobilization much like the United States experienced during World War II—except that this effort will need to be more comprehensive, several decades in duration rather than just five years, and globally integrated. Such a mobilization will allow us to fund the massive R&D effort needed to develop new energy and CO_2 absorption technologies, and to drive a rapid transformation of our power, water, industrial, housing, agricultural, and transportation systems.[49]

Of course, this will require changes in our lifestyles and in our economies, but it need not entail a degradation in the quality of life. The average US ecological footprint is 50% larger than that of the average person in most European countries, in part because the United States has more suburban sprawl, less public transportation, and uses more energy and water per person than most other developed countries. Clearly, however, our 50% larger footprint does not make for a correspondingly better quality of life.[50] For example: if you can get to and from work on foot or on a bike or on public transportation, you have a much smaller footprint than if you rely on a car—especially if you drive alone, as do over 75% of Americans, and especially if your car gets only 15 miles to the gallon, as is often the case today.[51] Vegetarians have a much smaller footprint than meat eaters. A house with a grass lawn has a bigger ecological footprint than one without, especially if the lawn is watered often and if it is treated with chemicals. Do any of these options reduce the quality of our lives—walking short distances rather than driving long ones, reducing meat consumption, or replacing grass lawns with drought-resistant plants? Hardly.

OVERCOMING SOCIAL DISINTEGRATION

The socialist transformation will aim to resolve the social crises provoked by capitalist development. The economic councils will work to overcome regional disparities and city-level dysfunctions that flow from our current political system's subservience to the private sector and to the uncontrolled dynamics of capitalist market competition. Investment will be directed to the regions that need it. No longer will localities have to bribe corporations with tax breaks and subsidies to stay or to invest. Real-estate industry interests will no longer dictate city building codes and permits.

We need such democratic management of the economy to enable people to get the education they require; to organize and fund childcare, elder-care, healthcare; to organize community security and restorative justice; and to manage public housing. We have already learned much about what is needed through the experiments of social-democratic countries and pro-gressive businesses and cities. Democratic socialism will apply more sys-tematically the results of those experiments.

Education: Beyond Human Capital

The post–World War II GI Bill paid returning veterans not only tuition but also living expenses to attend high school, college, or vocational/technical school, as well as providing low-cost mortgages, low-interest loans to start a business, and one year of unemployment compensation. The economic effects on the nation's economy and on these veterans' lives were momen-tous (despite the racial discrimination in its application and its limited benefits for women).[52]

But this democratizing step was soon reversed, and in our capitalist society today, education is a key mechanism ensuring the persistence of class and racial inequality across generations. Richer families can af-ford further education for their children, and these children have over-whelming advantages in getting into and graduating from the best schools and colleges and from there into better jobs. To eliminate this source of inequality, a socialist society not only will ensure that childcare, preschool, school, and college are free but also will pay a stipend while the student is studying.

Under these conditions, the cost of developing work-related skills—what some call today "human capital investment"—will be socialized. As a result, wage rates can be made far more equal. Indeed, so long as higher education is not truly free—because it requires paying fees and foregoing work income—jobs that require more education command a big pay pre-mium, otherwise the student has no way to repay the required investment or student loans. But if education is free, then there is no economic ra-tionale for these wage differentials. Education and career choice will no longer be constrained by parents' wealth. And people will be free to develop the types and levels of specialized skills for which they are most talented and in which they have the greatest interest.

Care: Beyond the Family

Care—childcare, eldercare, caring for the sick and the disabled—is important work, and caregivers will be recognized—and compensated—for their contribution to a critical societal function. This will be done in the first ring of the socialist economy by public agencies. It will be done in the second ring by socialized cooperatives. It will be done in the third ring by small private enterprises. And it will be done outside the formal economic sphere by neighbors helping each other.

People will earn decent wages undertaking such care, and they will bring authentic attention to the task because they are helping people who live in their own neighborhoods. These community service enterprises will be funded by the regional economic council based on a submission of their proposed budget and activities. Today, some communities organize local-exchange trading systems where people earn credits that can be exchanged for other local services.[53] In our socialist society, such activity could be compensated by neighborhood community councils in just the same way as work in any other part of the socialist economy.

Socialism can hardly be democratic if women's contributions continue to be devalued. And conversely, the socialization of many care activities will help clear the path toward greater gender equality. Indeed, gender discrimination will be addressed much more effectively once we leave behind the private-enterprise system. For example: pay equity efforts have been hobbled by lack of a standardized job classification system and by insufficient transparency about pay scales—capitalist employers naturally resist those policies. But such policies can be enacted easily in a system of socialized ownership.[54] Similarly, socialized ownership and democratic control will allow for much more aggressive action to remedy occupational and wage discrimination against African Americans and other minorities.

Our healthcare system is sick—sick with profit-seeking by insurance companies, for-profit hospitals, pharmaceutical and medical device companies, and doctors. A democratic-socialist society will transform healthcare into a public service under public control. There is no morally defensible reason why money should buy you more healthcare, and there is no political-economic reason to organize healthcare on that obscene principle.

Criminal Justice: Beyond Incarceration

Socialism will not do away with crime; but a socialist transformation of our economic system will do much to eradicate many of its common causes, most notably poverty and limited education options and job opportunities. Our response to the remaining criminality will be quite different from what we see around us today. The current system commits us to massive investments in crime detection, apprehension, and incarceration. Although our socialist society will still need some courts and prisons to sanction unacceptable behavior, we will replace this punitive retribution ethos with investment in community-level institutions for restorative justice and in genuinely rehabilitative prisons.[55]

Housing: Beyond Home Ownership

The US government has promoted and subsidized home ownership through the mortgage-interest tax deduction. This has been doubly problematic. On the one hand, that tax deduction is a massive subsidy for wealthier people and only of limited value to lower-income people. And on the other hand, to the extent that the encouragement has worked, it has discouraged worker militancy by raising the cost of job loss and by encouraging values of competitive individualism.[56]

As for renting, the capitalist housing market leaves renters vulnerable to rent increases, inadequate maintenance, and eviction when more lucrative options appear for the owners. This has prompted numerous heroic efforts to enact rent control. But the evidence is overwhelming that rent control leads at best to only very mixed outcomes. Rent controls are either too tight—making it unprofitable to build new housing and leaving just a tiny minority to benefit from their rent-controlled housing—or too loose—leading to rents that are too high for too many.[57]

The conclusion is clear: we cannot respect the human right to housing by attempting to subsidize or regulate a capitalist property market. We need a more thorough socialization of the ownership of land and housing. We will enact a vast program of high-quality public housing. Anyone who wants quality public housing at minimal rent will be able to access it without significant delay. Utopian? No. In Vienna, Austria, today—no socialist utopia—three out of five people live in municipal or cooperative housing, and much of it is architecturally beautiful.

Public housing has been stigmatized in the United States for decades as low-quality housing, only for the very poorest. But this stigma reflects the power of the real-estate and housing-construction industries over government policy. The demise of our country's big public housing projects was not due to the intrinsic limitations of modernist high-rise architecture, nor to the residents' neglect. It was due to persistent and ruthless budget cuts by local and federal housing agencies.[58]

Just like owners of other productive resources, under democratic socialism landlords will be expropriated (with compensation). The regional economic council will set rents. Basic—comfortable, dignified—housing will be either free or at minimal rent. The housing authority will charge correspondingly higher rents for housing with greater amenities or more desirable locations. With abundant high-quality public housing, there will be no reason to promote home ownership.

Such public housing will also provide the foundation for a richer communal life. Without imposing any collectivization on everyday life, local community councils will use public housing to ensure that neighborhoods have facilities for shared meals, childcare and eldercare, cooperative stores, and shared laundry facilities. The local councils will take responsibility for assuring the community's recreational needs as well as security and restorative justice processes. Neighborhoods will thus be transformed into living communities. These communities will become over time a primary unit of social organization alongside the family.

OVERCOMING INTERNATIONAL CONFLICT

Even absent a broader global shift to socialism, a movement in our own country toward democratic socialism is feasible. Yes, we should anticipate hostility from the international financial markets and the elites of other countries. As a result, we will need to plan for the corresponding international tensions. But we are a huge, wealthy economy, only modestly dependent on international trade and finance, so there is no reason to think this hostility will be debilitating.

In our trade with other countries, we will aim for international solidarity rather than nationalistic protection and imperialist domination. We will capitalize on opportunities to replace expensive domestic steel with cheaper imported steel (for example). Benefits will accrue to steel-using enterprises here, to the corresponding workers and consumers, and to the workers in the countries from which we are importing. But we will also have generous government investment to support the transition of steelworkers made redundant by those imports and to support the communities in which they live. While achieving that balance seems to be impossible in our capitalist system, it is not a difficult problem to solve in a socialist system.

If the prices of these imports are lower because the exporting countries are violating our environmental and labor standards, we can apply a tariff. Government can use that tariff to help fund the domestic trade-adjustment programs as well as to contribute to international efforts to improve environmental and labor conditions in the exporting countries. If other countries are willing to work with us on such environmental and labor issues, we will form "clubs" that give preferential trade terms based on environmental and social criteria.[59]

If adversaries attempt to inflict economic harm on our socialist economy, a democratic-socialist economic management system will buffer working people from the costs of those attacks. Capital controls will be an essential first, defensive step.[60] By contrast, such buffering was all but impossible for social-democratic reform efforts such as in France under President Mitterrand in the early 1980s, not only because the country was much less self-sufficient than the United States, but also because this reform path required continuous support from the French business community—which, predictably enough, saw no reason to oblige.

And even if we are isolated and under economic attack, our international relations will be radically reoriented to our higher goals. It is obvious that the 800 military bases that the United States has around the world are not intended to defend working people's interests, neither here nor there. A socialist America will scale back dramatically and repurpose the vast military-industrial complex at home and our vast military empire abroad. Scaled back, to free up most of the 3.5% of the national economy currently devoted to war. And repurposed, to focus on defensive capabilities at home and development assistance abroad. Some kind of (paid) national service will be a good way to ensure that the burden and opportunity of this work are fairly distributed.

Clearly, however, many more benefits of the democratic-socialist model would materialize if other countries also adopted it and if together we built the corresponding international governance system. Indeed, the socialization of production is now thoroughly global in scope, and the tension between socialized production and private property therefore plays out not only within national borders, but also in the international arena. The socialist resolution of this broader tension lies in the creation of correspondingly globalized forums for the democratic management of the global economy. Right-wing conservatives are appalled by the idea of a world government; socialists embrace it.

As other countries join us, we will be able to address challenges whose solutions lie out of reach in the current capitalist world. As more countries shift to the socialist model, we will eliminate trade in harmful but highly profitable industries such as drugs, toxic waste, and military equipment and firearms. We will begin to work together to allocate more fairly truly scarce, nonrenewable natural resources, such as fresh water and the minerals needed for modern industrial production. We will work together to overcome global inequalities in income, wealth, and health. We will progressively realize the bounty of modern technology for the benefit of humanity as a whole.

This sketch of a democratic-socialist America could be extended. We could address telecommunications and media policy, support for culture, the arts, sports, and many other important domains. But my goal has not been to draw a detailed blueprint. Instead, it has been simply to paint a picture of a plausible democratic-socialist system in just enough detail to allow you to assess its realism and desirability. We need to turn now to its feasibility.

CHAPTER 7

Getting There

The democratic-socialist model is so radically different from the neo-liberal model currently dominant in the United States, and indeed so different from the models we see or have seen in other countries, that it is hard to imagine how we get from here to there.

There are plenty of skeptics eager to convince us that there is no possible path. The *opportunity* for such a radical change is said to have dissipated as capitalist firms grow ever more powerful. People's *motivation* for making such a change is said to have shrunk as a result of the long-term rise in living standards and improvements in the social safety net. People's *ability* to fight for this change is said to have been weakened by the deskilling and fragmentation of their work as well as by a weakening of education standards. And the *path* to such a radical transformation is said to be blocked by the entrenched power of big business and the "deep state" in our political process, and by the decimation of the unions in the private sector.

The skeptics are wrong.

GROWING OPPORTUNITY

Capitalism's path of development is not random but instead reflects its basic features. And these features, most notably the progressive socialization of production, create ever-greater opportunity for a socialist transformation.

First, consider the evolution of industry structure. The idea of democratically managed *enterprises* has been around for centuries, but the idea of a democratically managed *economy* would have been absurdly un-realistic in the economic structure of early 19th-century America. Back then, our economy was dominated by small-scale farms and artisanal workshops that were geographically dispersed and largely isolated. But as capitalism has developed, smaller firms have been replaced by larger firms. Whereas socializing the ownership of tens of thousands of small retail firms would have been a herculean task, socializing the one big company that displaced them—Walmart—would be infinitely easier by comparison.

Second, the structure of property has shifted from individual and family proprietorships, to publicly traded corporations relying on dispersed investors, to financial markets dominated by a small number of institutional investors. Although this has led to ever-greater control of "Main Street" by "Wall Street," at the same time this evolution makes it much easier to bring both industry and finance under democratic control.

Third, capitalist development has led to an ever-larger role for govern-ment in the economy, funding a growing range of social and material infra-structure investments. Of course, conservatives encourage people to blame their problems on "big government." But most people's lives are very de-pendent on government—whether for schools or roads or Social Security pensions or Medicare support—and that creates a favorable context for progressives to argue for improving and expanding government rather than shrinking it or outsourcing it to private industry. Conservatives are desperately eager to discredit and defund government because they know all too well that the experience of effective government will encourage people to demand more of it.

Finally, capitalist enterprises are increasingly international. Economic activities are increasingly linked by conscious, strategically managed cooperation both within multinationals and between suppliers and customers across national borders. Not surprisingly, international gov-ernance structures—such as the UN, the World Trade Organization, the International Monetary Fund, and the various regional and bilateral trade agreements—have arisen to deal with the resulting tensions. Although this globalization of industry and the emergence of the corresponding gov-ernance systems have strengthened the hand of capital relative to labor, that should not lead us to overlook the opportunity this creates to give socialism a global form.

As capitalism develops, democratic control over the economy becomes, in this sense, objectively easier to implement. And subjectively, such con-trol appears increasingly plausible. Opportunity grows.

INCREASING MOTIVATION

As the economy evolves toward increasingly socialized production, it becomes ever more scandalous that control of the economy remains in the hands of the 1%. Government's unresponsiveness and our disempowerment in the workplace become more frustrating as monopolies swell, economic cycles recur, waste proliferates, the environmental crisis deepens, social crises multiply, and international conflicts persist.

Where once the negative features of capitalism might have been seen as the price we had to pay for its positive features, patience wears thin. Ever more powerful companies control ever vaster domains and capture ever more personal data. Employees see their efforts to create long-term value trashed in their employers' search for short-term profits. People are laid off because Wall Street analysts think their employer's payroll is too burdensome. Service levels offered to customers are lowered to reduce costs. R&D budgets are slashed to boost profits. People are left behind in periods of mass unemployment. Productive enterprises are dismantled because of overproduction in industry, and regions left in poverty as old industries decline. As citizens, we see government either serving the narrow interests of business or hamstrung in its efforts to serve broader societal interests and to respond to increasingly urgent environmental, social, and international crises.

The appearance of high-road firms adds fuel to the fire. Even if they often fail to live up to their promise of participation and engaging work, they offer a tantalizing prospect of a better workplace. People see a growing gap between, on the one hand, the promise of decent working conditions and social and environmental commitments of these high-road firms, and on the other hand, the abysmal conditions in their low-road competitors. And people see government acting to encourage rather than block that low road.

As capitalism develops, the contrast between how things work and how much better they could work in a different system becomes starker and more visible to the naked eye. Over time, this creates increasing, if latent, motivation for a system-wide transformation.

STRENGTHENING CAPABILITIES

Social change happens when the opportunities are ripe, when people stand up to change things, *and* when people have the capabilities required for effective action. Developing these capabilities is perhaps the most important positive feature of capitalist development: it is part of the broader process of the socialization of production. The experience of work in modern industry, especially but not only in high-road firms, equips employees with broader cognitive and social-organizational skills—skills of the kind they need to participate effectively in, and indeed to lead, our efforts to make a better world.

As we saw in our discussion of several high-road firms, mobilizing employees' creativity requires higher training investments in a wide range of technical and social skills. Recall the list: solving problems, leading teams, analyzing work processes, identifying improvement opportunities, dealing with conflicting views and divergent interests, and understanding the economics of industry. These skills equip working people to participate in and lead progressive social movements and political campaigns. The experience of participation in the workplace facilitates and encourages engagement in civic issues beyond the workplace.[1] At Kaiser Permanente, for example, unions such as the SEIU have been very successful in mobilizing members around issues well beyond their immediate wages and working conditions, in campaigns for the universal right to healthcare, for immigrants' rights, and for a higher minimum wage.

Even among low-road firms, many find that technology shifts force them to recruit more-skilled employees. True, these firms make little effort to mobilize the creativity of those employees, and they are opportunistic in exploiting their skills without being willing to invest in their further development or even pay fairly for them. Nevertheless, most of them rely on a workforce with ever-advancing literacy, numeracy, and social and technical skills. The development of these skills in the wider population has strengthened the organizational capacities of movements for labor, women's, LGBTQ, and civil rights.[2] These rising education and skill levels equip working people to be more effective in advancing progressive causes.

THREE SCENARIOS

How could we capitalize on these trends to achieve this democratic-socialist transformation? I see three scenarios—two that pass through crisis and the third that promises more gradual and cumulative, evolutionary change.[3] As I will explain, however, the third is very likely to collapse, and the path to socialism from there passes through crisis, too.

First, under conditions of economic crisis, at a future major downturn or financial crash, when many businesses are insolvent, there would be real popular resonance for a democratic-socialist call that insolvent firms and banks should be taken over by government and turned into either public enterprises or socialized cooperatives.

Second, the climate change process will soon come to be recognized more widely as a real emergency, akin to World War II. This could well happen if we have a season with, say, three or four major storms that swamp and cripple several major cities at once. People in Florida could start getting nervous about the inevitable effect of rising sea levels on the value of their real estate, and many of them could try to sell at the same time, thereby provoking a collapse of the housing market there that would ripple out into the broader financial markets. With effective leadership, this sense of emergency could be mobilized to create irresistible public pressure to transform radically and rapidly our economy in a more sustainable direction. At that point, a wide swath of industry could be pulled under government control so that an industrial-conversion economic council could orchestrate the requisite technological transformation and shift in consumption patterns.[4]

Alongside these two scenarios leading to socialism through economic crisis and environmental crisis, many progressives see a third scenario that promises a more gradual change. We could imagine that progressives build enough electoral support to implement some modest social-democratic reforms, such as a higher minimum wage, stronger environmental regulations, Medicare for all, and subsidized loans for college. Then, as our fellow citizens see what is possible, we could build support for taking further steps, such as mandatory worker representation on corporate boards, a national healthcare system, and free childcare and college education. And from there, we could take still further steps.

There is much to recommend this path, starting with the fact that it promises real, albeit modest, gains along the way. But this scenario is surely misleadingly incomplete if we forget that along this path, with every successful step, resistance from the private-sector business community will grow in intensity. Moreover, as we progress down this path, there is little we can do to weaken our opponents' structural power—our prosperity and government's capacity for action will, at each step, still depend on the business sector's profitability. Yes, we might succeed in taking money out of politics, but as we have seen, the power of the business sector is not fundamentally a matter of campaign contributions and lobbying—its roots are much deeper. Therefore, the path of gradual social-democratic reform too almost certainly leads to crisis—in this case, political crisis.[5] Such a crisis might open yet another pathway to socialism.

Crisis conditions—economic, environmental, or political—can create possibilities for radical transformation. But if crisis is to lead to a progressive transformation rather than to an authoritarian, reactionary outcome, we need to build wide support for our key ideas well in advance.

We must bring together the various progressive movements to formulate a common platform. It might look something like the "social and economic Bill of Rights for the 21st century" that has been proposed by the Democratic Socialists of America. The rights include: a living-wage job; enough nutritious and safe food; affordable and safe housing; preventive, acute, and long-term healthcare; free, high-quality public education; care for children and the elderly; income security throughout one's life; adequate leisure time; a healthy environment; and free association and unionization.[6]

One underlying principle here—informed by our diagnosis that sees capitalism itself as the root cause of our main problems—is that we should take out of the marketplace and turn into universal public services not only healthcare, childcare, eldercare, and education, but also housing, work, food, transportation, culture and leisure, etc. Our platform would thus aim to "decommodify" the resources we need to meet our basic needs—make them public goods rather than private, universally and freely available rather than for sale on the market—so that everyone has access to those resources, and we can fight to ensure that these services are under truly democratic control.

A second principle is international solidarity. The international dimensions to today's crises are too pressing for our focus to be exclusively domestic. Solidarity with "others" locally—reaching across differences of race, gender, sexual identity, and so on, to come together around common causes and support each other in our distinct causes—is cut from the same cloth as solidarity across borders and the fight against imperialism. It is all too obvious that xenophobia—whipped up by political demagogues against "foreigners" who would compete "unfairly" or immigrate "illegally"—is aimed at dividing working people here in the United States and at obscuring the real divergence of interests between us and the wealthy and powerful elite.

Clearly, it is not enough merely to enunciate these ideas: we need to agitate for them. How? There are at least four main arenas in which we must work: the political sphere, our workplaces, our schools, and our communities.

In Politics

It is important that we find organizational forms that can amplify our voices in the political sphere. Given the massive influence of business over government, we will need to work both outside and inside the electoral process. The Democratic Party is so deeply enmeshed with the business sector that it is difficult to imagine that it can become a consistent voice for progressive change. But that is not a reason not to try. Working to elect more progressives in Congress is an important part of our effort to popularize socialist ideas.

Winning elections means little if we do not have a mass movement to pressure our elected representatives. Therefore, at both the local and the national level, we need urgently to build an organization that gives us a capacity for more united, consistent agitation, education, and mobilization. We need an organization that is not merely an electoral get-out-the-vote machine, but one that is rooted in neighborhoods and workplaces, where people can discuss both local and national issues, act on them together, formulate proposals for wider discussion, elect leaders to represent them, express their views on proposals coming from that leadership, and thus form a coherent political organization with a shared purpose. Whether that organization looks much like any of the parties that shaped politics during the previous century remains an open issue.

With or without a unified organization of our own, there is much to be gained by working in coalition with other progressive movements, even if they aim to reform rather than replace capitalism. Such work can help us discover common ground through joint action and dialogue. It can give us an opportunity to present our views on where we should be headed. And it gives us a chance to learn where the levers for change lie.

The priority in these efforts must be to link up the various progressive movements. In recent years, we have seen growing tension between "identity-based" movements and movements that aim for more universalistic goals. Finding common ground here is a critical task for socialists. As a matter of principle, the struggle for socialism is a struggle for justice and equality for all. The struggles of the women's movements (such as #MeToo), of the movements of racial and ethnic minorities (such as BlackLivesMatter), of environmentalists (such as 350.org), and of the movements of immigrant and international solidarity—these are not "outside" the struggle for socialism. That much should be obvious from our discussion of the way capitalism erodes our environmental, social, and international conditions. And as a practical matter, the struggle for socialism cannot get far unless we find common cause with these other movements and join our energies with theirs.

Allied with these other movements, we will find ourselves working with people who are more attracted to one or other of the reform paths than to our radical path. But there is much common ground here, many opportunities for us to advance our ideas, and much we can learn.

With proponents of ethical capitalism, we can fight against destructive corporate practices and push firms to embrace more responsible principles and to put pressure on their peers. It is in joint struggles with these allies— better than lecturing them from afar—that we will find opportunities to highlight both the essential role of government regulation and the roadblocks to effective regulation created by the private-enterprise economic system. Yes, many of these people have given up on government as a vehicle for change, seeing it as hopelessly incompetent; but we should nevertheless be able to engage them in the struggle to get local and national government to block the low road and to clear the way for high-road firms and for local social innovation. And as socialists, we have much to learn from these experiences, in particular about the more enlightened and the more deplorable corporate practices that shape our lives.

With proponents of regulated capitalism, we can fight together for higher minimum wage, stronger environmental protections, limits on gerrymandering and on the role of money in elections, and so forth. These struggles are a powerful crucible in which people come to see more clearly the nature and limits of capitalism. It is in these joint struggles—here too, better than lecturing people from afar—that we can point to the structural power of business to limit what we can accomplish through conventional electoral politics and regulatory mechanisms. We should be able to interest these allies in the struggle to strengthen political democracy against plutocracy. And as socialists, we have much to learn from these struggles, in particular about how to make government more responsive to people's concerns.

With proponents of social-democratic reform, we can go further, and fight together for labor law reform, subsidized childcare, single-payer healthcare, free college tuition, public housing, government investment in job creation, and so forth. In these fights together, we can help social democrats see that implementing these reforms will not create a stable, self-reinforcing, path of progressive change. We can help them see that if we limit our goals to those that the business sector can support, we will never get where we need to go. If we are part of these struggles, we can help people find the courage to formulate goals that garner popular support even if they prompt elite fears. To take an example: we should fight together with social democrats for a single-payer healthcare system; but a victory here will immediately create new tensions, which we will be able to resolve only by bringing doctors into a public healthcare system as salaried employees, and then by bringing pharmaceutical and medical device industries under public ownership.

With our friends who are focused on the opportunities and threats posed by the current wave of technological revolution, we can fight for Internet neutrality, against the privatizing of the information commons by big corporations that control access to research journals and other cultural and civic resources, against the irresponsible monopolistic profiteering of monopolies such as Google and Facebook, and for the rights of workers displaced by automation. We can celebrate together the emancipatory potential of these new technologies and help mobilize anger that the capitalist private-property system fails to capitalize on them. We can learn how the new technologies can help us to organize and eventually to govern.

In Our Workplaces

Our workplaces are a second arena of contestation. Union-organizing campaigns, just like political and workplace campaigns organized by established unions, are contexts in which socialists can help others develop a critical understanding of capitalism and sharpen our own critique.

Although unions have lost almost all foothold in the private sector and although they are under threat in the public sector, the demand for worker representation has strengthened rather than shrunk. We have every reason to hope that with persistent and creative effort, that demand can be met with organizing appeals that resonate. We have not been successful so far in efforts to organize unions at giant monopolies such as Walmart or Amazon, but many dedicated activists continue to look for ways to help employees in these firms organize. This is not an insurmountable challenge. It may take a change in our outmoded labor laws to do it, but that too is feasible. Even as we struggle to organize workers into existing unions, we should be open to the possibility that the old institutional forms of unionism are perhaps obsolete.[7]

In high-road firms, employees and unions can organize to seize the opportunities afforded by more-enlightened management practices. While unions should guard their capacity for independent action, they can explore ways to move from a reactive and purely defensive response vis-à-vis new management practices toward a more proactive posture. Instead of only critiquing the limits to management's commitment to social responsibility and employment fairness, progressive forces can challenge management to make these commitments more real, and socialists can help allies see the systemic reasons for these firms' failures to deliver.[8]

In Our Schools

The education system is another critical strategic arena for us. We can mobilize the frustrations created by the neoliberal transformation of our education system—ever more expensive for families, oriented to training rather than education, and starved for resources. We need to fight for education funding and to strengthen the professional status of teachers—defending the teachers' unions and upgrading teachers' education and salary levels.

Teachers at all levels have considerable influence in shaping young students' minds and hearts. It's not for nothing that the right wing has sustained such an energetic attack on public education and on the "liberal bias" of universities. So we need to fight for progressive reforms in the curriculum. In our primary and secondary schools, we can fight to strengthen humanities and civics education. If many people have lost confidence in democracy—and if they are therefore skeptical about our ideas about extending democracy to the governance of enterprises and to the management of the whole economy—it surely has something to do with the limited opportunities they have had to debate and differentiate the principles of democracy from the sordid reality of the sham democracy they see in practice in the United States today.

Most states require at least one course related to civics education, but only nine states and the District of Columbia require even one full year of civics. Not surprisingly, students' knowledge is abysmal. According to the federal government's National Assessment of Educational Progress (NAEP), in 2014, only 23% of eighth graders performed at or above even the *proficient* level in civics. In the 2010 NAEP assessment (the last time it was done at 12th-grade level) only 24% of 12th graders performed at or above this *proficient* level. Fully 36% failed to reach even the *basic* level.[9] The national average Advanced Placement exam on "US Government" score is 2.64 (out of 5.0 maximum), which is lower than the average AP score of all but three of the other 45 AP exams.[10]

In Our Communities

Finally, in our communities, we can create opportunities for our fellow citizens to experience concretely what democratic socialism might look like.

Earlier chapters discussed a range of possibilities, such as the efforts that link worker cooperatives to local government and anchor institutions.

Some progressives have suggested that if prospects are so dim at the national level, we might have more success with initiatives such as these, at a local level.[11] Indeed, some argue that the superior economic performance and quality of life of cities that embrace this model will spark a wave of imitation in other cities across the country. In this bottom-up way, they argue, we can encourage the national-level changes we need so badly. It would certainly be a wonderful thing to see more cities adopt a community-wealth-building approach.

But the localist idea—that competition between cities could transform the country—suffers from the same flaws as the ethical-capitalism model's reliance on competition between firms. Yes, cities and states can serve as "laboratories of democracy"—but the results will not diffuse far unless we have a national government willing and able to support these experiments, to block other localities from taking the low road, and to take the successful models to scale. Without a radical change in our country's broader political-economic structure, these local experiments alone cannot yield the change we need.

Building islands of progressive policy in our local communities may not be the royal road to the societal transformation we need; however, local communities are a critical arena for our educational and organizing work. Our political struggle needs roots in people's everyday lives, not just in electoral get-out-the-vote efforts. The socialist movement was strongest in the United States a century ago, when it had roots in local communities—in union locals, but also in churches, bars, ethnic associations, youth clubs, sports teams, summer camps. The progressive left has lost most of such anchoring. We need to rebuild these roots. Without them, our political arguments are just empty abstractions, and our organizing efforts lack traction.

But we must rebuild these community ties on new foundations. Capitalism has helped to sweep away the traditional forms of community, based on hierarchies of ethnicity, race, and gender. The conservative right clings to what remains of these old forms and activates fears that the old order and its privileges have been lost. Our efforts should embrace the positive aspects of capitalism's legacy, including the emergence of new, more egalitarian forms of community.

INSTEAD OF A CONCLUSION

I wrote in the Introduction that this book's message is at once urgent, hopeful, and optimistic. In the intervening chapters, I have tried to give substance to those three elements. Let's reprise them in reverse order.

Progressives have reason to be optimistic about the prospects for democratic socialism in the twenty-first century. Yes, we confront huge challenges in finding a way past the economic, workplace, political, environmental, social, and international crises we face, but we have means with which to meet these challenges. Yes, this will require a fundamental change in our form of society, but we already have both technological and managerial foundations on which this new form can be built. Yes, it is frustrating that this change has not happened yet, but over the longer term, capitalism's own development toward increasingly socialized production makes democratic socialism progressively more feasible and more necessary.

We can be hopeful. Even when prospects for radical change look slim, capitalism's failures and crisis tendencies fuel deepening and widening frustration. The contrast between the opulent wealth of the one percent and the precarious condition of the rest of us, the 99 percent, is ever more obscene. The contrast between the promise of advanced technologies and the abject conditions around us is ever more absurd. This means that opportunities for a radical rupture might open at any moment, surprising us all. While there is a real danger that reactionary demagogues might capitalize on these frustrations, progressive activists can tap them too—in our efforts in the political arena, workplaces, schools, and communities—to work toward a better world.

But this transformation is urgent. While the development of capitalism has brought many benefits, it also engenders crises, and that development itself ensures that these crises deepen and multiply over time. Given the unnecessary suffering already created by this increasingly obsolete capitalist system and given the likelihood that this suffering will be magnified in coming years, socialist transformation—the creation of an economy for the 99%—is urgent, desperately urgent.

ACKNOWLEDGMENTS

This book is based on a series of three public lectures I was invited to give at the Saïd Business School, Oxford University—the Clarendon Lectures in Management Studies—in October 2015. The annual lecture series is organized jointly by the Business School and Oxford University Press. I thank the colleagues at Saïd Business School and David Musson of OUP, who invited me to give these lectures and hosted me so graciously. And I thank David Pervin, who took over responsibility for the manuscript in OUP's New York office, for his generous editing guidance.

I am indebted to the many friends and colleagues who have helped me over the years to develop the ideas I express here. To name just those who saw various versions of this book in its gestation and who helped so generously with comments and criticisms, sometimes in sympathy with the basic argument and sometimes not: Gar Alperovitz, Eileen Appelbaum, John August, Zlatko Bodrožić, Paul Cockshott, Tom Cummings, Rick Delbridge, Andrew Dettmer, Pat Devine, Nancy DiTomaso, Paul Edwards, Nate Fast, Bill Fletcher Jr., John Bellamy Foster, Doug Gamble, Paul Goldman, Nina Gregg, Charles Heckscher, Sue Helper, Rebecca Henderson, Bob Howard, Jonas Ingvaldsen, Tom Kochan, David Laibman, David Levy, Paul Lichterman, Mike Lounsbury, Richard Marens, Jasper McAvoy, Anita McGahan, Chris Nyland, Max Ogden, Alain Othenin-Girard, Don Palmer, Danny Pollitt, Lee Price, Larry Prusak, Philine Qian, Shaun Richman, Mari Sako, Julie Schor, Jason Schulman, David Schweickart, Randy Schutt, Richard Smith, Tony Smith, Carroll Stephens, Dan Swinney, Eero Vaara, Marc Ventresca, Patrick Venturini, Matt Vidal, Judy Wajcman, Rick Wartzman, Mark Wilson, and Mike Yates.

I owe special thanks to my colleagues in the Management and Organization Department at the University of Southern California, who have helped make my academic home such an intellectually enriching place. And thanks too to my students, who have taught me so much.

This book would never have materialized without the urgings of my sister Louise, whom I thank for her sage advice along the way.

Its deepest origins I owe to my parents, Ruth and Jacques, who made a passion for justice and equality feel like a minimum criterion for human decency.

Finally, I thank my most critical critics and most enthusiastic supporters—my children, Laura, Zully, and David, and my wife, Ruth Kremen. They make everything possible.

NOTES

INTRODUCTION
1. See Moorhead (2012).
2. Jameson (2003, p. 76).
3. Wilde (2007 [1891]).

CHAPTER 1
1. On the distinctive features of neoliberalism, see Streeck (2014), Harvey (2007), Fine and Saad-Filho (2017).
2. A list of recessions is at Wikipedia under "List of recessions in the United States."
3. According to the *Forbes* 2018 rankings: Jeff Bezos, head of Amazon and owner of the *Washington Post*; Bill Gates of Microsoft fame; Warren Buffett, the investor and head of Berkshire Hathaway; Bernard Arnault, who owns a family of high-fashion brands such as Louis Vuitton; Mark Zuckerberg, the founder of Facebook; Amancio Ortega, the founder of the Spanish fashion chain Zara; Carlos Slim Helú, the Mexican telecom tycoon and owner of conglomerate Grupo Carso; Charles and David Koch, who own Koch Industries, the United States' second-largest privately held firm, and who fund conservative think tanks such as the Cato Institute, the Heritage Foundation, and the American Enterprise Institute; and Larry Ellison, CEO of the technology firm Oracle.
4. Wolff (2013).
5. Board of Governors of the Federal Reserve System (2018).
6. United States Department of Agriculture (2018).
7. This is what the Bureau of Labor Statistics calls the "U6" measure of labor underutilization, incorporating people "marginally attached to the labor force"— those who currently are neither working nor looking for work but indicate that they want and are available for a job and have looked for work sometime in the past 12 months.
8. Rose (2017).
9. Employment under capitalist conditions has always been somewhat precarious. Recently we have heard much concern about an increase in this precariousness, due to outsourcing, technology change, employer policies that favor "independent contractor" status, etc. However, it is not clear that precariousness is increasing much or that it will increase much further. The distribution of job tenure seems to be largely unchanged. According to the Bureau of Labor Statistics, the median tenure with the current employer has in fact risen, with a few bumps along the way, from 3.5 years in 1983 to 4.2 years in 2016. That

increase is visible among both private- and public-sector employees. Among younger workers under 35 years old, median tenure has remained essentially the same. The one group where there has been a decline is among men over 35. The rate of "turnover" in jobs—the proportion of workers starting or ending a job— was flat during most of the 1990s and has trended downward quite regularly since then. Part-time employment grew between 1960 and the mid-1980s, but it has remained at about 17% of the nonagricultural workforce since then. Involuntary part-time work shows no upward trend since 1960, bouncing around between 2% and 5% of total employment depending on the business cycle. The proportion of workers holding more than one job has declined regularly since the late 1990s. Temporary agency employment rose from about 0.5% of employment in 1982 to 2% in the late 1990s, but shows no further increase since then. So, while employment precariousness is a real concern and always has been, the available data do not suggest it is worsening significantly (see Henwood 2018).

10. One study concluded, "The earnings of displaced workers do not catch up to those of their nondisplaced counterparts for nearly 20 years. The effect of unemployment on earnings is even more substantial for workers unemployed 26 weeks or more. [. . .] In particular, after 10 years the wages of long-term unemployed workers were roughly 32 percent lower than nondisplaced workers, while the wages of short-term unemployed workers were only about 9 percent lower" (Cooper 2014).

11. Brenner (1979).

12. Roelfs et al. (2011).

13. We can divide the past 50 years into three successive periods. Even in the best years in the 1965–1980 period, about 12% of economy-wide capacity was idle, and in the worst years, that proportion rose to 25%. In 1980–2000, the best years saw 15% of the country's capacity idle, and the worst, 30%.

14. See Federal Reserve Bank of St. Louis (2018). Capacity utilization indexes are based on data for 71 industries in manufacturing, 16 in mining, and 2 in utilities. Why it shows this long-term declining pattern is a bit of a mystery. (I called the experts who collect the data, and they had no explanation.) There is some question as to whether things have worsened as much as this over the longer period, or the data are somehow biased (see Shaikh and Moudud 2004). But the main fact remains unchanged: cyclical downturns are very wasteful, leaving much productive capacity underutilized.

15. Krones (2016).

16. Woolhandler and Himmelstein (2017).

17. I have not found any recent studies, but in the 1950s, the cost of purely cosmetic design changes account for fully 25% of the cost of the average new model car (Fisher, Griliches, and Kaysen 1962). Planned obsolescence is still a major factor in many other industries, for example in textbook publishing (Iizuka 2007).

18. Balasegaram (2014).

19. See Greenhouse (2009), Kusnet (2008). Some observers downplay this crisis, pointing to many surveys showing that employees are in large majority "satisfied" with their jobs. But being satisfied does not mean that mean that you would not leap at an opportunity to change jobs—or at an opportunity to change the management you work under. "Job satisfaction" surveys capture many things, including people's stoic acceptance of things when they see no alternatives.

20. Freeman and Rogers (2006).

21. Kochan et al. (2018).
22. Godard and Frege (2013).
23. A study by Eaton, Rubinstein, and McKersie (2004) listed the General Motors–United Automobile Workers partnership at Saturn, the ATT–Communications Workers of America in their Workplace of the Future program, Kaiser Permanente and a coalition of unions (which I discuss in a later chapter), the steel industry and the United Steelworkers of America, and in the federal government under President Clinton a partnership with the American Federation of Government Employees (AFGE) and the National Treasury Employees Union (NTEU). The earlier history of such efforts is summarized in Slichter, Healy, and Livernash (1960, Ch. 28).
24. Pew Research Center (2016).
25. Gallup (2017), Pew Research Center (2016).
26. Soon after NAFTA was negotiated, public opinion was opposed, 46% to 38% (*Los Angeles Times* 1993).
27. See Kiley (2018). On the parallels between Obama's program and the Massachusetts program under Republican Mitt Romney, see Holan (2012).
28. Saad (2013).
29. Saad (2009).
30. Teixeira (2010).
31. A host of mainstream economists and "public choice" theorists have contributed to this cynicism about democracy, by encouraging us to accept the assumption that self-interest is the only significant motivation among both voters and politicians.
32. Pew Research Center (2015).
33. Pew Research Center and Associated Press (2006).
34. Pew Research Center (2014).
35. World Wildlife Fund (2014).
36. Stockholm Resilience Center (2018).
37. Oerlemans (2016), Kolbert (2014).
38. Huntingford and Mercado (2016).
39. Climate Vulnerability Monitor (2012). For a sketch of the implications of the less optimistic scenarios, see Wallace-Wells (2018).
40. Brauer (2016).
41. See Strauss, Kulp, and Levermann (2015).
42. Lin et al. (2016).
43. See poll results at Langer (2017).
44. On children: in 2014, 37% of youth experienced a physical assault, and 9% of youth experienced an assault-related injury. Of girls 14 to 17 years old, 4.6% experienced sexual assault or sexual abuse. Overall, 15.2% of children and youth experienced maltreatment by a caregiver, including 5.0% who experienced physical abuse (Finkelhor et al. 2015). On the extraordinary rates of violence toward LGBTQ people, see Park and Mykhyalyshyn (2016).
45. Working full-time but taking short periods off for the birth of a couple of children also leads to the huge cumulative salary losses relative to women's male counterparts (see Rose and Hartmann 2004).
46. Maestas et al. (2017, p. xiii): "Some 70 percent of workers report actual work hours that are more than 5 percent higher or lower than their ideal number of hours, and more than half of these (39 percent of the working population) rate having the right number of hours as essential or very important."

47. American Psychological Association (2016).
48. Hochschild (2016).
49. On the job market, see Borowczyk-Martins, Bradley, and Tarasonis (2017). On housing, see Reardon, Fox, and Townsend (2015).
50. While 67 percent of non-Hispanic whites are very or somewhat satisfied "with how blacks are treated," only 47% of non-Hispanic blacks feel the same way. Asked if "blacks have as good a chance as whites in your community to get any kind of job for which they are qualified," 74% of the whites agree, and only 40% of blacks do. See Gallup Editors (2014).
51. Massey, Rothwell, and Domina (2009); Stolle, Soroka, and Johnston (2008); Howard, Gibson, and Stolle (2005).
52. Population Reference Bureau (2017).
53. Vagins and McCurdy (2006).
54. Bezruchka (2010).
55. Braveman et al. (2010).
56. Urban Institute (2018).
57. Joint Center for Housing Studies of Harvard University (2018).
58. National Law Center on Homelessness and Poverty (2018).
59. OECD (2016).
60. Scott-Clayton (2018).
61. Foster and McChesney (2004), Chomsky (2010).
62. See a listing at Swanson (2018).
63. Vine (2015), Johnson (2007, 2011).
64. See Union of Concerned Scientists (2018).
65. OECD (2018).

CHAPTER 2

1. If we accounted for the value of housework rather than counting only market transactions, this would have added about 26% to the official gross domestic product in 2010 (Bridgman et al. 2012). That figure has been declining—it was 39% in 1965—as more women work outside the home and more household goods and services are purchased rather than produced at home.
2. See for example Gnanasambandam, Miller, and Sprague (2017) and Dunne, Roberts, and Samuelson (1989). Some small enterprises remain small and successful by dominating a narrow market niche, but this is not the general pattern.
3. On violence: Davis (2002) argues that the integration of peasants from China, India, and Brazil into the world capitalist system disrupted the stability of peasant communities in these regions, and that this disruption played a key role in the huge famines of the late 19th century—with a death toll of somewhere between 30 and 60 million people. The El-Nino Southern Oscillation was the trigger for droughts and floods, but it was probusiness government policies that explain why these events led to mass starvation.
4. See Zijdeman and Ribeira da Silva (2015). We might note that most of the medical breakthroughs that brought us such improvements in mortality and health are attributable to scientific research conducted outside the orbit of the capitalist economy—by government or philanthropically funded research.
5. Economic Innovation Group (2017).
6. US Bureau of Census, 2015 SUSB Annual Data Tables by Enterprise Industry. In 1988, the earliest period for which there are comparable data, the ratio was

45.4%. Firm size (and establishment size) have been growing in each major industry group except manufacturing, which now represents only about 11% of the private-sector workforce.

7. See for example Leung, Meh, and Terajima (2008).

8. Stone (2013).

9. See Khan (2016), Schmitz (2016).

10. Council of Economic Advisors (2016).

11. Externalities are the unpriced consequences of one enterprise's activities for other enterprises or people or resources. Sometimes externalities can be positive, such as when a large firm offers well-paying jobs and thereby creates customers for other retail businesses in the local community. But as concerns the natural environment, these externalities are far more often devastatingly negative.

12. In a system where firms and their investors base their decisions on expected profits, future costs and benefits are inevitably "discounted." Discounting is based on a simple idea: people usually prefer to get $100 now over even the most credible promise of $100 a year from now. More generally: the benefit you get from a payment in the distant future is worth less to you than the benefit you could get from that same payment right now. This is partly because we are impatient. But it is also because the $100 we get now could be put to work and therefore generate benefits for us over the year. We could, for example, simply invest it and let the interest payments compound. But notice how debilitating such discounting becomes when we are worried about the very-long-term impact of decisions we make today on the lives of our children and grandchildren. Imagine that we are running an environmentally responsible manufacturing company, and we are choosing between two production technologies for our factory. The two technologies produce the same quality and quantity of our product at a similar cost, but one, although more expensive, produces less CO_2 emissions. Since we care about our emissions and their impact on the lives of our children and grandchildren, and we put a value on this reduction of emissions—let us say that this reduction is worth $1,000 per year. How much more should we be willing to pay today for the equipment that emits less over many years to come? That depends on the discount rate—the rate at which we discount future benefits. If our discount rate is 3%, that $1,000 annual benefit to our grandchildren 50 years in the future is only worth $220 to us today. So even large, long-term future benefits of the environmentally superior technology do not justify more than a small additional outlay today. Moreover, under capitalist conditions, we do not get to choose the discount rate: our investors force one on us, since if our firm uses a discount rate that is lower than the rate of return our investors can get from other investment opportunities, investors will desert us. And in practice, that means firms are forced to use a discount rate of around 7%–10%, and at a 10% rate, a $1,000 benefit in 50 years' time is worth just $8.50 today. Even though we care about the environment, if we operate in a capitalist world, we end up almost entirely ignoring the effects that our decisions today are going to have on the environment that our grandchildren will inherit.

13. Mainstream economists ignore this intrinsic instability, preferring to assume that competitive markets naturally converge to a socially optimal equilibrium, and that this happy outcome eludes us only because of random "exogenous shocks" and/or poor "macroeconomic management" by government and the Federal Reserve (as noted by Romer forthcoming; Beaudry, Galizia, and Portier

2015). The ideological incentive to adopt this view is obvious. An older tradition of economic analysis acknowledged that markets were by nature unstable, and that booms produced their own busts: see for example Kaldor (1940), Kalecki (1937), Hicks (1950). Shaikh (1978) presents a good overview of various theories.

14. See also Hayek (1945).

15. Several further points on this. First, even if they knew their competitors' plans, firms would still have no way to coordinate to deal with the conflicts they observed among those plans. Since they are in competition with each other, there is no way to find a mutually agreeable plan . . . except if there are just a few firms and they can collude to extract monopoly profits from hapless customers. Second, many firms do indeed cooperate with suppliers and customers in planning for the future; but these interfirm networks are in competition with other interfirm networks, which leads to the same type of coordination failure at the inter-network level. Toyota, for example, has a close cooperative relationship with many of its first-tier suppliers, and many of Toyota's competitors have tried to follow Toyota in creating such networks, but these networks are locked in a ferocious competitive struggle for market share in the auto industry. Finally, we should note that the dilemma I note in the text here can be somewhat softened by the creation of a futures market: farmers can buy futures contracts to mitigate their worries about the impact of changing weather and of their competitors' production choices on the price they are likely to get for their crop next year. But these contracts are costly, and they only work to smooth out cycles in very circumscribed settings, ones where changes are incremental and there is some foundation for prediction. By way of counterexample: the futures market did not anticipate or mitigate the 2008 crash.

16. In principle, the liquidation of excess capacity could happen in a more gradual, rational way through bankruptcy proceedings. But the only way to conduct an orderly bankruptcy process for such a wide swath of overcapacity all at once would require nationalizing vast proportions of the economy—which is hardly compatible with the capitalist model. The United States did effectively nationalize General Motors and Chrysler in 2009, and there was even talk of nationalizing the banks—and even though this was seen as only a temporary measure to ensure an orderly liquidation of their unpayable debts, screams of horror resonated across the corporate boardrooms and golf clubs across the country. See for example Gattuso (2009), *Wall Street Journal* (2009), Newman (2009).

17. Ghilarducci et al. (2016), Wolff (2017).

18. Thorne et al. (2018).

19. This was the conclusion also reached by former head of the Federal Reserve, Alan Greenspan, reflecting on the 2008 crash: "Unless there is a societal choice to abandon dynamic markets and leverage for some form of central planning, I fear that preventing bubbles will in the end turn out to be infeasible" (Greenspan 2010, p. 243). On the mechanisms of this financial instability, see Minsky (1980) and Cassidy (2009). Each individual financial crisis also involves, of course, context-specific factors. The 2008 crash was made almost inevitable by the accumulation of giant pools of financial assets unable to find profitable investment opportunities in the nonfinancial sector, wandering the globe looking for speculative opportunities in financial markets.

20. See Baker (2016), Epstein (2018).

21. On cigarettes, Campaign for Tobacco-Free Kids (2014). On food, see Moss (2013).
22. See Baker (2016). Baker notes further that this 2% of national income is more than five times the total government budget for food stamps and nearly twenty times the budget for Temporary Assistance for Needy Families (TANF). And this 2% would grow to about 5% if we added the costs due to the patents on medical equipment, software, and other items.
23. In universities, innovative researchers earn status, rather than financial profits, from being the first to come up with an idea. And when they publish it, they earn further status the more people use their idea and cite them for it.
24. Heller (2010), Boldrin and Levine (2013), Williams (2013).
25. Boldrin and Levine (2013): "The case against patents can be summarized briefly: there is no empirical evidence that they serve to increase innovation and productivity, unless productivity is identified with the number of patents awarded—which, as evidence shows, has no correlation with measured productivity."
26. This was not the way capitalism formed in other parts of the world. In most other regions, peasant farmers under feudal lords' control were forced off the land and into urban factories.
27. Although the conventional wisdom is that anyone with a good idea should be able to start their own business, in reality those without already accumulated wealth find it is very difficult to do that. It is very difficult to accumulate enough savings, or to mobilize the savings of enough other people, or to access sufficient credit to start a business (Gentry and Hubbard 2004). As a result, most people have no choice but to work as employees.
28. The Census estimates that the self-employed (including both unincorporated and incorporated) represent 10% of the labor force. But some of these are only self-employed in their legal status: they are actually employees who are paid as independent contractors so their employer can avoid taxes and benefits. And 30% of the self-employed are small-scale employers, albeit typically with fewer than five employees. See Hipple and Hammond (2016).
29. It is often said that the impact of social class on outcomes like job satisfaction, life happiness, and political orientation has declined in the United States over the past decades. However, social class—measured simply by whether you are an employer versus employee versus self-employed, and if employed, whether you supervise anyone—remains a powerful predictor of such outcomes (as compared to alternative predictors such as occupation and status), and its impact has not declined significantly since the 1970s. See Wodtke (2016).
30. Heath and Mobarak (2015) and Foo and Lim (1989) reach this same conclusion from very different political starting points.
31. Benmelech, Bergman, and Kim (2018).
32. Schor and Bowles (1987).
33. See Lindert and Williamson (2016). Income inequality was relatively low in colonial America in the late 18th and early 19th century. The top 1% received only 8.5% of total income in 1774, compared to over 20% today. But this was mainly because at that time Europeans were colonizing the continent, destroying the native American population, and the government was making land freely available to the colonizers. By 1860, the United States had caught up to the level of inequality (as measured by the Gini coefficient) of England at the time—a

level that would prevail until the Great Depression, and a level to which we have returned since the last part of the 20th century.

34. See Kiatpongsan and Norton (2014); Mishel, Schmitt, and Shierholz (2013); Saez and Zucman (2016).

35. The literature on "varieties of capitalism" contrasts "coordinated market economies" such as Germany or Sweden with "liberal market economies" such as the United States and the United Kingdom (Hall and Soskice 2001). The main factor differentiating these varieties is the relative weight of government in the economy. But government in both types is largely subservient, for the reasons I explain later.

36. See Ferguson (1995), Winters and Page (2009), Woll (2016), Gough (2000). There is a long-running scholarly and political debate on the relationship between government and society in capitalist societies. The view presented here sees government as largely constrained by the basic structure of our economy. I give less weight to both the autonomy of government and the maneuvering of elites to pressure government. Those latter factors loom larger when we focus on smaller-scale issues of less general concern.

37. Hiltzik (2018). For further information, see https://muninetworks.org/.

38. Estimates of municipal broadband users from Mitchell (2018).

39. Ferguson (1995).

40. Winters and Page (2009), Gilens (2012).

41. The mass-based interest groups included a wide range, running from the AARP and the AFL-CIO to the Christian Coalition and the American Rifle Association. The business-oriented interest groups included a wide range of industry lobbying organizations such as the American Bankers Association.

42. The revolving door is where regulators and legislators are offered lucrative private-sector jobs on leaving the public sector, and when people move from the private sector into government roles regulating the industries they came from. For a searchable database, consult http://www.opensecrets.org/revolving/.

43. Not that the banks needed to apply much pressure. President Obama and his senior administration officials—many of whom came straight out of Wall Street—were falling over themselves to help the banks return to profitability, even if it meant lying to Congress, reneging on promises to legislators, and ignoring legislation and public commitments about how the bailout funds were to be used. See Taibbi (2013).

44. Comstock (2011b, 2011a), Clark and Stewart (2011).

45. Morray (1997), Singer (1988).

46. More generally on capital strikes and flight, see Young, Banerjee, and Schwartz (2018); Epstein (2005); Przeworski and Wallerstein (1988).

47. Observing this "structural dependence" of government on capitalist interests, some commentators differentiate businesses' "capture" of government—when businesses organize to dominate the agencies that are supposed to regulate them—from the bigger problem of "deep capture"—where business interests not only deliberately shape legislators' and regulators' action but also frame the way issues and possibilities are formulated in the media, by academics, and more broadly in civil society (Hanson and Yosifon 2003).

48. Shapira and Zingales (2017) examine a prototypical case—that of Dupont's emissions of a toxic chemical named C8 used in the production of Teflon. These emissions had terrible effects on the health of neighboring residents, farm animals, and wildlife. For these emissions, Dupont was eventually fined

$670 million by the EPA on top of tens of millions paid out in previous litigation. Using internal company documents disclosed in trials, the authors show that this bad outcome was not due to ignorance, an unexpected turn of events, or bad corporate governance. Even though Dupont knew of a cost-effective way of disposing of the C8 safely, polluting was simply the best option for the company's bottom line. Neither individually nor jointly were the legal risks, regulatory risks, and risks to the reputation of the corporation or its managers enough to outweigh the cost advantages.

49. On plunder, see Ray Anderson, now deceased former head of Interface, a carpet company, in his segment of the movie *The Corporation*, available at https://www.youtube.com/watch?v=Tf9yWNiIEZU.

50. See Agyeman et al. (2016).

51. See Smith (2016), Klein (2014), Magdoff and Foster (2011).

52. See Ostrom et al. (1999).

53. For a collection of articles on this theme, see Bhattacharya (2017).

54. For an overview see Satz (2017), Fraser (2016a).

55. The story was different in other countries. Where capitalism emerged out of feudal society, such as in England and most of western Europe, it was often by force that people were pulled out of family production and into wage labor. And in that violent process, both women and men (and often children too) were dragged into primitive factories and capitalist agriculture. It was only in a subsequent phase that children were sent to school rather than work and women were pushed back into the domestic sphere (Horrell and Humphries 1995).

56. This estimate (20%) understates married women's engagement with the market economy. Married women in this period often took in boarders and piecework, even if this did not register as wage employment (Folbre 1993).

57. Men's participation rates have been steadily falling from about 87% in 1950 to about 69% today, while women's participation has been rising over the course of the 20th century and seems to have leveled off since 2000 at about 57%.

58. Pew Research Center (2013).

59. See Burnham and Theodore (2012). The global migrations that bring domestic workers from less affluent regions to the US and other affluent countries have deeply contradictory effects on the women who migrate as well as on their families and communities in their home countries (Parreñas 2015; Hochschild 2001). A similar global migration chain is also prominent in nursing, where healthcare systems in the United States and other developed countries experience a constant shortage that is filled by migration of nurses from less affluent countries rather than by improved local wages and conditions (Yeates 2012, 2005).

60. See Dawson (2016), Fraser (2016b).

61. For a journalistic account, see Farrow, Lang, and Frank (2006).

62. Take the case of home care (Osterman 2017). Home-care aides and nurses are currently paid very low wages. The quality of care suffers accordingly. Low wages reduce the current costs of these services, but low quality adds to our healthcare costs in the future. In a capitalist system, those future healthcare costs are a source of profit for other players in the economy (pharmaceutical and insurance companies, hospitals, and physicians), so there is little impetus to change things—other than the struggles of home-care workers themselves and the voice of their patients and patients' families.

63. Another sad example of government's subservience to industry was the Obama administration's capitulation to the fast-food industry: see Wilson and Roberts (2012).
64. See comments from several urban economy specialists at Citylab (2018).
65. Dwyer-Lindgren et al. (2017).
66. As with the broader category of environmental sustainability, there is no automatic market process that rectifies supply-and-demand imbalances in the market for land. That is because land is not a commodity in the political-economy sense of the word: it is not something produced for sale and profit, so it is not generally something of which more could be produced in response to price increases. (The exceptions are rare, such as when artificial land-fill expands the shoreline.) If housing is in demand, developers will want to build more, but the land on which they build is a limited resource and its owners enjoy monopoly rents. Ignoring the distinctive nature of land, much mainstream analysis of zoning and rent regulations assumes that such regulations are the main cause of our housing problem—reducing the supply of new housing without any compensating benefits to those looking to rent or buy (see, for example, Jenkins 2009). A classic statement of this mainstream view is presented by Friedman and Stigler (1946). Land is implicitly treated as just another form of capital, ignoring the intrinsic non-reproducibility that differentiates the supply of land from that of products and services that are produced for sale. Moreover, on the demand side, land and housing are unlike the other elements of the ordinary family's budget, which are at least somewhat flexible. If food prices rise, we cut back on more expensive items, and if clothes cost more, we buy fewer. But if the rent or the mortgage payment increases, you have little choice but to pay, especially if alternative affordable housing is in short supply.
67. Allegretto and Mishel (2016).
68. Kennedy (2010).
69. The history makes for sad reading. I cite just a few examples. In 1953, in response to the decision by the democratically elected parliament in Iran to nationalize their country's oil industry, the United States covertly overthrew the government, installed the Shah, and supported the resulting repression for decades (Abrahamian 2001). In 1954, the United States invaded Guatemala to stop the Guatemalan government from taking unused land belonging to the United Fruit Company for redistribution to peasants (Swamy 1980). In the early 1970s, International Telephone and Telegraph (ITT) tried to mobilize the US Central Intelligence Agency to defeat the social-democratic candidate, Salvador Allende, in Chilean national elections. The CIA initially refused; Allende was elected; and ITT kept pushing the US government and other US businesses to deny credit and aid to the new government and to support Allende's political rivals. After the Allende government nationalized copper mines owned by American firms, the US government supported a violent military coup by the military that overthrew the Allende government and led to years of brutal authoritarian rule (Barnet and Muller 1975).
70. There is a vast literature on this, but some starting points would include Wallerstein (2004) and Arrighi (1994).
71. On the shape and evolution of global inequality, see Alvaredo et al. (2018). On the variety of trajectories of individual companies, see for example Amsden (2001) and Evans (2012). These authors show that a key factor is the capacity of national governments to orchestrate investment. Even though formally

independent, the periphery countries' governments are typically weak, lacking much of a tax base, and dependent on their ability to attract foreign investment.

72. Now (2016).
73. Zucman (2015).
74. Li and Zhou (2017).
75. I cite just three examples. At the urging of tobacco companies, the US trade representative threatened sanctions against Thailand if that government went ahead with an effort to block cigarette imports in the hope of curbing smoking and limiting the costs of the resulting disease (MacKenzie and Collin 2012). The Trans-Pacific Partnership negotiations were eventually cut short by the election of a more unilateralist president in the United States, but the course of the negotiations was shaped by the US representatives' dedication to advancing US industry's interests at the expense of other countries' business interests and political sovereignty (Public Citizen 2018). The United States' diplomatic and military support for the extraordinarily destructive Saudi war in Yemen in 2017–2018 appears to be motivated by US economic interests associated with continued arms sales to Saudi Arabia and reliance on this repressive regime in regional geopolitical rivalries (Nissenbaum 2018).
76. See the Doomsday clock updated regularly by the Bulletin of Atomic Scientists at https://thebulletin.org/doomsday-clock/.

CHAPTER 3

1. See Maddison (2007).
2. The idea that capitalist development creates increasing interdependence of economic activity has been central to a broad range of capitalism's earliest chroniclers, from Adam Smith to Karl Marx (from whom I borrow the term "socialization"), to Emile Durkheim, and beyond.
3. The term "socialization" is also used to refer to two other distinct but related processes: first, the process of shifting ownership from the private to the public sector (an idea to which we will return later), and second, the process by which people, especially young children, absorb the cultural resources of the broader society.
4. The story starts from a different place in Europe and other regions of the world, of course, but the main lines of development point in the same direction. In the United States, capitalism arose through a process of settler-colonialism, the eradication of the original inhabitants, and the importation of millions of slaves. In England, by contrast, capitalism developed more "organically" from feudalism, with the emergence in rural areas of a class of capitalist farmers and a class of dispossessed agricultural workers, and the expansion in the cities of commercial trade and productive investment.
5. In 1852, Massachusetts was the first state to pass compulsory education laws. Mississippi was the last, in 1918.
6. For a sketch of the history of some of the managerial and technological innovations that enabled firms to manage and coordinate this expanding array of activities, see Nightingale et al. (2003).
7. This evolution took time, of course: the market for goods did not become integrated across the nation until the late 1800s; markets for investment capital, in the early 1900s; and the labor market became truly national only after World War II. Over this same period, a growing proportion of firms engaged in international trade. Today, nearly a quarter of all manufacturing companies

export outside the United States, and nearly 40% of those with more than 20 employees do so (Lincoln and McCallum 2018).

8. This is not to imply that government was irrelevant to the American economy of the late 18th and early 19th century (see, for example, Novak 2008): my point is simply that it has become progressively more important over time.

9. See Mazzucato (2015) and Block and Keller (2015).

10. See US Bureau of the Census (1975, P-20). We should note too that the school year was considerably shorter and absences were considerably more frequent back then. In 1870 the school year was only 132 days long (compared to about 180 today), and the attendance rate averaged about 59% (compared to about 90% today).

11. As argued, for example, by Bowles and Gintis (1976) and reiterated more recently by Bowles and Gintis (2002). See also Stevens (2009), Khan (2010).

12. For a review of the available evidence on this upgrading tendency, see Handel (2012). On the United States, see Vidal (2013). One concern with efforts to assess trends in skill levels is how to account for tacit, experience-based skills that are not acquired in formal education or training. Traditional peasant agriculture, for example, relies on a remarkably rich body of know-how— much of which is being lost. But we should not romanticize such know-how to the point of forgetting the benefits of farmers' education in modern science and technology in increasing crop yields, developing new crop varieties, improving the efficiency of fishing, poultry, and cattle operations, and so on. Note too that the economy's need for higher skills does not mean that our education system has kept up. That is one reason why people without any college education have had a hard time finding jobs, or keeping jobs, or finding jobs with adequate pay, while those with higher degrees are generally (depending on the specialty) in much greater demand and their earnings have grown so much more rapidly (Goldin and Katz 2009). Nor does industry's need for higher skills mean that there are no mismatches: I earlier noted the prevalence of overqualified college graduates. But closer examination suggests that, frustrating as it surely is, this overeducation is mostly transitory, as most college graduates eventually transition to more appropriate jobs (Sloane 2014).

13. As a result, the share of government *expenditures* in the economy has continued to rise since 1980, albeit with ups and downs and at a slower average rate, while the share of government in nonfarm *employment* (excluding armed forces and intelligence agencies, but including the postal service) rose from about 13% in 1950 to about 19% till 1975, but fell pretty regularly from then to about 15% in 2000 (and has bumped around between 15% and 17% since then). On employment, see Federal Reserve Bank of St. Louis (2015).

14. See the description in Genoways (2017).

15. President Obama put it well in a widely quoted presidential campaign speech on July 13, 2012, where he said: "[L]ook, if you've been successful, you didn't get there on your own. [. . .] If you were successful, somebody along the line gave you some help. There was a great teacher somewhere in your life. [. . .] Somebody invested in roads and bridges. If you've got a business—you didn't build that. Somebody else made that happen. The Internet didn't get invented on its own. Government research created the Internet so that all the companies could make money off the Internet." Obama's analysis was accurate, even if the Republican candidate Mitt Romney ridiculed Obama and curried favor with

business by truncating the quote down to "If you've got a business—you didn't build that. Somebody else made that happen" (Kiely 2012).

16. A paper by Jordà et al. (2018) shows that across the 17 "advanced" economies, the integration of both their "real" economies and their finance sectors has grown rather steadily over the past 150 years. Reinhart and Rogoff (2009) show that since 1800 (although with an important interruption between the two world wars), financial capital has tended to become more mobile globally, and the number of countries drawn into banking crises in each downturn has tended to grow.

17. For a review of recent research on this, see https://promarket.org/connection-market-concentration-rise-inequality/.

18. See for example Harrigan (1981).

19. Arthur (1996).

20. Khan (2017).

21. Gallup (2017).

22. Gallup (2017).

23. Mazzucato (2015) shows that the US federal government has been instrumental in funding and otherwise promoting a range of technologies that were critical for the Internet, basic medicines, shale gas, space missions, etc. Her argument is compelling that the government has long played a role in the economy that goes well beyond the traditional one of remedying market failures and setting the legal framework for market interactions. But it is striking that the initiatives she describes are so oriented to national defense and to support for highly profitable industries. The ability of government in a capitalist society to act outside those parameters—our ability to direct government investment toward other types of democratically determined goals—is terribly limited. She cites one nice example of this limitation: yes, the NIH funds a lot of basic medical research, but most of it is aimed at facilitating (highly profitable) therapeutic drugs and far too little at (unprofitable) areas like diagnostics, surgical treatments, and lifestyle changes (Mazzucato 2015, 10). Moreover, our subservient government is entirely committed to the trickle-down idea of "socialization of risk and privatization of rewards" (195ff): the profits from the deployment of the technologies whose development government has funded flow to private industry rather than going back into the public coffers (see also Lazonick and Mazzucato 2013). She paints an inspiring vision of the role that a more "entrepreneurial state" could play in directing innovation toward green and inclusive growth, but she has little to say about where the political will would come from to pursue this vision. Her vision fits far more easily into the democratic socialist model I propose in chapter 6 than into any variant of capitalism.

CHAPTER 4

1. Gibson (1999).

2. See https://bcorporation.net/.

3. See, for example, McWilliams (2015), Mackey and Sisodia (2014), Porter and Kramer (2011).

4. On corporate social and environmental responsibility (CSR), the literature is enormous: for starting points, see Dahlsrud (2008), McWilliams (2015). On the high-road model, see Rogers (1990), Wright and Rogers (2011, Ch. 9), Kochan et al. (2013), Helper (2009), Helper and Noonan (2015).

5. Margolis and Elfenbein (2008).

6. For a devastating critique of the comforting illusion that noble efforts by the powerful and wealthy can help solve our problems without threatening these people's privilege, see Giridharadas (2018).

7. The argument advanced by many libertarians comes close to this "optical illusion" view. They do not deny that externalities might exist, but argue (1) that government efforts to resolve them by regulation or taxes are liable to do more harm than good, (2) that the better way to resolve them would be to privatize more of these social and natural resources, and (3) that those of us who see positive potential in government regulation exaggerate the negative impact of externalities to justify an expansion of government's role. See for example Adler (2008), Lane (2009).

8. Note however that Patagonia's founder, Yvon Chouinard—a hero to the corporate social responsibility community—estimates that only 10% of Patagonia's customers buy the company's products because they like the company's values. The other 90% buy these products, he says, because they like the styles (see interview at https://www.youtube.com/watch?v=O3TwULu-Wjw).

9. Kitzmueller and Shimshack (2012) summarize the literature on environmental responsibility, saying, "the preponderance of empirical economic studies favor a mild negative relationship between environmental performance and overall competitiveness (Jaffe et al. (1995), Ambec and Barla (2006), Pasurka (2008).) [. . .] Margolis, Elfenbein, and Walsh (2007) meta-analysis found a median correlation between social performance and financial performance of just 0.08, which is small in practical terms. Further, the average correlation shrinks significantly when only studies that include basic controls like industry, firm size, and risk were reviewed. Margolis, Elfenbein, and Walsh also note that the detected positive average correlation between corporate social responsibility and corporate financial performance (CFP) is 'at least as attributable to causation from CFP to CSR as the reverse'" (70–71).

10. Fair Trade coffee is a good example: see Hainmueller, Hiscox, and Sequeira (2015).

11. See the collection of papers in Michie, Blasi, and Borzaga (2017).

12. Pencavel, Pistaferri, and Schivardi (2006) found that worker-owned cooperatives in Italy had on average 14% lower wages than otherwise similar capitalist enterprises, and their wages were more volatile, because when business conditions were bad, they adjusted wages rather than laying off workers. The authors argue—rather plausibly—that their results should be generalizable to other countries.

13. See the discussion on the range of factors that block the expansion of cooperatives in Artz and Kim (2011).

14. Kitzmueller and Shimshack (2012): "Despite consistent qualitative survey results that suggest that CSR may influence labor markets, the quantitative empirical literature generally fails to reject a null hypothesis of small or no labor market effect" (72). That is true for executive compensation and even for the broader labor markets: "Recent economy-wide studies of comprehensive datasets demonstrate, on average, no systematic difference between wages in the nonprofit and for-profit sectors after controlling for individual, job, and workplace attributes [citations omitted]. Some studies even discover premiums in the nonprofit sector [citations omitted]. In sum, while more evidence is needed, workers at socially responsible firms do not appear to be sacrificing

wages or other forms of compensation. It therefore appears unlikely that labor market effects systematically drive observed CSR" (72–73).

15. People in the SRI community often quote data from the Social Investment Forum to the effect that over 20% of all assets under management in the United States today are invested in funds that use some form or other of SRI strategy (Investment 2016). But this figure seems vastly inflated. As best I can tell, it counts all the assets in any portfolio that offers any SRI fund within it—no matter how small the proportion actually invested in those SRI funds, and no matter how modest the SRI commitments of those funds.

16. See the various contributions in Porter et al. (2007).

17. The failures of the ethical-capitalism approach to global supply chain governance are demonstrated by Locke (2013). Nike, under pressure from activists, made unusually serious efforts to improve labor conditions in its global supply chain. Based on detailed data made available by Nike, Locke shows that these efforts have come to naught: there are just too many conflicting pressures within Nike and on its suppliers. He makes a compelling case that complementary efforts by government—for example, through a well-designed program of labor inspectors—are essential if we want to improve labor conditions in such global supply chains.

18. In his 2009 book, Judge Richard Posner offers an eloquent argument for this conclusion, one that is all the more convincing because this arch-conservative reached it so reluctantly (Posner 2009). From a business point of view, Porter and Van der Linde (1995) offer another influential argument in favor of (well-designed) regulation.

19. The Federal Reserve is a key actor of any stimulus program. By statute, the Federal Reserve has three goals—maximum employment, stable prices, and moderate long-term interest rates. But closer analysis shows that the employment commitment is at best a very half-hearted one. It is not to eliminate unemployment, but only to ensure "maximum" employment, by which they mean the maximum that is compatible with the other two goals. And why is there a trade-off between employment and the other two goals? I show in the following paragraphs that the reason does not lie in some mystery of the machinery of macroeconomics: it lies in the deep resistance of the business community to the loss of profits and power.

20. The classic analysis is offered by Kalecki (1943).

21. Smith (2016).

22. This analysis is supported even by the libertarian Cato Institute: see Thrall and Dorminey (2018).

23. Among many articles on this theme, readers might start with Stiglitz (2017) and Rhaman (2018). For more in-depth treatment, see Drahos and Braithwaite (2017), Dutfield (2017), May (2015).

24. On the idea of "corporatism," see Siaroff (1999). On "co-determination," see Streeck (1983), FitzRoy and Kraft (2005). I focus on social democracy as we see it in the Nordic countries, and leave aside countries such as the Netherlands, Germany, and France, where the role of government lies midway along the spectrum stretching between this Nordic model and the market-oriented model in the United States and the United Kingdom. For a review of the problems facing the social-democratic model viewed more broadly, see Palley (2018).

25. For a balanced view of the Nordic model's successes and failures in relation to gender and the social crisis of care, see Lister (2009).

26. Those who are skeptical of Nordic social democracy as a model often cite another factor against its applicability in the United States: these are relatively very small countries and their populations are relatively homogeneous. Indeed, these countries are so small that the leaders of every major business can meet with the government cabinet members around a modest-sized conference table. That makes it difficult to draw strong conclusions that would apply on the larger scale of the United States.

27. For an insightful essay on how Finland's social-democratic compromise was undermined by its (initially) successful efforts to join the arena of global technological competition, see Ornston (2014). For an analysis of the demise of Sweden's social-democracy under the pressure of neoliberal policy and global financialization, see Belfrage and Kallifatides (2018).

28. Credit Suisse (2016). Similarly, the rate of intergenerational mobility in Sweden is similar to that of the supposedly less-mobile economies of the United Kingdom and the United States. It is only a little higher today than in the preindustrial era. See Clark (2012).

29. See Minx et al. (2008).

30. Aggestam and Bergman-Rosamond (2016).

31. Sullivan (2014).

32. Vucetic (2018).

33. McKinnon, Muttitt, and Trout (2017).

34. A good starting point for further reading is the Wikipedia entry "Technological Utopianism" and Huesemann and Huesemann (2011).

35. For a useful review of the issues, see Davis (2016).

36. Alcorta (1994).

37. Some environmentalists see great merit in localism, but the evidence is accumulating that it would mean more-expensive food and/or more extensive use of chemicals in agriculture. And it would not save much in CO_2 emissions, because transport is just 11% of the food system emissions. See Sexton (2011).

38. The music industry has, naturally, fought back, to reassert property rights. See, for example, Fassler (2011).

39. Frenken (2017) offers a useful contrast of three models of the sharing economy—capitalist, state-dominated, and cooperative.

40. True, there is no guarantee in a capitalist market system that jobs lost to automation in one firm or one industry will reappear magically in another industry in just the right number and occupational mix. True also: we have already seen that government in a capitalist society is very unlikely to step in as an "employer of last resort." But on the other hand, big improvements in productivity in an industry typically lead to lower prices for the products of that industry, and this leaves customers with more money to spend on the products of other industries, which in turn leads these other industries to expand production and hire more employees. That is why, over the last two centuries of capitalism, we have seen so little impact on aggregate employment caused by prior waves of technological revolution See Arntz, Gregory, and Zierahn (2016), Mishel and Bivens (2017).

41. Part of the appeal of universal basic income is the idea that it moves us toward the abolition of wage labor, which is, after all, a means of exploitation and a form of domination. But it only does this for the minority who would be willing and able to live on the modest income it would provide. Far better to reduce work time for everyone. Another part of the appeal is that, as compared

with a socialist program of political-economic transformation, universal basic income seems like a relatively modest policy reform—more easily implemented, embraced even by those on the right who see it as a way to slash social welfare benefits—even though, were it implemented, it would open up an exciting path for social and economic development. However, while it may seem like a simpler policy reform, its implementation in the context of an ongoing capitalist economy would rapidly encounter strong resistance—without doing much to build the movement for more fundamental change. It puts the cart before the horse. We should also note the right-wing supporters of the idea, who hope that the introduction of a universal basic income (equivalently: a negative income tax) would legitimate the elimination of all other existing social welfare programs. As they see it, there would be no need for a government-run social security program, for example, if everyone has been assured of a basic income allowing them—if they so choose—to save for their own pension. See, for example, Friedman (2009 [1962]).

42. For a rich historical and philosophical discussion of universal basic income in the context of the American tradition of "labor republicanism," see Gourevitch (2013).

43. Paul, Darity, and Hamilton (2017).

CHAPTER 5

1. An overview of Aristotle's view of democracy and other political systems is at Miller (2017).

2. Ronald Coase postulated that firms are more effective than markets when the organizational costs of managing within a firm are less than the transaction costs required for the corresponding set of market relations relying on competition and price comparisons (Coase 1937). Oliver Williamson argued that the key factor explaining whether the transaction costs of accessing an asset via the market are greater or smaller than the organizational costs of accessing that asset from a sister unit within the same organization is whether the asset in question is more or less specific to the user's needs (Williamson 1975). To illustrate: if a steel company needs generic paper clips, it should buy them rather than make them; but if it needs specialized components whose production requires capabilities that are not used by any other firm, it should probably make rather than buy these components—otherwise, the supplier firm could leverage its monopoly position to raise its price at the steel company's expense. This argument from comparative transaction/organizational costs, however, is only about the sourcing decision facing the individual firm: it is not about how best the overall economy should be structured. Williamson therefore ignores all the systemic dysfunctions of the market that we have discussed—its instability, monopoly tendencies, the costs of negative externalities and opportunity costs of foregone positive externalities.

3. We should note that some large firms organize themselves internally along market lines. Their main units are set up as independent businesses, which charge market rates for the products and services that they sell to each other, and which compete for funding from headquarters much as firms compete for investment funds on the stock market. In this "holding company" model, strategic management is kept to a minimum. This market model of internal organization works reasonably well so long as the business units are independent in their core activities. If, however, these activities are more

interdependent—and if headquarters wants to develop and exploit potential synergies among the businesses—the misfit between interdependent cross-unit production and independent unit control generates many of the same dysfunctions that we see in the wider market-based economy. See, for example, Eccles (1985).

4. In many companies, not only internal operations but also relations with suppliers and customers are strategically managed (see for example Hansen [2009], Fawcett, Jones, and Fawcett [2012]). Instead of arms-length market relations, where the firm would select components from a supplier's catalog on an as-needed basis, the firm negotiates a long-term contract with one or two suppliers, which stipulates prices, quantities, quality, delivery dates, contingencies, penalties, and so forth. Such contracts embody a mix of market competition and joint strategic management. High-road companies go further in this joint strategic management. In their attempts to leverage the creativity of their suppliers as well as their employees, they often cooperate with suppliers in the design of components, in determining the best production processes, and in resolving design, production, and delivery problems. Such interfirm joint strategic management has been shaped by the same four organizational principles as the high-road firms' intrafirm management. It thus holds lessons for horizontal contracting between enterprises in a democratic-socialist economy, even if in practice today such joint efforts must contend with the corrosive effects of capitalist market competition.

5. We can distinguish this *collaboration* from *coordination*, which is what we do in situations where the goals and the means of attaining them are specified in advance (as in highly routinized operations). And we can distinguish collaboration from *cooperation*, which is what we do where the goals are specified but the means are not (as in a team working to reach a prespecified goal such as the introduction of a new product).

6. Like material technologies, management techniques function in capitalist firms simultaneously as productive tools and as weapons of domination and exploitation, with sometimes one aspect predominating and sometimes the other (see Adler 2012). For a historical perspective on the evolution of these innovations in management, see Bodrožić and Adler (2018). For another perspective on the development of management (and on the corresponding growth of managers as an occupational category) as an outgrowth of the socialization of production, see Duménil and Lévy (2018).

7. In the literature on socialism, this set of activities is often referred to as "planning," and socialism is understood as a system of "centralized planning," in contrast with capitalism as a system of "decentralized market coordination." Planning, however, is only one phase of a broader process we need—a process that would identify goals, develop plans for reaching them, allocate resources for the fulfillment of these plans, assess performance, and revise goals and plans over time. And the relative roles of central agencies versus local actors in the socialist economy is an open issue, not a predetermined one. Outside the specialized literature on the economics of socialism, such a broad process with variable responsibilities for central and local units is commonly referred to as "strategic management." The Wikipedia entry "Strategic Management" offers a good overview.

8. To take an example: you may be free from government strictures to read what you want, but that is not much empowerment if you have not had the

opportunity to learn how to read. A good place to start on positive versus negative freedom is Carter (2018). See also Sen (1993) and Nussbaum (2011). One alternative approach agrees that freedom is essentially a matter of freedom-from, but that such freedom is worth little if people don't have the ability to exercise it for lack of resources. A second alternative is proposed by Gourevitch (2015), who argues that what I am calling positive freedom can also be construed as another form of negative freedom—freedom from institutional constraints on our opportunities to participate in decisions that affect us.

9. The management literature on this issue is sometimes confused, defining centralization and participation in ways that make them seem mutually exclusive. But the more robust definitions can be summarized simply. Centralization is about how far *up* an authority hierarchy someone lower down needs to take a proposal before they reach a person or committee who can decide to accept or reject the proposal without needing to consult anyone even higher. Participation is about how far *down* or *across* the hierarchy someone takes their proposal for consultation and approval before the decision is made. Participation can, of course, vary in intensity, ranging from fully shared authority, to the obligation to consult, and to the right to be informed at the weakest end of the range. We want centralization in an organization when we need strong consistency of action across all the organization's subunits. We want participation when the knowledge required to define goals and plans for reaching them is more dispersed further down or further across the hierarchy. On centralization, see Pugh and Hickson (1976); on participation, see Heller (1998), Glew et al. (1995).

10. Skeptics of participative centralization often refer to what has been called the "iron law of oligarchy"—the idea that as organizations grow, no matter how democratic they start out, they inevitably succumb to the domination of a self-interested few (the classic statement is Michels 1966 [1911]). True, there are many cases that fit this generalization. But history also teaches us that there is also a powerful countertendency, one that has been called an "iron law of democracy" (Gouldner 1955). Whether at the national or organizational level, when leaders become autocratic—when they lead for their own benefit and at the expense of others—we often see those others rebel, challenge leaders, and reassert democratic principles. (In some settings, people can also encourage change by voting with their feet and leaving: see Hirschman (1970).) To decree that a degeneration toward oligarchy is inevitable is to dress up cynicism as some kind of wisdom or social theory.

11. There is a considerable body of management and accounting research on the effects of participation in strategy and budgeting processes on organizational performance. The evidence is mixed, but on balance mostly shows benefits for business performance. See for example Wooldridge, Schmid, and Floyd (2008); Wooldridge and Floyd (1990); Gerbing, Hamilton, and Freeman (1994); Vilà and Canales (2008); Derfuss (2009).

12. A vivid if fictitious portrait of the power of these systems is presented in Austin, Cotteleer, and Escalle (2003).

13. Paralleling the skepticism concerning socialist planning, when enterprise resource planning (ERP) systems were first proposed by software services companies such as SAP, many observers expressed skepticism these systems would ever be successful. The implementation of these systems requires a massive, organization-wide effort to bring into a single, coherent database all

the information used in every department. The cost is high, and implementation efforts are often delayed and sometimes fail, but the benefits have been impressive. After an initial period of skepticism, ERP is now a taken-for-granted, standard feature of good management practice in large businesses (see Davenport (2000), Thomé et al. (2012)). Moreover, it appears that the implementation of ERP systems enhances rather than detracts from the enterprise's flexibility (Qu et al. 2014).

14. Specifically: Kaiser is organized as a consortium of regional entities, each bringing together Kaiser Foundation Health Plans for insurance (chartered as a nonprofit public-benefit corporation), Permanente Medical Groups (which are for-profit physician partnerships or professional corporations that do business almost exclusively with Kaiser), and, in regions where Kaiser has a bigger presence, Kaiser Foundation Hospitals (also not-for-profit, and funded by the Health Plans).

15. See Schilling et al. (2011).

16. This dashboard was not a ground-breaking innovation: many big corporations have developed similar management tools. Kaiser was somewhat unusual in sharing the information widely and in treating all four dimensions as equally important, where many other businesses treat the other dimensions merely as possible contributors to success on the financial dimension.

17. See Smillie (2000), Hendricks (1993).

18. By far the largest of the unions in the partnership was the Service Employees International Union (SEIU): the full list of participating unions is available at http://www.unioncoalition.org.) On the partnership, see Kochan (2013), Kochan et al. (2009), Kochan (2008). For more critical views of the partnership, see Borsos (2013) and Early (2011). The California Nurses Association refused to participate in the partnership. In 2018, the coalition began coming apart, with SEIU attempting to assert more control and to get the coalition to adopt a more adversarial stance, prompting in turn 22 Locals, representing about one-third of the members in the coalition, to pull out of the coalition. The future of the labor-management partnership was uncertain at that time.

19. Schilling, Chase, et al. (2010), Whippy et al. (2011).

20. Kochan (2013).

21. If Kaiser was so committed to this matrix form, it was probably because that form was needed in the world of healthcare delivery. Here, many working units are tightly interdependent. Sharing authority and resources was therefore critical in ensuring these units' effective coordination.

22. At the top level, the ultimate governing body of the labor–management partnership is the Labor Management Strategy group, composed of regional presidents from Kaiser Permanente's eight regions, executives from Kaiser Permanente's national leadership, the leaders of the Permanente Medical Groups, and union leaders in the Coalition (including at least one representative from each of the Coalition's 11 affiliated unions). See Kaiser Permanente and Coalition of Kaiser Permanente Unions (2012).

23. See August (n.d.). We should note in passing that the union Coalition did not shy away from the question of economic effectiveness. The unions understood that their industry and employer were under great pressure to improve efficiency and quality. This pressure was not simply coming from low-road competitors: it also represented mounting frustration with the deep dysfunction of the American healthcare system. That dysfunction means that our healthcare system costs

Americans far more than in any other advanced economy while achieving poorer health outcomes. Unions and management agreed that the partnership should aim to demonstrate a high-road path to solving these national affordability and quality challenges.

24. See Kaiser Permanente (2010), Pearl (2017), Berwick (2010), and Litwin (2010).

25. See for example Matzler et al. (2016); Stieger et al. (2012); Gast and Zanini (2012); Whittington, Cailluet, and Yakis-Douglas (2011); Whittington, Hautz, and Seidl (2017). Open strategy is modeled on the "open innovation" model, in which firms look outside their boundaries—to suppliers, customers, online communities—for innovative ideas (Chesbrough 2006). The focus here has been on horizontal, not vertical, participation, and on involving people outside the firm's boundaries. In characterizing these horizontal relations, much of this literature ignores the profound differences between competitive, self-interested market relations and communal relations based on generalized reciprocity. And this literature pays little attention to the centralization dimension. On that last issue, Sibony (2012) notes that when this open strategy process lacks centralization, it fails to help the "strategist identify the need for radical shifts in direction, wrestle through difficult trade-offs between options that seem similarly attractive, or develop plans for working through intensely competitive circumstances. . . . [C]rowd-based mechanisms are a powerful engine to produce groupthink on a grand scale, encouraging people to stick to predefined anchors that become more and more powerful as other contributors appear to confirm them."

26. Oligarchy is not inevitable (see note 10 above), but there is a risk of oligarchy in any system of elected representation, and this leads some theorists of democracy to advocate the ancient Greek system based on "sortition," where political officials are selected by random sampling from a larger pool of candidates. See the corresponding Wikipedia entry for some entry points to the literature.

27. This is the foundation for a famous argument in favor of socialism advanced by Joseph Schumpeter (1976 [1942]): big firms, he argued, could "routinize" innovation (plan for it, and provide specialized personnel and dedicated funding for it) by creating centralized R&D units instead of relying on the unplanned emergence of innovation in the decentralized market process. Note, however, that today, instead of investing in R&D, many big established companies such as Microsoft, Google, Facebook, and Apple use their monopoly profits to sweep up small firms that have developed promising innovations. It is through such acquisitions rather than internal R&D that these monopolies acquire the new technologies they need to maintain their dominance and suppress the emergence of rival technologies that might reduce the profitability of their industry.

28. The classic reference here is Hayek (1956 [1944]). For a particularly cogent critique, see Cockshott and Cottrell (1997).

29. Schilling, Deas, et al. (2010).

30. McCreary (2010).

31. Cohen, Ptaskiewicz, and Mipos (2010). Training is available to help employees and managers work effectively in these teams, and a staff of facilitators is available to coach them. The progress of teams toward higher levels of team effectiveness is tracked, and goals are codified in the collective bargaining agreement. For example, by 2019, 87% of UBTs were supposed to reach Level 4 or 5 of the 5-level assessment rubric. See the Partnership website for more

information on this "Path to performance" effort: https://www.lmpartnership.org/path-to-performance.

32. Cohen, Ptaskiewicz, and Mipos (2010).

33. Bjelland and Wood (2008).

34. The Collaborative Innovating principle bears some similarity to the open innovation model referred to earlier. And as with open strategy, the focus of open innovation models is horizontal communication of innovative ideas across organizational boundaries, in a process somewhere between market exchange and communal reciprocity. It thus affords little insight into the question at hand here, which is how to facilitate communication across levels in a complex, hierarchical organization.

35. The NIH's intramural research arm is the largest biomedical research institution in the world: it employs some 1,200 principal investigators and over 4,000 postdoctoral fellows in basic, translational, and clinical research. Its extramural arm is much larger again: it provides 28% of the biomedical research funding spent annually in the United States. Those who fear the stultification of research creativity in such centralized national research enterprises should be reassured by the stellar record of the NIH in driving radical innovation. Our investment in NIH-sponsored research has yielded a rate of return somewhere between 25% and 40% per year by reducing the economic cost of illness in the United States. Among the 21 drugs with the highest therapeutic impact on society introduced between 1965 and 1992, public funding was instrumental for 15 of them (Joint Economic Committee 2000). On DARPA, see Azoulay et al. (2018).

36. See a sketch of such a program at Janda and Moezzi (2014) and See et al. (2015).

37. David (2015).

38. While this view of how firms achieve high levels of efficiency is largely a matter of common sense, it is rather different from that found in most economic treatments, where the emphasis has been on the role of incentives rather than on the procedures that shape work processes. In reality, while both incentives and processes have an impact on business performance, the average impact of processes is much greater—roughly an order of magnitude greater—than that of incentives (Knott and McKelvey 1999). Getting financial incentives "wrong"— using pay and bonuses that do not reward the dimensions of individual performance that matter for the firm's overall performance—can badly hurt the firm's performance; but getting them "right" makes little positive contribution, at least as compared to getting people to use best practices rather than relying on their own judgment.

39. As research on industrial quality has repeatedly shown, it is difficult to improve a process that is not standardized. That is true not only where that process is basically repetitive (Adler and Cole 1993, 1994) but also where it is not, as shown in the cases below of Kaiser's clinical guidelines and the CMM at CSC (Adler et al. 2005).

40. One of the best-known theories of work motivation focuses on the characteristics of work that make it more versus less motivating, specifically: skill variety, task identity, task significance, autonomy, and feedback (Hackman and Oldham 1980). For a critique and an alternative approach, see Adler and Chen (2011).

41. The plant was closed in 2010, as Toyota confronted a global over-capacity problem and decided to consolidate production at their (nonunion) plant in Kentucky. For a fuller discussion of NUMMI and its high-road practices, see

Adler (1993). Toyota is not generally taken as exemplary of high-road practices. Their management system has often been criticized as highly stressful for workers (Parker and Slaughter 1988). But the strength of the union at NUMMI and Toyota's eagerness to create a positive labor climate in this, their first North American plant, led the plant to adopt many high-road features.

42. The 1985 collective bargaining agreement stipulated that "New United Motor Manufacturing, Inc. recognizes that job security is essential to an employee's well-being and acknowledges that it has a responsibility, with the cooperation of the Union, to provide stable employment to its workers. The Union's commitments in Article II of this Agreement are a significant step towards the realization of stable employment. Hence, the Company agrees that it will not lay off employees unless compelled to do so by severe economic conditions that threaten the long-term viability of the Company. The Company will take affirmative measures before laying off any employees, including such measures as the reduction of salaries of its officers and management, assigning previously subcontracted work to bargaining unit employees capable of performing this work, seeking voluntary layoffs, and other cost saving measures."

43. The British industrial psychologist Baldamus (1961) theorized this effect under the heading "traction"—the feeling of being pulled along by the steady rhythm of the work. It is striking that concerns about work intensity ranked very low on the union Local's priority list of concerns. The main exceptions were in the context of some new model introduction periods, when poor planning left some assembly-line workers struggling for months on end with too much work and too many defects to handle in too little time, sometimes with serious ergonomic consequences (see Adler, Goldoftas, and Levine 1997).

44. Whippy et al. (2011), Bisognano and Kenney (2012, Ch. 7), Davino-Ramaya et al. (2012).

45. Sometimes Kaiser's guidelines have been attacked by consumer-rights groups for clinical guidelines that are based on cost considerations and that risk sacrificing patients' health. As a capitalist enterprise, it would hardly be surprising if Kaiser's guidelines or the implementation of these guidelines were sometimes biased to suit the organization's bottom-line interests. Overall, however, their record seems very positive.

46. See https://www.lmpartnership.org/sites/default/files/10-essential-tips-huddles.pdf, and https://www.lmpartnership.org/tools/daily-huddles.

47. See, for example, Standish Group (1994), Gibbs (1994), Lieberman and Fry (2001), Jones (2002). Things have not improved much in the intervening years: in 2015, the Standish Group estimated that 66% of projects end in partial or total failure (based on their analysis of 50,000 projects globally).

48. Humphrey (2002).

49. The CMM was created to support the development of large-scale, integrated systems. At the other end of the spectrum, we find small-scale, modular systems, where "Agile" or "Scrum" development approaches have proven effective. The two can be combined easily enough (Anderson 2005; Lukasiewicz and Miler 2012; Brown, Ambler, and Royce 2013).

50. Fishman (1996).

51. Adler (2006), Adler et al. (2005), Adler (2015).

52. On cost, see Berwick and Hackbarth (2012), and on errors, see Daniel and Makary (2016).

53. This is essentially what the UK National Health System does with its National Institute for Health and Care Excellence. See de Joncheere, Hill, and Klazinga (2006) and Drummond (2016) for evaluations.
54. Individualism here refers to a preference for a loosely knit social framework in which individuals are expected to take care of only themselves, and collectivism means a preference for a tightly knit framework in which individuals expect everyone to take care of each other. It is reflected in whether people's self-image is defined in terms of "I" or "we." See Hofstede (1980). Inglehart and Welzel (2005) argue that "modernization" implies a shift from collectivism to individualism, and that this shift toward individualism is a key precondition for the emergence of democracy. But they (like many other scholars who study individualism and collectivism) use a concept of collectivism that is very traditionalistic. I will argue that collectivism need not be so traditionalistic.
55. On the psychology of collectivism, individualism, and creativity, see Goncalo and Staw (2006).
56. Firms have been driven to try to achieve this synthesis because it would obviate the trade-off between innovation and efficiency that is commonly experienced in low-road firms. Low-road firms rely on a coercive approach to achieving efficiency, so pushing the people doing creative work to become more efficient would alienate them and hamper innovation. And in these firms, the people doing the more routine work live under the burden of this coercion and therefore have little interest in contributing to innovation efforts. As a result, management is typically left with a stark choice between imposing standardization to ensure efficiency or allowing the flexibility needed to ensure innovation. This is one of the main reasons that the mainstream business-strategy literature—such as in Porter (1985)—urges firms to choose between a cost-leadership strategy and a differentiation strategy. If a low-road firm wants both efficiency and innovation, its best choice is to create a centralized R&D unit; but this inevitably creates tensions between the innovation-oriented R&D unit and the firm's efficiency-oriented operations units. These tensions are common in industry, where the operations units resent the disruption occasioned by the introduction of innovative products, and the R&D units are unconcerned about the "manufacturability" of their product designs. Because of these difficulties, this combined strategy (the "Analyzer" strategy described by Miles and Snow [1978]) represents a compromise and typically achieves only modest levels of efficiency and only modest levels of innovation. High-road firms, however, can overcome this tradeoff between innovation and efficiency by using Collaborative Innovating and Collaborative Learning. These firms encourage employees in innovation-oriented units to bring forward ideas aimed at improving efficiency in their innovation activity, and encourage employees in production-oriented units to bring forward innovative ideas aimed at improving efficiency as well as new products and services. In the management literature, the ability of an organization to excel at both innovation and efficiency is referred to as "ambidexterity." See Adler, Goldoftas, and Levine (1999) for an analysis of NUMMI's success in building this capability. At stake in the present section is what kind of employee motivation is required to assure this ambidexterity.
57. For a particularly insightful analysis of this, see Macpherson (1962).
58. Stephens, Markus, and Townsend (2007).

59. For a more theoretical discussion of the idea of shared purpose, see Adler and Heckscher (2018).

60. For some supporting evidence on deliberation's effects, see Gastil, Bacci, and Dollinger (2010).

61. See Brown, Deletic, and Wong (2015), Hansen and von Oetinger (2001). High-road firms bet that personal development opportunities will attract higher-quality personnel, even if the new skills they acquire make it easier for some employees to leave subsequently to other employers.

62. http://www.lmpartnership.org/stories/safe-speak.

63. The bonus system for Kaiser's unionized employees was less tailored to interdependence. Under the partnership agreement, employees received bonuses paid out in equal amounts to all the region's employees. These bonuses were based on whether the region has met targets that have been negotiated between unions and management and that reflect a mix of variables from the various points on the Value Compass, such as attendance, safety, service, and clinical outcomes.

64. Yaun (2006), Palmisano (2004).

65. Heckscher et al. (2017).

66. Heckscher et al. (2017). See also Heckscher (2007).

67. Heckscher et al. (2017).

68. Charles Heckscher (2018), personal communication.

69. e-reward.co.uk (2016).

70. See for example the discussion prompted by a post by Olah (2013).

71. See Adler, Goldoftas, and Levine (1997).

CHAPTER 6

1. Absent public ownership, economy-wide economic management is limited to the range of options that are profitable for the private sector. We would be back on the regulated capitalism or social-democratic models discussed and critiqued in chapter 4. On the experience of such "indicative" forms of planning in a range of countries, see Yülek (2015).

2. This socialist idea has had a long history in the United States. Wikipedia has a quick survey, "History of the Socialist Movement in the United States." Contemporary discussion in the United States can be sampled at the Democratic Socialists of America website (http://www.dsausa.org/toward_freedom). For a sampling that is less focused on the United States, see the symposia in the journal *Science and Society* published in Spring 1992, Spring 2002, and April 2012.

3. Gar Alperovitz (2013, 2005) offers a particularly useful survey of these innovations. I borrow extensively from his account here, and refer readers to his books for the relevant references. See also the work assembled by Erik Wright under the heading "real utopias" at https://www.ssc.wisc.edu/~wright/ERU.htm.

4. On cooperatives and other forms of socialized ownership in the United States, see Schneiberg (2010) and Hanna (2018).

5. Mondragon was unable, however, to absorb all the 5,600 workers whose jobs were threatened with the financial collapse of its largest group, Fagor, in 2014. The firm was sold to Cata, a Spanish domestic appliance company.

6. Mishel and Schieder (2017).

7. Forcadell (2005). The Catholic roots of Mondragon leave a legacy of suspicion toward centralization. The Catholic principle of "subsidiarity"—the idea that

issues should be decided at the most local level that is competent, rather than by a central authority—is attractive, but in Catholic thought and in Mondragon it has been paired with celebration of the market as a decentralized coordination mechanism. In part, this is a relic of the ideological struggle of the church against Communism and of the practical struggle for independence from governments that might threaten the church's autonomy.

8. See https://www.cincinnatiunioncoop.org/ and an early evaluation by Schlachter (2017).

9. Kelly and McKinley (2015).

10. See https://democracycollaborative.org/.

11. Fung and Wright (2003), Ansell and Gash (2008), Innes and Booher (2010), Roberts (2004), Wainwright (2003), Curato et al. (2017). Some socialists are skeptical of deliberative democracy, but their main concern is not whether democracy under socialism should embrace deliberative procedures but whether deliberative democracy today, in the interstices of contemporary capitalism, holds much emancipatory potential (see, for example, Hauptmann 2001).

12. The public sector expands our understanding not only of Collaborative Strategizing (Baiocchi and Ganuza 2014) but also of Collaborative Learning and Working. Collaborative Learning through enabling standardization has come to the fore in some recent studies of public sector management, showing how "green tape" differs from "red tape" and how the former can support effective public administration. Five general characteristics of Collaborative Learning have emerged from public sector organizations' green tape efforts. Procedures should be written rather than only oral, to ensure that they are open to scrutiny. They should be logical and comport with common sense. They need to be consistently applied. They should allow for an appropriate degree of flexibility—neither too stringent nor too lax. And their purposes should be clear to the people they affect. This research suggests that the lessons on Collaborative Learning we culled from high-road firms have been validated in public sector organizations too. See on this DeHart-Davis (2009b, 2009a), DeHart-Davis, Davis, and Mohr (2014). Collaborative Working has also emerged recently as a key issue in the public sector, in the proliferating scholarship on "public service motivation." The motivation we often find—and that we would want to find even more often—among public sector employees is similar to that cultivated in the high-road firms: one that is both willingly compliant with standards and policies, and eager to contribute individually to the refinement of those standards and to the advancement of the organization's mission. See Ritz, Brewer, and Neumann (2016), Anderfuhren-Biget, Varone, and Giauque (2014).

13. See Benkler (2006), Kostakis and Bauwens (2014), O'Mahoney and Ferraro (2007).

14. See Weinstein (1967) and the Wikipedia entry "List of Elected Socialist Mayors in the United States."

15. Radford (2003) reviews this history. A similar fate has befallen municipal socialism in the United Kingdom—see for example Quilley (2000).

16. See McKibben (2016), Delina (2016), Silk (2016).

17. On poverty, see Plotnick et al. (1998).

18. Labor leaders, too, encouraged conversion. In 1940, Walter Reuther, a leader in the United Auto Workers, launched a campaign to force the major automakers to convert to aircraft production. The literature on this period is enormous: some starting points include Hooks (1993), Wilson (2016). World War II is much more interesting for our purposes here than World War I. In the earlier war,

government intervention in the economy was relatively minor and the war was much shorter.

19. Leftist historians (such as Koistinen 1973) bemoan the fact that unions did not play as big a role as they would have liked in the mobilization, and these historians point to the powerful alliance of Southern Democrats and business-friendly Republicans determined to suppress labor's influence. But even by this account, it is clear that the war period brought about a dramatic increase in the capacity of workers to influence decisions in the workplace and in the political sphere (see also Lichtenstein 2000). For a portrait of one workplace, see Lee (2004).

20. The business community was virulently antiunion, and employers accused the Board of trying to "sovietize" industry. Charles Wilson, president of General Motors, expressed the prevailing view, "There will be none of this equal voice bunk at GM" (quoted in Guzda, 1984). Although some 4,800 such committees, covering about 40% of the workforce in manufacturing and mining, were registered by 1944, only about 500 of them actually functioned. See also De Schweinitz (1949).

21. Quoted in Wilson (2016, 241).

22. One notable instance: Karl Polanyi (1968 [1944]).

23. This chapter sketches a distinctively democratic form of socialism because the alternative, undemocratic forms have been so discredited. There are nevertheless things we can learn from the experience of the former USSR and its allies and from China, too. I summarize those lessons very briefly here, and then summarize the democratic alternatives that have been proposed and from which I draw inspiration.

    In the standard model of economic planning developed in the USSR, a central agency planned output and investment for major industries. The planners ensured the balance of supply and demand across interdependent industries using physical rather than monetary units. For example, steel-using industries sent to the planners their projections for the tons of steel they would need in the coming year; the steel industry authority was instructed to produce this amount of steel; and then this output target was divided up among the various steel plants in the country.

    Notwithstanding considerable inefficiency and waste, this system allowed the centrally planned economies to maintain an impressive rate of investment and economic growth, and to make impressive improvements in people's material living standards too. (On the USSR, see Ofer 1987; Brainerd 2010; and Ellman 2014.) One strength of this system: from the central planners' vantage point, the value of "human capital" was immediately obvious, and these countries made commitments to public education and public health that even critics of the system saw as superior to the haphazard policies prevalent in advanced capitalist economies at the time.

    However, top-down planning in authoritarian political systems such as the USSR became less effective as those economies shifted from "extensive" development—based on bringing into production more natural and human resources—to "intensive" development—based on technological innovation. Aware of this slippage, leaders in the USSR and its Eastern European allies undertook various reform efforts. These reforms aimed primarily to give enterprises more local autonomy and more incentive to contribute to the achievement of the plan's higher-level goals.

Soviet reforms starting in the late 1970s thus focused the central planners on a smaller set of high-level goals, and devolved down to enterprise managers and production teams the task of specifying more-detailed goals. (A lively literature followed these innovations in the West: see for example the compilation by Shaffer [1984].) In practice, however, the authoritarian legacy of Stalinism hobbled these efforts, and eventually the political collapse of the USSR cut short all reform efforts.

In China and Vietnam, economic planning now plays a more limited role. The big state-owned enterprises take guidance from central planning authorities, but the overall direction of economic development also reflects the great weight of the private sector and the ruling party's commitment to integration into the world capitalist economy. (On this, see Ellman 2014, Ch. 2.).

Turning to proposals for a more democratic form of socialism, we find three main variants. The primary issue on which they differ is the extent to which the overall coordination of economic activity should be centrally planned versus left to decentralized competition.

At the centralization end of the spectrum, some argue that all enterprises should be managed as if they were units of one big integrated enterprise organized on a "functional" rather than "multi-divisional" basis. Here, centralized, democratic, strategic management would entirely displace competition. For particularly cogent presentations of how such a system would work, see Cockshott and Cottrell (1993) and Mandel (1986).

At the decentralization end of the spectrum lie proposals for "market socialism." Proponents of market socialism accept the general socialist premise that ownership should be democratized somehow to ensure a more equitable sharing of accumulated wealth, but they see this democratization taking the form of widely distributed, private ownership, rather than socialized, public ownership. Many recommend worker cooperatives as the appropriate structure for each socialist enterprise, but want to see these cooperatives compete in markets for their own profits, rather than contributing to an economy-wide plan. Market socialists are fearful of allowing central authorities too much control, and doubtful that these authorities could master the massive amount of data needed for comprehensive planning. They therefore propose a system where strong government regulation is counterbalanced by strong market forces, where market competition determines prices and wages, and where profitability guides decentralized enterprise decisions on production and investment. Market socialism models are presented in Bardhan and Roemer (1992), Wright (1996), Schweickart (2011), Wolff (2012).

Intermediate positions along this spectrum allow for the coexistence of an economy-wide strategic plan with a subordinate role for competition and some kind of market process. These models resemble the strategic management process of many multi-divisional corporations, where some degree of autonomy for the individual subunits is balanced with an overarching commitment to shared strategic goals. More scope can be left for enterprises to contract with their choice of suppliers or customers than in the fully centralized model. And central planning can be replaced by horizontal relations between workers' councils and consumers' councils without markets (Albert and Hahnel, 1991); by multilevel (central and local) iteration within planning, also without markets (Laibman, 2002, 2013); or by a mix of strategic planning and market outcomes (Devine, 2002).

Much of the debate among proponents of these various models will be resolved by practical experimentation rather than theoretical argument. That said, my presentation represents a combination of the centralized and the intermediate positions because we have several reasons to be skeptical of the market socialism models.

First, to deal with the various crises we face—most notably, the environmental one—we urgently need a concerted, coordinated effort led by a strong central authority to reorient radically and rapidly our production and investment. Once we escape these turbulent waters, it might make sense to give more weight to local decision-making as compared to central, higher-level priorities. And perhaps in that context the market process could play a bigger role. But in the foreseeable future, these higher-level priorities will need to play the primary role in our strategic management process.

Second, even in the longer-term, we must ensure that prices that are used in planning include environmental and social externalities and that they reflect our concerns for the distant future. The market process typically fails in both these respects, and the bigger the role left to the market, the greater the discrepancy between socially optimal "full" prices and the prices that emerge through market competition. To take one example: we do not want to allow wage levels and workers' basic income security to be dependent on market competition. The market socialist model relies on government regulation and taxes to remedy these deficiencies of the market process—a poor substitute for democratic control.

Third, we need to ensure that the production and investment plans for each enterprise taken individually add up to a whole economy that is consistent—rather than leaving us with shortages and surpluses—and that this aggregate supports our strategic goals. This implies that higher-level regional, industry, or national councils might need to push enterprises to change their proposed plans—just as headquarters in a multidivisional firm might push its business units to revise their proposed plans.

And finally, over time, a system dominated by market competition, even one that starts with a socialistic egalitarian distribution of ownership, seems likely to generate massive inequalities. The mathematics (based on thermodynamic systems) get complicated, but Foley (2010) demonstrates that because trades in a decentralized market typically happen at disequilibrium rather than equilibrium prices, such systems tend spontaneously toward highly unequal distributions of wealth and income. Foley (2017) gives a compelling example: in the 1990s, several eastern European countries privatized most of their state assets by distributing "vouchers" or shares on an egalitarian basis. But once people were allowed to buy and sell the vouchers, ownership very rapidly became highly concentrated.

A basic question underlying these debates over the relative roles of centralized strategic planning versus decentralized market processes seems to be whether we think people can engage seriously in a process of strategic deliberation over economic goals at the regional, industry, and national levels. Skeptics worry that the scope of people's social identification is inevitably narrower, focusing on their individual well-being or, at its widest, that of their immediate community or work unit. But we have no valid reason to accept that unproven assumption.

24. For reviews, see Murrell (1991); Trujillo, Estache, and Perelman (2005); and European Federation of Public Service Unions (2014).

25. A similar process is common in organizations that create new communication channels through which employees can voice concerns (for example about quality or safety, or supervisor or coworker behavior). Invariably, the number of concerns registered rapidly increases—not because things have gotten worse, but because there is now a way to raise concerns.

26. For a balanced, mainstream view of the history and pros and cons of bank nationalization, see Elliott (2009).

27. This strategic management effort relies on three key informational inputs that will come from the bottom-up expression of needs from citizens (in their neighborhood, city, and regional councils) and workers (in their work-team, enterprise, and industry councils). First, an estimate of household consumer demand. After all, that should be the main purpose of economic activity—to provide what we all need to live by. Many enterprises will have launched new products in the prior year, and we will need information on how well these products meet people's needs. Proposals for new consumption items could also be vetted ahead of time, perhaps by electronic voting.

    The second key input is the amount of investment we want to make in things that will make our lives better and our economy more effective. Some of these priorities will be decided directly in the national economic council, and others will come up for deliberation from regional and industry councils.

    And the third key input is government-sector demand for goods and services that do not reach the household sector even indirectly. This will be a much larger share of the economy than it is today because a socialist government will offer a much richer variety of services. Government agencies will send to the higher-level economic councils proposals for expenditures and investments in the coming year.

    Once they have in hand the forecasts of consumer, investment, and government demand, the economic councils will use detailed models of the technologies of production and information on the resources available in each of industries to quantify the outputs and inputs required of all the industries. This is not all that different from the enterprise resource planning systems we reviewed in the prior chapter. Technically, this is done using a detailed input-output matrix, which shows, for each industry, all the inputs it requires from the others. Once we know the desired final demand (i.e., consumer, investment, and government needs) of the economy, we can use this matrix to calculate the outputs required of every industry. (The US government's Bureau of Economic Analysis already creates such a matrix, albeit at a high level of industry aggregation.) The results will "cascade down" to industry and regional councils as proposals, much as in a high-road capitalist firm headquarters would propose targets for the firm's main divisions.

    In the terms used in the earlier discussion of the varieties of socialism, proponents of centralization argue that specific production goals derived from the national economic strategy should then be sent out to enterprises as physical quantities (Mandel 1986; Cockshott and Cottrell 1993). Proponents of what I called the intermediate position argue that the strategy should specify goals—some specific, and some more aggregate, depending on the sector—and benchmark prices, and leave enterprises more flexibility in deciding how to respond to the national priorities (Laibman 2015).

    The intermediate approach would work as follows. (For simplicity, I focus on the industrial side of planning—we will have a parallel process on the regional side; and I simplify the multiple levels down through which the plan will cascade both down and up, as if there were only the national and the enterprise levels.) The national economic council will set goals and benchmark prices for the economy's main products. These benchmark prices will be what I referred to earlier as "full" prices. They will aim to assign to each product not just the "private" costs that would be relevant for decision-making in capitalist firms, but also the indirect economic, social, and environmental costs, including housing, education, medical care, emissions, and so on.

Enterprises will respond to the national council's goals and benchmark prices by developing proposals for their own local production and investment. (These proposals will be developed through dialogue between higher and lower levels within enterprises, and among the stakeholders on their respective governing councils.) Depending on the degree to which their choices are consequential for the whole society (by virtue of their positive or negative externalities) enterprises will be free to choose their products, technologies, and suppliers, but they will be required to communicate to the national council any contracts they established with suppliers or customers, to allow other enterprises to adjust their plans accordingly. This approach leaves enterprises more flexibility and makes more use of locally available information, but it makes it more important to develop accurate and effective economic, social, and environmental indicators of enterprise performance (discussed below).

We will allow enterprises to adjust the sales price of their output where demand exceeds or falls below the plan's expectations. That price flexibility will help avoid rationing and surpluses. And it will provide useful information to other enterprises so they can adjust their plans in the current period, and to the national council so it can adjust next year's plan. But these enterprises' performance will be rewarded based on the benchmark prices set in the strategic management process, not on the adjusted, market prices. The underlying principle is simply that there is no reason to reward or penalize the enterprise for outcomes that the strategic planning process did not anticipate.

Basic goods that we deem everyone's birthright will be free—like water from public water fountains today. Other, non-basic goods will be offered for sale. In a socialist system, where incomes are relatively egalitarian, there will be no rich people able to bid up the prices of preferred products to the level that excludes poor people's access to them. So, consumer goods' prices here, unlike in a capitalist society, will reflect a legitimate form of consumer voting, and neither subsidies nor rationing will be necessary or useful.

Revenues and costs will not be the only basis on which these enterprises' performance will be assessed: environmental and social dimensions of performance will also be important, even if some are difficult to quantify. We have learned much about the limits of quantified measures of environmental and social performance from recent efforts in the United States and Europe to develop "triple-bottom-line" accounting. (A good survey is available in Epstein and Buhovac 2014.) Under capitalist conditions, triple bottom-line accounting efforts fall terribly short, for two main reasons. First, profitability pressures push firms to count only those social and environmental costs that are "material" to their own profitability. And second, some of the social and environmental dimensions of life are simply not amenable to quantification: the cost of lost biodiversity, or of the loss of neighborhood ethnic diversity, for example, cannot be reduced to measurements in dollars.

The economic, social, and environmental goals and performance of enterprise will all be the object of ongoing stakeholder dialogue in the economic councils and enterprise boards. Enterprises in the socialist core will earn bonuses (and prestige) for superior performance on social and environmental dimensions, even if those dimensions do not add to the firm's economic efficiency. For one model of what that might look like, see Laibman (2015). If achieving superior performance on social and environmental dimensions require sacrificing the firm's economic efficiency, that wisdom of that trade-off will be assessed in these stakeholder dialogue forums. For some examples of such dialogues and the way they have developed and used quantitative indicators, see Fraser et al. (2006), Scipioni et al. (2009).

28. This skepticism was expressed particularly cogently by Alec Nove (2004), notwithstanding his sympathy for socialism. For a rebuttal, see Cottrell and Cockshott (1993) and Cockshott and Cottrell (1997). This debate was just one phase of a debate started in the early 20th century on the feasibility and efficiency of a planned economy. In a first round, Von Mises (2008 [1920]) argued that public ownership would render impossible any rational economic planning because planners would have no market price information. In fact, this objection had already been preemptively refuted by Barone (1935 [1908]), who showed how in principle planners could develop a system of simultaneous equations to reach a result mirroring that which would be provided by market prices. In a second round, Hayek (1935) retreated a step to argue that Barone's solution might be possible in principle but would be too computationally difficult in practice. In the third round, Lange (1938) defeated this objection by showing how shadow prices could be calculated through an iterative procedure and how the planned economy could thus replicate the efficiency claimed by neoclassical economists for the capitalist economy. This debate, framed in the terms set by neoclassical economics, showed that market socialism could be efficient, notwithstanding the absence of private ownership. Subsequently, a more radical argument emerged among "Austrian" economists inspired by Hayek, aiming to invalidate any argument for either socialism or capitalism that was based on efficiency, and aiming to focus attention entirely on the idea that even if socialist planning were efficient, the weight of government would be contrary to our "liberty" interests. The literature is large, but for a succinct presentation and defense of socialist planning, see Adaman and Devine (1996).

29. In the literature on the economics of socialism, this is known as the problem of "soft budget constraint" (see Kornai 1979, 1986). This is a major challenge within the capitalist enterprise too: the annual budgeting process within corporations is notoriously corrupted by gaming. Under capitalism, market competition enforces some (variable) degree of budget discipline. Under socialism, we will rely on the robustness of democratic accountability.

30. See Schor (2008), Alperovitz (2005, Ch. 17).

31. Coote, Franklin, and Simms (2010), Smith (1989).

32. For a simple explanation of the logic of venture capital, see Zider (1998) and for discussion of how entrepreneurship fits into a democratic-socialist system, see Adaman and Devine (2002), Kotz (2002).

33. Altringer (2013).

34. See Sundgren et al. (2005). In this context, it is useful to recall the findings of McClelland (1961), confirmed in the meta-analysis by Collins, Hanges, and Locke

(2004), that entrepreneurs—even in capitalist societies—are motivated by need for achievement rather than desire for money. While people with low need for achievement perform better when offered greater financial rewards, these rewards have no effect on people with a high need for achievement.

35. The history of previous waves of technological revolution shows that, even in capitalist economies, active government policy has become increasingly important in energizing and orienting the deployment of revolutionary new technologies, that is, technologies with big and pervasive effects across the economy. Consider the policies needed to capitalize on the wave of technologies associated with the automobile, oil, and mass production. Government investment in ensuring access to home ownership, encouraging workers' wage growth commensurate with productivity, and highway construction were critical in creating a context that allowed these technologies to come together and fuel the post–World War II boom. Perez (2015) and Mazzucato (2015) sketch inspiring visions of how we could manage the current wave of technological revolution—the new digital revolution currently underway—so that its elements can be mobilized to meet our environmental challenges while simultaneously creating a more equitable global economy. Their accounts, however, elide the question of the broader structures of control and ownership that would be required for government to take up this responsibility effectively. There is therefore reason to doubt their proposals could be implemented: they would be a more realistic guide for action in a democratic-socialist society of the kind sketched here.

36. I use the term "workers" to refer to people working in socialist enterprises, whatever type of job they are doing, and I reserve the term "employee" to refer to people employed by capitalist firms.

37. See, for example, Malleson (2013), Corcoran and Wilson (2010).

38. Laliberte (2013), Witherell, Cooper, and Peck (2012).

39. See Adams and Freedman (1976), Adams (1965).

40. For some fruitful ideas on the form of government that fits our democratic socialist ideas, see Hind (2018).

41. See for example Parkinson and Mansbridge (2012), Fung (2015), Mansbridge (1983).

42. Dahl (2008, 71).

43. Cohen (1989), Sanders (1997).

44. One way to think about this is as "agonistic pluralism" (Mouffe 1999).

45. See Meadow and Randers (1992).

46. Anderson and Bows (2011).

47. Jacobson and Delucchi (2011), Delucchi and Jacobson (2011). These studies' estimates of the associated economic costs have been challenged as far too optimistic (Clack et al., 2017), but my argument is not weakened by such objections. Indeed, it seems abundantly clear that we cannot overcome the climate crisis in a way that preserves the private sector's profitability, and this is a powerful argument for socialist transformation.

48. Heinberg and Fridley (2016) estimate the cost for a global transition to renewable energy at $200 trillion. Rezai, Foley, and Taylor (2012) point out that such investment in mitigation may change the *pattern* of consumption but need not reduce current *levels* of consumption. If mitigation measures such as a carbon-tax impact consumers, government can rebate the tax income to these consumers. The funding for that investment can come from borrowing (so that

future generations pay the cost of the improvements they will enjoy), and if this borrowing raises current interest rates, this will not reduce current consumption expenditure but instead displace some of conventional investment, replacing it with mitigation investment—which is precisely what is needed.

49. A sketch of a plan along these lines has been developed by a group called the Climate Mobilization: see Silk (2016). Their plan is explicitly modeled after the World War II economic mobilization. It does not propose any socialization of property, but I do not see how it can proceed very far without comprehensive socialization.

50. As noted by http://www.sustainablemeasures.com/node/102.

51. US Census Bureau, 2013 American Commuting survey, Table S0801.

52. Some 51% of GIs took advantage of the education support: 2.2 million of them to attend college and another 5.6 million for vocational training (Stanley 2003).

53. The associated Wikipedia entry offers a starting point for reading further on such systems.

54. Even today, the federal government's job classification systems cover an enormous range of occupations and skill gradations within occupations; pay levels are public information; and as a result, the public sector has been far more effective in addressing gender pay inequity than the private sector. See Yoder (2014).

55. For opposing but ultimately complementary visions, see Lancaster (2017) and Davis (2011). In this as with other arenas, socialist policies can build on the success of some social-democratic countries—in this case, Finland's criminal justice system. See for example Lahti (2017).

56. The research results are compelling: controlling for a host of other factors, home ownership encourages more conservative political attitudes: see Adler (2017), Ansell (2014).

57. Even discounting for the promarket bias of many economists, it is very difficult to find evidence in favor of the effectiveness of rent control: see the review by Turner and Malpezzi (2003). Rent control is an example of how difficult it is to find a way within capitalism beyond the double-binds created by reliance on the market.

58. Austen (2018).

59. Keohane, Petsonk, and Hanafi (2017).

60. Crotty and Epstein (1996).

CHAPTER 7

1. Godard (2007); Budd, Lamare, and Timming (2018); Pateman (1970).

2. Across a wide range of countries, and compared to those with less education, college-educated individuals have more than twice the level of engagement with both "old" social movements (political parties, trade unions, and professional associations) and "new" ones (environmental associations, Third World development associations, women's organizations, and peace organizations) (Schofer and Fourcade-Gourinchas 2001).

3. The first and third are adapted from the scenarios sketched by Schweickart (2011, Ch. 6).

4. One sketch of what this might look like is Silk (2016).

5. Proponents of social democracy sometimes refer to the famous essay by Karl Polanyi, "The Great Transformation" (1968 [1944]), to argue that capitalism's

emergence involved the "disembedding" of the market process from the societal constraints characteristic of precapitalist forms of society, and that this disembedding provoked so much turmoil that it eventually led to a "re-embedding" countermovement in the form of social democracy. They extrapolate from there to argue that the current wave of neoliberalism will similarly provoke a new wave of social-democratic reform. I think this reading of Polanyi misses one of his key points: that if the core of the economy remains capitalist, such a re-embedding process will inevitably provoke another round of disembedding as the market mechanism stalls under regulatory constraints, and as the capitalist class fights to preserve its social dominance and privileges. Yes, Polanyi defended regulated capitalism and social-democratic reform against the barbarism of a disembedded, "every man for himself" type of capitalism; but his basic argument was that so long as the core of the economy remains capitalist, this "double movement" is a seesaw between dis- and re-embedding—indeed, an "infernal pendulum" (the phrase is from Dale 2010, 233) from which humanity cannot escape. The only escape, he argued, is via a fundamental socialist transformation.

Sweden offers an object lesson in the limits of the path of social-democratic reform. In 1976, when social democracy was already well established, the main Swedish union confederation (LO) proposed what was called the Meidner plan (named after one of its authors). This plan would have required all companies above a certain size to issue new voting stock amounting to 20% of each year's profits to a wage-earners' fund. There was to be one fund per industry, administered by a union-dominated board, which was to allocate funds to training, research, and revitalizing failing companies. These funds were to be controlled by industry-specific union organizations. Over a period of a few years, such a plan would have gradually but effectively socialized ownership and control. Despite popular support, implementation of the plan was stalled by massive opposition from the business sector—since it was clear that this path would lead to the elimination of their privilege and wealth—as well as from the conservative parties. Facing this opposition, the Swedish Social Democratic party turned against it too. Here in the United States, it is hard to imagine any organized force capable of credibly advancing such a plan, but if we overcame that hurdle, we should expect similarly forceful opposition from the business sector. For Meidner's own account of the plan and its failure, see Meidner (1993). For a proposal to update it and bring it to the United States, see Gowan and Viktorsson (2017).

6. See Democratic Socialists of America (2012).
7. See, for example, Rolf (2018), Burns (2014), and McAlevey (2016).
8. One strand of progressive thought argues that participation in the workplace will develop both the capacity and motivation to engage in wider political activity. Others worry that such workplace participation will distract people from the bigger problems in society. The evidence is fragmentary, presumably because a lot depends on the specific organizational circumstances, but it tends to support the former view: see, for example, Timming and Summers (2018).
9. National Center for Education Statistics (2015).
10. Shapiro and Brown (2018). Most colleges require a score of 3.0 or higher to qualify for college credit, and some require a score of 4.0 or higher.

11. Rogers (2009, 2015) makes a particularly attractive case for local transformation efforts, by marrying it with a case for strong government regulation at the national level. If the federal government set a high floor for social and economic policies across all the localities—blocking the low road—then, he argues, competitive markets would support rather than undermine widespread prosperity. We would still be left, however, with the constraints imposed by the capitalist structure of the economy. The crises of capitalism would not be overcome.

REFERENCES

Abrahamian, Ervand. 2001. "The 1953 coup in Iran." *Science and Society*, 65 (2): 182–215.

Adaman, Fikret, and Pat Devine. 1996. "The economics calculation debate: Lessons for socialists." *Cambridge Journal of Economics*, 20 (5): 523–537.

Adaman, Fikret, and Pat Devine. 2002. "A reconsideration of the theory of entrepreneurship: A participatory approach." *Review of Political Economy*, 14 (3): 329–355.

Adams, J. Stacy. 1965. "Inequity in social exchange." In *Advances in Experimental Social Psychology*, edited by L. Berkowitz, 267–299. New York: Academic Press.

Adams, J. Stacy, and Sara Freedman. 1976. "Equity theory revisited: Comments and annotated bibliography." In *Advances in Experimental Social Psychology*, edited by Leonard Berkowitz and Elaine Walster, 43–90. New York: Academic Press.

Adler, David R. K. 2017. "The Waitrose effect: Boom times for homeowners but evictions for tenants." *Guardian*, October 2. https://www.theguardian.com/inequality/2017/oct/02/the-waitrose-effect-boom-times-for-homeowners-but-evictions-for-tenants.

Adler, Jonathan. 2008. "Environment." *Encyclopedia of Libertarianism*, accessed May 28, 2018. https://www.libertarianism.org/encyclopedia/environment.

Adler, Paul S. 1993. "The 'learning bureaucracy': New United Motor Manufacturing, Inc." In *Research in Organizational Behavior*, edited by Barry M. Staw and Larry L. Cummings, 111–194. Greenwich, CT: JAI.

Adler, Paul S. 2006. "Beyond hacker idiocy: A new community in software development." In *The Firm as a Collaborative Community: Reconstructing Trust in the Knowledge Economy*, edited by Charles Heckscher and Paul S. Adler, 198–258. New York: Oxford University Press.

Adler, Paul S. 2012. "The ambivalence of bureaucracy: From Weber via Gouldner to Marx." *Organization Science*, 23 (1): 244–266.

Adler, Paul S. 2015. "Community and Innovation: From Tönnies to Marx." *Organization Studies*, 36 (4): 445–471.

Adler, Paul S., and Clara X. Chen. 2011. "Combining creativity and coordination: Understanding individual creativity in large-scale collaborative creativity." *Accounting, Organizations and Society*, 36 (2): 63–85.

Adler, Paul S., and Robert E. Cole. 1993. "Designed for learning: A tale of two auto plants." *Sloan Management Review* (Spring): 85–94.

Adler, Paul S., and Robert E. Cole. 1994. "Rejoinder." *Sloan Management Review* (Winter): 45–49.

Adler, Paul S., Barbara Goldoftas, and David I. Levine. 1997. "Ergonomics, employee involvement, and the Toyota production system: A case study of NUMMI's 1993 model introduction." *Industrial and Labor Relations Review*, 50 (3): 416–437.

Adler, Paul S., Barbara Goldoftas, and David I. Levine. 1999. "Flexibility versus efficiency? A case study of model changeovers in the Toyota production system." *Organization Science*, 10 (1): 43–68.

Adler, Paul S., and Charles Heckscher. 2018. "Collaboration as an organization design for shared purpose." In *Research in the Sociology of Organizations*, edited by Petra Hiller, Leopold Ringel, and Charlene Zietsma, 81–111. Bingley, UK: Emerald.

Adler, Paul S., Frank E. McGarry, Wendy B. Irion-Talbot, and Derek J. Binney. 2005. "Enabling process discipline: Lessons on implementing the capability maturity model for software." *MIS Quarterly: Executive*, 4 (1): 215–227.

Aggestam, Karin, and Annika Bergman-Rosamond. 2016. "Swedish feminist foreign policy in the making: Ethics, politics, and gender." *Ethics and International Affairs*, 30 (3): 323–334. doi: 10.1017/S0892679416000241.

Agyeman, Julian, David Schlosberg, Luke Craven, and Caitlin Matthews. 2016. "Trends and directions in environmental justice: From inequity to everyday life, community, and just sustainabilities." *Annual Review of Environment and Resources*, 41: 321–340.

Albert, Michael, and Robin Hahnel. 1991. *Looking Forward: Participatory Economics for the Twenty First Century*. Boston, MA: South End Press.

Alcorta, Ludovico. 1994. "The impact of new technologies on scale in manufacturing industries: Issues and evidence." *World Development*, 22 (5): 755–769.

Allegretto, Sylvia A., and Lawrence Mishel. 2016. *The Teacher Pay Gap Is Wider than Ever*. Washington, DC: Economic Policy Institute.

Alperovitz, Gar. 2005. *America beyond Capitalism: Reclaiming Our Wealth, Our Liberty, and Our Democracy*. Hoboken, NJ: John Wiley.

Alperovitz, Gar. 2013. *What Then Must We Do? Straight Talk about the Next American Revolution*. White River Junction, VT: Chelsea Green.

Altringer, Beth. 2013. "A new model for innovation in big companies." *Harvard Business Review*, November 19.

Alvaredo, Facundo, Lucas Chancel, Thomas Piketty, Emmanuel Saez, and Gabriel Zucman (eds.). 2018. *World Inequality Report*. Cambridge, MA: Belknap Press.

Ambec, Stefan, and Philippe Barla. 2006. "Can environmental regulations be good for business? An assessment of the Porter hypothesis." *Energy Studies Review*, 14 (2): 42.

American Psychological Association. 2016. *Stress in America: The Impact of Discrimination*. Washington, DC: American Psychological Association.

Amsden, Alice Hoffenberg. 2001. *The Rise of "The Rest": Challenges to the West from Late-Industrializing Economies*. New York: Oxford University Press.

Anderfuhren-Biget, Simon, Frédéric Varone, and David Giauque. 2014. "Policy environment and public service motivation." *Public Administration*, 92 (4): 807–825.

Anderson, David J. 2005. *Stretching Agile to Fit CMMI Level 3-The Story of Creating MSF for CMMI/SPL Reg/Process Improvement at Microsoft Corporation*. Agile Conference. Proceedings, Washington, DC.

Anderson, Kevin, and Alice Bows. 2011. "Beyond 'dangerous' climate change: Emission scenarios for a new world." *Philosophical Transactions* of the Royal Society A: Mathematical, Physical and Engineering Sciences, 369 (1934): 20–44.

Angell, Marcia. 2005. The Truth about the Drug Companies: How They Deceive Us and What to Do About It. New York: Random House.

Ansell, Ben. 2014. "The political economy of ownership: Housing markets and the welfare state." American Political Science Review, 108 (2): 383–402.

Ansell, Chris, and Alison Gash. 2008. "Collaborative governance in theory and practice." Journal of Public Administration Research and Theory, 18 (4): 543–571.

Arntz, Melanie, Terry Gregory, and Ulrich Zierahn. 2016. The Risk of Automation for Jobs in OECD Countries. OECD Social, Employment and Migration Working Papers, No. 189. Paris: OECD.

Arrighi, Giovanni. 1994. The Long Twentieth Century: Money, Power, and the Origins of our Times. London: Verso.

Arthur, W. Brian. 1996. "Increasing returns and the new world of business." Harvard Business Review (July–August): 100–109.

Artz, Georgeanne M., and Younjun Kim. 2011. Business Ownership by Workers: Are Worker Cooperatives a Viable Option? Iowa State University, Department of Economics, Ames, IA.

August, John. n.d. "Transforming US healthcare through workplace innovation." European Workplace Innovation Network (EUWIN) website. Last modified November 12, 2016. http://portal.ukwon.eu/File%20Storage/4694176_7_ John_August_Article.pdf.

Austen, Ben. 2018. High-Risers: Cabrini-Green and the Fate of American Public Housing. New York: Harper.

Austin, Robert D., Mark J. Cotteleer, and Cedric X. Escalle. 2003. Enterprise Resource Planning: Technology Note. Boston, MA: Harvard Business School.

Azoulay, Pierre, Erica Fuchs, Anna Goldstein, and Michael Kearney. 2018. Funding Breakthrough Research: Promises and Challenges of the "ARPA Model." National Bureau of Economic Research, Cambridge, MA.

Baiocchi, Gianpaolo, and Ernesto Ganuza. 2014. "Participatory budgeting as if emancipation mattered." Politics and Society, 42 (1): 29–50.

Baker, Dean. 2016. Rigged: How Globalization and the Rules of the Modern Economy Were Structured to Make the Rich Richer. Washington, DC: Center for Economic and Policy Research.

Balasegaram, Manica. 2014. "Drugs for the poor, drugs for the rich: Why the current R&D model doesn't deliver." Speaking of Medicine, November 7, 2018. https:// blogs.plos.org/speakingofmedicine/2014/02/14/drugs-poor-drugs-rich-current-rd-model-doesnt-deliver/.

Baldamus, Wilhelm. 1961. Efficiency and Effort: An Analysis of Industrial Administration. London: Tavistock.

Bardhan, Pranab, and John E. Roemer. 1992. "Market socialism: A case for rejuvenation." Journal of Economic Perspectives, 6 (3): 101–116.

Barnet, Richard J., and R. M. Muller. 1975. Global Reach: The Power of the Multinational Corporations. London: Jonathan Cape.

Barone, E. 1935 [1908]. "The ministry of production in the collectivist state." In Collectivist Economic Planning, edited by F. A. Hayek, 245–290. London: Routledge and Kegan Paul.

Beaudry, Paul, Dana Galizia, and Franck Portier. 2015. Reviving the Limit Cycle View of Macroeconomic Fluctuations. National Bureau of Economic Research, Cambridge, MA.

Belfrage, Claes, and Markus Kallifatides. 2018. "Financialisation and the new Swedish model." *Cambridge Journal of Economics*, 42 (4): 875–900.

Benkler, Y. 2006. *The Wealth of Networks: How Social Production Transforms Markets and Freedom*. New Haven, CT: Yale University Press.

Benmelech, Efraim, Nittai Bergman, and Hyunseob Kim. 2018. *Strong Employers and Weak Employees: How Does Employer Concentration Affect Wages?* National Bureau of Economic Research, Cambridge, MA.

Berwick, D. M., and A. D. Hackbarth. 2012. "Eliminating waste in us health care." *JAMA*, 307 (14): 1513–1516. doi: 10.1001/jama.2012.362.

Berwick, Donald M. 2010. *Connected for Health: Using Electronic Health Records to Transform Care Delivery*. New York: John Wiley & Sons.

Bezruchka, Stephen. 2010. "Health equity in the USA." *Social Alternatives*, 29 (2): 50.

Bhattacharya, Tithi. 2017. *Social Reproduction Theory: Remapping Class, Recentering Oppression*. London: Pluto Press.

Bisognano, Maureen, and Charles Kenney. 2012. *Pursuing The Triple Aim: Seven Innovators Show the Way to Better Care, Better Health, and Lower Costs*. New York: John Wiley & Sons.

Bjelland, Osvald M., and Robert Chapman Wood. 2008. "An inside view of IBM's 'Innovation Jam.'" *MIT Sloan Management Review*, 50 (1): 32.

Block, Fred L., and Matthew R. Keller. 2015. *State of Innovation: The US Government's Role in Technology Development*. New York: Routledge.

Board of Governors of the Federal Reserve System. 2018. *Report on the Economic Well-Being of U.S. Households in 2017*. Washington, DC.

Bodrožić, Zlatko, and Paul S. Adler. 2018. "The evolution of management models: A neo-Schumpeterian theory." *Administrative Science Quarterly*, 63 (1): 85–129.

Boldrin, Michele, and David K. Levine. 2013. "The case against patents." *Journal of Economic Perspectives*, 27 (1): 3–22.

Borowczyk-Martins, Daniel, Jake Bradley, and Linas Tarasonis. 2017. "Racial discrimination in the US labor market: Employment and wage differentials by skill." *Labour Economics*, 49: 106–127.

Borsos, John. 2013. "The Surrender of Oakland: The 2012 National Agreement between the Coalition of Kaiser Permanente Unions and Kaiser Permanente." *WorkingUSA*, 16 (2): 269–276.

Bowles, Samuel, and Herbert Gintis. 1976. *Schooling in Capitalist America*. New York: Basic Books.

Bowles, Samuel, and Herbert Gintis. 2002. "Schooling in capitalist America revisited." *Sociology of Education*, 75 (1): 1–18.

Brainerd, Elizabeth. 2010. "Reassessing the standard of living in the Soviet Union: An analysis using archival and anthropometric data." *Journal of Economic History*, 70 (1): 83–117.

Brauer, Michael. 2016. "Poor air quality kills 5.5 million worldwide annually." Institute for Health Metrics and Evaluation (IHME), accessed November 7, 2018. http://www.healthdata.org/news-release/poor-air-quality-kills-55-million-worldwide-annually.

Braveman, Paula A., Catherine Cubbin, Susan Egerter, David R. Williams, and Elsie Pamuk. 2010. "Socioeconomic disparities in health in the United States: What the patterns tell us." *American Journal of Public Health*, 100 (Suppl 1): S186–S196. doi: 10.2105/AJPH.2009.166082.

Brenner, M. Harvey. 1979. "Influence of the social environment on psychopathology: The historic perspective." In *Stress and Mental Disorder*, edited by James E. Barrett, 161–177. New York: Raven Press.

Bridgman, Benjamin, Andrew Dugan, Mikhael Lal, Matthew Osborne, and Shaunda Villones. 2012. "Accounting for household production in the national accounts, 1965–2010." *Survey of Current Business*, 92 (5): 23–36.

Brown, Alan W., Scott Ambler, and Walker Royce. May 18–26, 2013. "Agility at scale: Economic governance, measured improvement, and disciplined delivery." In *Proceedings of the 2013 International Conference on Software Engineering*. San Francisco, CA, 873–881.

Brown, Rebekah R., Ana Deletic, and Tony H. F. Wong. 2015. "Interdisciplinarity: How to catalyse collaboration." *Nature*, 525 (7569): 315–317.

Budd, John W., J. Ryan Lamare, and Andrew R. Timming. 2018. "Learning about democracy at work: Cross-national evidence on individual employee voice influencing political participation in civil society." *Industrial and Labor Relations Review*: 956–985.

Burnham, Linda, and Nik Theodore. 2012. *Home Economics: The Invisible and Unregulated World of Domestic Work*. New York: National Domestic Workers Alliance. Center for Urban Economic Development and University of Illinois at Chicago Data Center.

Burns, Joe. 2014. *Strike Back: Using the Militant Tactics of Labor's Past to Reignite Public Sector Unionism Today*. Brooklyn, NY: Ig Publishing.

Campaign for Tobacco-Free Kids. 2014. *Designed for Addiction*. Washington, DC.

Carter, Ian. 2018. "Positive and negative freedom." In *The Stanford Encyclopedia of Philosophy*, edited by Edward N. Zalta. https://plato.stanford.edu/archives/sum2018/entries/liberty-positive-negative/.

Cassidy, John. 2009. *How Markets Fail: The Logic of Economic Calamities*. New York: Farrar, Straus and Giroux.

Chesbrough, Henry William. 2006. *Open Innovation: The New Imperative for Creating and Profiting from Technology*. Boston, MA: Harvard Business School Publishing.

Chomsky, Noam. 2010. "US Savage Imperialism." *Z Magazine* (November 30).

Citylab. 2018. "What to do about HQ2." https://www.citylab.com/equity/2018/01/what-to-do-about-hq2/551486/.

Clack, Christopher T. M., Staffan A. Qvist, Jay Apt, Morgan Bazilian, Adam R. Brandt, Ken Caldeira, Steven J. Davis, et al. 2017. "Evaluation of a proposal for reliable low-cost grid power with 100% wind, water, and solar." *Proceedings of the National Academy of Sciences*, 114 (26): 6722–6727.

Clark, Andrew, and Heather Stewart. 2011. "If the banks forsake London, where might they go?" *Guardian*, April 9.

Clark, Gregory. 2012. "What is the true rate of social mobility in Sweden? A surname analysis, 1700–2012." Unpublished manuscript, University of California, Davis.

Climate Vulnerability Monitor. 2012. *A Guide to the Cold Calculus of a Hot Planet*. Madrid: DARA and the Climate Vulnerable Forum.

Coase, Ronald. 1937. "The nature of the firm." *Economica*, 4: 386–405.

Cockshott, W. Paul, and Allin F. Cottrell. 1993. *Towards a New Socialism*. Nottingham: Spokesman.

Cockshott, W. Paul, and Allin F. Cottrell. 1997. "Information and economics: A critique of Hayek." *Research in Political Economy*, 16: 177–202.

Cohen, Joshua. 1989. "The economic basis of deliberative democracy." *Social Philosophy and Policy*, 6 (2): 25–50.

Cohen, Paul M., Mark Ptaskiewicz, and Debra Mipos. 2010. "The case for unit-based teams: A model for front-line engagement and performance improvement." *Permanente Journal*, 14 (2): 70–75.

Collins, Christopher J., Paul J. Hanges, and Edwin A. Locke. 2004. "The relationship of achievement motivation to entrepreneurial behavior: A meta-analysis." *Human Performance*, 17 (1): 95–117.

Comstock, Courtney. 2011a. "Jamie Dimon stunningly confronts Ben Bernanke, suggests excessive financial regulations are slowing the recovery." *Business Insider*, June 7.

Comstock, Courtney. 2011b. "Jamie Dimon: Wall Street's new hero for ambushing Bernanke." *Business Insider*, June 8.

Cooper, Daniel. 2014. *The Effect of Unemployment Duration on Future Earnings and Other Outcomes*. Working Paper 13–8. Boston, MA: Federal Reserve Bank of Boston.

Coote, Anna, Jane Franklin, and Andrew Simms. 2010. *21 Hours: Why a Shorter Working Week Can Help Us All to Flourish in the 21st Century*. London, UK: New Economics Foundation.

Corcoran, Hazel, and David Wilson. 2010. *The Worker Co-operative Movements in Italy, Mondragon and France: Context, Success Factors and Lessons*. Calgary, Canada: Canadian Worker Cooperative Federation.

Cottrell, Allin F., and W. Paul Cockshott. 1993. "Calculation, complexity and planning: the socialist calculation debate once again." *Review of Political Economy*, 5 (1): 73–112.

Council of Economic Advisors. 2016. *Benefits of Competition and Indicators of Market Power*. Washington, DC.

Credit Suisse. 2016. *Credit Suisse Global Wealth Databook 2016*. Zurich.

Crotty, James, and Gerald Epstein. 1996. "In defence of capital controls." *Socialist Register*, 32 (32).

Curato, Nicole, John S. Dryzek, Selen A. Ercan, Carolyn M. Hendriks, and Simon Niemeyer. 2017. "Twelve key findings in deliberative democracy research." *Daedalus*, 146 (3): 28–38.

Dahl, Robert A. 2008. *On Democracy*. New Haven, CT: Yale University Press.

Dahlsrud, Alexander. 2008. "How corporate social responsibility is defined: An analysis of 37 definitions." *Corporate Social Responsibility and Environmental Management*, 15 (1): 1–13.

Dale, Gareth. 2010. *Karl Polanyi: The Limits of the Market*. Cambridge: Polity.

Daniel, Michael, and Martin A. Makary. 2016. "Medical error—the third leading cause of death in the US." *BMJ*, 353 (i2139): 476636183.

Davenport, Thomas H. 2000. *Mission Critical: Realizing the Promise of Enterprise Systems*. Boston, MA: Harvard Business Review Press.

David, H. 2015. "Why are there still so many jobs? The history and future of workplace automation." *Journal of Economic Perspectives*, 29 (3): 3–30.

Davino-Ramaya, Carrie, L. Kendall Krause, Craig W. Robbins, Jeffrey S. Harris, Marguerite Koster, Wiley Chan, and Gladys I. Tom. 2012. "Transparency matters: Kaiser Permanente's national guideline program methodological processes." *Permanente Journal*, 16 (1): 55–62.

Davis, Angela Y. 2011. *Are Prisons Obsolete?* New York: Seven Stories Press.

Davis, Gerald F. 2016. "Can an economy survive without corporations? Technology and robust organizational alternatives." *Academy of Management Perspectives*, 30 (2): 129–140.

Davis, Mike. 2002. *Late Victorian Holocausts: El Niño Famines and the Making of the Third World*. London: Verso.

Dawson, Michael C. 2016. "Hidden in plain sight: A note on legitimation crises and the racial order." *Critical Historical Studies*, 3 (1): 143–161.

de Joncheere, K., S. Hill, and N. Klazinga. 2006. *The Clinical Guideline Programme of the National Institute for Health and Clinical Excellence (NICE)*. Copenhagen, Denmark: World Health Organization.

De Schweinitz, Dorothea. 1949. *Labor and Management in a Common Enterprise*. Cambridge, MA: Harvard University Press.

DeHart-Davis, Leisha. 2009a. "Green Tape and Public Employee Rule Abidance: Why Organizational Rule Attributes Matter." *Public Administration Review*, 69 (5): 901–910.

DeHart-Davis, Leisha. 2009b. "Green tape: A theory of effective organizational rules." *Journal of Public Administration Research and Theory*, 19 (2): 361–384.

DeHart-Davis, Leisha, Randall S. Davis, and Zachary Mohr. 2014. "Green tape and job satisfaction: Can organizational rules make employees happy?" *Journal of Public Administration Research and Theory*, 25 (3): 849–876.

Delina, Laurence L. 2016. *Strategies for Rapid Climate Mitigation: Wartime Mobilisation as a Model for Action?* New York: Routledge.

Delucchi, Mark A., and Mark Z. Jacobson. 2011. "Providing all global energy with wind, water, and solar power, Part II: Reliability, system and transmission costs, and policies." *Energy Policy*, 39 (3): 1170–1190.

Democratic Socialists of America. 2012. "A social and economic Bill of Rights." Accessed November 7, 2018. http://www.dsausa.org/a_social_and_economic_bill_of_rights.

Derfuss, Klaus. 2009. "The relationship of budgetary participation and reliance on accounting performance measures with individual-level consequent variables: A meta-analysis." *European Accounting Review*, 18 (2): 203–239.

Devine, Pat. 2002. "Participatory planning through negotiated coordination." *Science and Society*, 66 (1): 72–85.

Drahos, Peter, and John Braithwaite. 2017. *Information Feudalism: Who Owns the Knowledge Economy?* New York: Taylor and Francis.

Drummond, Michael. 2016. "Clinical guidelines: A NICE way to introduce cost-effectiveness considerations?" *Value in Health*, 19 (5): 525–530. doi: https://doi.org/10.1016/j.jval.2016.04.020.

Duménil, Gérard, and Dominique Lévy. 2018. *Managerial Capitalism: Ownership, Management, and the Coming New Mode of Production*. London: Pluto Press.

Dunne, Timothy, Mark J. Roberts, and Larry Samuelson. 1989. "The growth and failure of US manufacturing plants." *Quarterly Journal of Economics*, 104 (4): 671–698.

Dutfield, Graham. 2017. *Intellectual Property Rights and the Life Science Industries: A Twentieth Century History*. New York: Routledge.

Dwyer-Lindgren, Laura, Amelia Bertozzi-Villa, Rebecca W. Stubbs, Chloe Morozoff, Johan P. Mackenbach, Frank J. van Lenthe, et al. 2017. "Inequalities in life expectancy among US counties, 1980 to 2014: Temporal trends and key drivers." *JAMA Internal Medicine*, 177 (7): 1003–1011.

e-reward.co.uk. 2016. *IBM co-creates a radical new approach to performance management*. Reward Blueprints 113. https://www.e-reward.co.uk/research/case-studies/ibm-co-creates-a-radical-new-approach-to-performance-management.

Early, Steve. 2011. *The Civil Wars in U.S. Labor: Birth of a New Workers' Movement or Death Throes of the Old?* Chicago, IL: Haymarket.

Eaton, Susan C., Saul A. Rubinstein, and Robert B. McKersie. 2004. "Building and sustaining labor-management partnerships: Recent experiences in the US." *Advances in Industrial and Labor Relations*: 137–156.

Eccles, Robert G. 1985. *The Transfer Pricing Problem: A Theory for Practice*. Lexington, MA: Lexington Books.

Economic Innovation Group. 2017. *Dynamism in Retreat: Consequences for Regions, Markets, and Workers*. Washington, DC.

Elliott, Douglas J. 2009. "Bank Nationalization: What is it? Should we do it?" In *Initiative on Business and Public Policy*. Washington, DC: Brookings Institution.

Ellman, Michael. 2014. *Socialist Planning*. Cambridge: Cambridge University Press.

Epstein, Gerald. 2018. "On the social efficiency of finance." *Development and Change*, 49 (2): 330–352.

Epstein, Gerald A. 2005. *Capital Flight and Capital Controls in Developing Countries*. Cheltenham, UK: Edward Elgar.

Epstein, Marc J., and Adriana Rejc Buhovac. 2014. *Making Sustainability Work: Best Practices in Managing and Measuring Corporate Social, Environmental, and Economic Impacts*. San Francisco, CA: Berrett-Koehler.

European Federation of Public Service Unions. 2014. *Public and Private Sector Efficiency: A Briefing for the EPSU Congress*. Brussels: European Federation of Public Service Unions.

Evans, Peter B. 2012. *Embedded Autonomy: States and Industrial Transformation*. Princeton, NJ: Princeton University Press.

Farrow, Anne, Joel Lang, and Jenifer Frank. 2006. *Complicity: How the North Promoted, Prolonged, and Profited from Slavery*. New York: Random House Digital.

Fassler, Joe. 2011. "How Copyright Law Hurts Music, From Chuck D to Girl Talk." *The Atlantic*, April 12.

Fawcett, Stanley E., Stephen L Jones, and Amydee M. Fawcett. 2012. "Supply chain trust: The catalyst for collaborative innovation." *Business Horizons*, 55 (2): 163–178.

Federal Reserve Bank of St. Louis. 2015. "Government employment in context." *The FRED Blog*, November 7, 2018, accessed January 26, 2019. https://fredblog. stlouisfed.org/2015/08/government-employment-in-context/.

Federal Reserve Bank of St. Louis. 2018. "Capacity utilization: Total industry." Accessed November 7, 2018. https://fred.stlouisfed.org/series/TCU.

Ferguson, Thomas. 1995. *Golden Rule: The Investment Theory of Party Competition and the Logic of Money-Driven Political Systems*. Chicago: University of Chicago Press.

Fine, Ben, and Alfredo Saad-Filho. 2017. "Thirteen things you need to know about neoliberalism." *Critical Sociology*, 43 (4-5): 685–706.

Finkelhor, D., H. A. Turner, A. Shattuck, and S. L. Hamby. 2015. "Prevalence of childhood exposure to violence, crime, and abuse: Results from the national survey of children's exposure to violence." *JAMA Pediatrics*, 169 (8): 746–754. doi: 10.1001/jamapediatrics.2015.0676.

Fisher, Franklin M., Zvi Griliches, and Carl Kaysen. 1962. "The costs of automobile model changes since 1949." *Journal of Political Economy*, 70 (5, Part 1): 433–451.

Fishman, Charles. 1996. "They write the right stuff." *Fast Company*, 6 (95).

FitzRoy, Felix, and Kornelius Kraft. 2005. "Co-determination, efficiency and productivity." *British Journal of Industrial Relations*, 43 (2): 233–247.

Folbre, Nancy. 1993. "Women's informal market work in Massachusetts, 1875–1920." *Social Science History*, 17 (1): 135–160.

Foley, Duncan K. 2017. *Socialist Alternatives to Capitalism II: Vienna to Santa Fe.* Working Paper. New York: New School for Social Research.

Foley, Duncan K. 2010. "What's wrong with the fundamental existence and welfare theorems?" *Journal of Economic Behavior and Organization*, 75 (2): 115–131. doi: https://doi.org/10.1016/j.jebo.2010.03.023.

Foo, Gillian H. C., and Linda Y. C. Lim. 1989. "Poverty, ideology and women export factory workers in South-East Asia." In *Women, Poverty and Ideology in Asia: Contradictory Pressures, Uneasy Resolutions*, edited by Haleh Afshar and Bina Agarwal, 212–233. London, UK: Palgrave Macmillan.

Forcadell, Francisco Javier. 2005. "Democracy, cooperation and business success: The case of Mondragón Corporación Cooperativa." *Journal of Business Ethics*, 56 (3): 255–274.

Forum for Sustainable and Responsible Investment. 2016. *Report on US Sustainable, Responsible and Impact Investing Trends 2016.* Washington, DC.

Foster, John Bellamy, and Robert W. McChesney. 2004. *Pox Americana: Exposing the American Empire.* New York: Farrar, Straus and Giroux.

Fraser, Evan D. G., Andrew J. Dougill, Warren E. Mabee, Mark Reed, and Patrick McAlpine. 2006. "Bottom up and top down: Analysis of participatory processes for sustainability indicator identification as a pathway to community empowerment and sustainable environmental management." *Journal of Environmental Management*, 78 (2): 114–127.

Fraser, Nancy. 2016a. "Contradictions of capital and care." *New Left Review* (100): 99–117.

Fraser, Nancy. 2016b. "Expropriation and exploitation in racialized capitalism: A reply to Michael Dawson." *Critical Historical Studies*, 3 (1): 163–178.

Freeman, Richard B., and Joel Rogers. 2006. *What Workers Want.* Ithaca, NY: Cornell University Press.

Frenken, Koen. 2017. "Political economies and environmental futures for the sharing economy." *Philosophical Transactions of the Royal Society A: Mathematical, Physical and Engineering Sciences*, 375 (2095): 20160367.

Friedman, Milton. 2009 [1962]. *Capitalism and Freedom.* Chicago: University of Chicago Press.

Friedman, Milton, and George J. Stigler. 1946. *Roofs or Ceilings? The Current Housing Problem.* Irvington-on-Hudson, NY: Foundation for Economic Education.

Fung, Archon. 2015. "Putting the public back into governance: The challenges of citizen participation and its future." *Public Administration Review*, 75 (4): 513–522.

Fung, Archon, and Erik O. Wright. 2003. *Deepening Democracy: Institutional Innovations in Empowered Participatory Governance.* London: Verso.

Gallup. 2017. *State of the American Workplace.* Washington, DC: Gallup.

Gallup Editors. 2014. *Gallup Review: Black and White Differences in Views on Race.* Washington, DC: Gallup.

Gast, Arne, and Michele Zanini. 2012. "The social side of strategy." *McKinsey Quarterly*, 2 (1): 82–93.

Gastil, John, Chiara Bacci, and Michael Dollinger. 2010. "Is deliberation neutral? Patterns of attitude change during 'The Deliberative Polls™.'" *Journal of Public Deliberation*, 6 (2): 3.

Gattuso, James L. 2009. "General Motors bankruptcy and nationalization: Exit strategy needed." Heritage Foundation, accessed November 7, 2018. https://www.heritage.org/government-regulation/report/ general-motors-bankruptcy-and-nationalization-exit-strategy-needed.

Genoways, Ted. 2017. *This Blessed Earth: A Year in the Life of an American Family Farm.* New York: Norton.

Gentry, William M., and R. Glenn Hubbard. 2004. "Entrepreneurship and household saving." *Advances in Economic Analysis and Policy*, 4 (1).

Gerbing, David W., Janet G. Hamilton, and Elizabeth B. Freeman. 1994. "A large-scale second-order structural equation model of the influence of management participation on organizational planning benefits." *Journal of Management*, 20 (4): 859–885.

Ghilarducci, Teresa, Siavash Radpour, Bridget Fisher, and Anthony Webb. 2016. *Household Economic Shocks Increase Retirement Wealth Inequality.* New York: Schwartz Center for Economic Policy Analysis (SCEPA), The New School.

Gibbs, WW. 1994. "Software's chronic crisis." *Scientific American*, 271 (3): 72–81.

Gibson, William. 1999. "'The science in science fiction': NPR interview, November 30, 1999." http://www.npr.org/templates/story/story.php?storyId=1067220.

Gilens, Martin. 2012. *Affluence and Influence: Economic Inequality and Political Power in America.* Princeton, NJ: Princeton University Press.

Giridharadas, Anand. 2018. *Winners Take All: The Elite Charade of Changing the World.* New York: Knopf.

Glew, David J., Anne M. O'Leary-Kelly, Ricky W. Griffin, and David D. Van Fleet. 1995. "Participation in organizations: A preview of the issues and proposed framework for future analysis." *Journal of Management*, 21 (3): 395–421. doi: http://dx.doi.org/10.1016/0149-2063(95)90014-4.

Gnanasambandam, Chandra, Allen Miller, and Kara Sprague. 2017. "Grow fast or die slow: The role of profitability in sustainable growth." McKinsey & Company, accessed November 8, 2018. https://www.mckinsey.com/industries/high-tech/our-insights/ grow-fast-or-die-slow-the-role-of-profitability-in-sustainable-growth.

Godard, John. 2007. "Is good work good for democracy? Work, change at work and political participation in Canada and England." *British Journal of Industrial Relations*, 45 (4): 760–790.

Godard, John, and Carola Frege. 2013. "Labor unions, alternative forms of representation, and the exercise of authority relations in US workplaces." *Industrial and Labor Relations Review*, 66 (1): 142–168.

Goldin, C. D., and L. F. Katz. 2009. *The Race between Education and Technology.* Cambridge, MA: Harvard University Press.

Goncalo, J. A., and B. M. Staw. 2006. "Individualism-collectivism and group creativity." *Organizational Behavior and Human Decision Processes*, 100 (1): 96–109.

Gough, Ian. 2000. "The enhanced structural power of capital: A review and assessment with Kevin Farnsworth." In *Global Capital, Human Needs and Social Policies: Selected Essays, 1994–99*, edited by Ian Gough, 77–102. New York: Palgrave.

Gouldner, Alvin W. 1955. "Metaphysical pathos and the theory of bureaucracy." *American Political Science Review*, 49 (469–505).

Gourevitch, Alex. 2013. "Labor republicanism and the transformation of work." *Political Theory*, 41 (4): 591–617.

Gourevitch, Alex. 2015. "Liberty and its economies." *Politics, Philosophy and Economics*, 14 (4): 365–390.

Gowan, Peter, and Mio Tastas Viktorsson. 2017. "Revising the Meidner plan." *Jacobin*, November 7, 2018. https://www.jacobinmag.com/2017/08/sweden-social-democracy-meidner-plan-capital.

Greenhouse, Steven. 2009. *The Big Squeeze: TOUGH times for the American Worker*. New York: Knopf.

Greenspan, Alan. 2010. "The Crisis." *Brookings Institution Papers on Economic Activity* (Spring): 201–261.

Guzda, Henry P. 1984. "Industrial democracy: Made in the U.S.A." *Monthly Labor Review* (May): 26–33.

Hackman, J. Richard, and Greg R. Oldham. 1980. *Work Redesign*. Reading, MA: Addison-Wesley.

Hainmueller, Jens, Michael J. Hiscox, and Sandra Sequeira. 2015. "Consumer demand for fair trade: Evidence from a multistore field experiment." *Review of Economics and Statistics*, 97 (2): 242–256.

Hall, Peter A., and David W. Soskice. 2001. *Varieties of Capitalism: The Institutional Foundations of Comparative Advantage*. New York: Oxford University Press.

Handel, Michael J. 2012. *Trends in Job Skill Demands in OECD Countries*. OECD Social, Employment and Migration Working Papers. Paris: OECD.

Hanna, Thomas M. 2018. *Our Common Wealth: The Return of Public Ownership in the United States*. Manchester, UK: Manchester University Press.

Hansen, Jared M. 2009. "The evolution of buyer-supplier relationships: An historical industry approach." *Journal of Business and Industrial Marketing*, 24 (3/4): 227–236.

Hansen, M. T., and B. von Oetinger. 2001. "Introducing T-shaped managers: Knowledge management's next generation." *Harvard Business Review*, 79 (3): 106–116.

Hanson, Jon, and David Yosifon. 2003. "The situation: An introduction to the situational character, critical realism, power economics, and deep capture." *University of Pennsylvania Law Review*, 152 (1): 129–346.

Harrigan, Kathryn Rudie. 1981. "Barriers to entry and competitive strategies." *Strategic Management Journal*, 2 (4): 395–412.

Harvey, David. 2007. *A Brief History of Neoliberalism*. New York: Oxford University Press.

Hauptmann, Emily. 2001. "Can less be more? Leftist deliberative democrats' critique of participatory democracy." *Polity*, 33 (3): 397–421.

Hayek, Friedrich A. von. 1935. "The present state of the debate." In *Collectivist Economic Planning: Critical Studies on the Possibilities of Socialism,* edited by Friedrich A. von Hayek, Ludwig Mises, George N. Halm, Enrico Barone, and Nikoloas G. Pierson, 201–243. London: Routledge and Kegan Paul.

Hayek, Friedrich A. von. 1945. "The use of knowledge in society." *American Economic Review*, 35 (4): 519–530.

Hayek, Friedrich A. von. 1956 [1944]. *The Road to Serfdom*. Chicago: University of Chicago Press.

Heath, Rachel, and A. Mushfiq Mobarak. 2015. "Manufacturing growth and the lives of Bangladeshi women." *Journal of Development Economics*, 115: 1–15.

Heckscher, Charles. 2007. *The Collaborative Enterprise: Managing Speed and Complexity in Knowledge-Based Businesses*. New Haven, CT: Yale University Press.

Heckscher, Charles, Clark Bernier, Hao Gong, Paul Dimaggio, and David Mimno. 2017. "'Driving Change by Consensus': Dialogue and Culture Change at IBM." Academy of Management Proceedings. Atlanta, GA.

Heinberg, Richard, and David Fridley. 2016. *Our Renewable Future: Laying the Path for One Hundred Percent Clean Energy*. Washington, DC: Island Press.

Heller, Frank A. 1998. *Organizational Participation: Myth and Reality*. New York: Oxford University Press.

Heller, Michael. 2010. *The Gridlock Economy: How Too Much Ownership Wrecks Markets, Stops Innovation, and Costs Lives*. New York: Basic Books.

Helper, Susan. 2009. "The high road for US manufacturing." *Issues in Science and Technology*, 25 (2): 39–45.

Helper, Susan, and Ryan Noonan. 2015. *Taking the High Road: New Data Show Higher Wages May Increase Productivity, Among Other Benefits*. ESA Issue Brief. Washington, DC: US Department of Commerce.

Hendricks, Rickey. 1993. *A Model for National Health Care: The History of Kaiser Permanente*. New Brunswick, NJ: Rutgers University Press.

Henwood, Doug. 2018. "The gig economy fantasy." https://www.jacobinmag.com/2018/06/precarity-american-workplace-gig-economy, accessed Jan 7, 2019.

Hicks, John Richard. 1950. *A Contribution to the Theory of the Trade Cycle*. Oxford: Clarendon Press.

Hiltzik, Michael. 2018. "An FCC commissioner attacks municipal broadband systems by falsely claiming they're a threat to free speech." *Los Angeles Times*, November 1. http://www.latimes.com/business/hiltzik/la-fi-hiltzik-fcc-broadband-20181031-story.html.

Hind, Dan. 2018. "The constitutional turn: Liberty and the cooperative state." Next System Project, last modified September 7, 2018. https://thenextsystem.org/learn/stories/constitutional-turn-liberty-and-cooperative-state.

Hipple, Steven F., and Laurel A. Hammond. 2016. *Self-Employment in the United States*. Washington, DC: Bureau of Labor Statistics.

Hirschman, A. O. 1970. *Exit, Voice, and Loyalty: Responses to Decline in Firms, Organizations, and States*. Cambridge, MA: Harvard University Press.

Hochschild, Arlie Russell. 2016. *Strangers in Their Own Land: A Journey to the Heart of the American Right*. New York: New Press.

Hochschild, Arlie R. 2001. "The nanny chain: Mothers minding other mothers' children." *The American Prospect* (January 3): 32–36.

Hofstede, Geert. 1980. *Culture's Consequences: International Differences in Work-Related Values*. Beverly Hills, CA: Sage.

Holan, Angie Drobnic. 2012. "RomneyCare & ObamaCare: Can you tell the difference?" Politifact, accessed November 7, 2018. https://www.politifact.com/truth-o-meter/article/2011/may/18/romneycare-and-obamacare-can-you-tell-difference/.

Hooks, Gregory. 1993. "The weakness of strong theories: The US state's dominance of the World War II investment process." *American Sociological Review*, 58 (1): 37–53.

Horrell, Sara, and Jane Humphries. 1995. "Women's labour force participation and the transition to the male-breadwinner family, 1790–1865." *Economic History Review*, 48 (1): 89–117. doi: 10.2307/2597872.

Howard, Marc M., James L. Gibson, and Dietlind Stolle. 2005. *The US Citizenship, Involvement, Democracy Survey*. Washington, DC: Center for Democracy and Civil Society (CDACS), Georgetown University.

Huesemann, Michael, and Joyce Huesemann. 2011. *Techno-Fix: Why Technology Won't Save Us or the Environment*. Gabriola Island, Canada: New Society Publishers.

Humphrey, W. S. 2002. "Three process perspectives: Organizations, teams, and people." *Annals of Software Engineering*, 14 (1): 39–72.

Huntingford, Chris, and Lina M. Mercado. 2016. "High chance that current atmospheric greenhouse concentrations commit to warmings greater than 1.5°C over land." *Scientific Reports*, 6: 30294. doi: 10.1038/srep30294.

Iizuka, Toshiaki. 2007. "An empirical analysis of planned obsolescence." *Journal of Economics and Management Strategy*, 16 (1): 191–226.

Inglehart, Ronald, and Christian Welzel. 2005. *Modernization, Cultural Change, and Democracy: The Human Development Sequence*. New York: Cambridge University Press.

Innes, Judith E., and David E. Booher. 2010. *Planning with Complexity: An Introduction to Collaborative Rationality for Public Policy*. New York: Routledge.

Jacobson, Mark Z., and Mark A. Delucchi. 2011. "Providing all global energy with wind, water, and solar power, Part I: Technologies, energy resources, quantities and areas of infrastructure, and materials." *Energy Policy*, 39 (3): 1154–1169.

Jaffe, Adam B., Steven R. Peterson, Paul R. Portney, and Robert N. Stavins. 1995. "Environmental regulation and the competitiveness of US manufacturing: What does the evidence tell us?" *Journal of Economic Literature*, 33 (1): 132–163.

Jameson, Fredric. 2003. "Future city." *New Left Review*, 21: 65.

Janda, Kathryn B., and Mithra Moezzi. 2014. "Broadening the energy savings potential of people: From technology and behavior to citizen science and social potential." *ACEEE Summer Study on Energy Efficiency in Buildings*, 7:133–7:146.

Jenkins, Blair. 2009. "Rent control: Do economists agree?" *Econ Journal Watch*, 6 (1): 73–112.

Johnson, Chalmers. 2007. *The Sorrows of Empire: Militarism, Secrecy, and the End of the Republic*. New York: Metropolitan Books.

Johnson, Chalmers. 2011. *Dismantling the Empire: America's Last Best Hope*. New York: Metropolitan Books.

Joint Center for Housing Studies of Harvard University. 2018. *The State of the Nation's Housing 2018*. Cambridge, MA: Harvard University.

Joint Economic Committee, United States Senate. 2000. *The Benefits of Medical Research and the Role of the NIH*. Washington, DC.

Jones, C. 2002. "Defense software development in evolution." *Crosstalk* (November): 26–9.

Jordà, Òscar, Moritz Schularick, Alan M. Taylor, and Felix Ward. 2018. *Global Financial Cycles and Risk Premiums*. Cambridge, MA: National Bureau of Economic Research, Working Paper 24677.

Kaiser Permanente. 2010. *Kaiser Permanente Completes Electronic Health Record Implementation*. Accessed January 26, 2019. https://share.kaiserpermanente. org/article/kaiser-permanente-completes-electronic-health-record-implementation/.

Kaiser Permanente, and Coalition of Kaiser Permanente Unions. 2012. *National Agreement*. Accessed January 26, 2019. https://www.lmpartnership.org/2012-national-agreement.

Kaldor, Nicholas. 1940. "A model of the trade cycle." *Economic Journal,* 50 (197): 78–92.

Kalecki, Michal. 1937. "A theory of the business cycle." *Review of Economic Studies*, 4 (2): 77–97.

Kalecki, Michal. 1943. "Political aspects of full employment." *Political Quarterly*, 14 (4): 322–330.

Kelly, Marjorie, and Sarah McKinley. 2015. *Cities Building Community Wealth*. Washington, DC: Democracy Collaborative.

Kennedy, Paul. 2010. *The Rise and Fall of the Great Powers*. New York: Vintage.

Keohane, Nathaniel, Annie Petsonk, and Alex Hanafi. 2017. "Toward a club of carbon markets." *Climatic Change*, 144 (1): 81–95.

Khan, Lina M. 2017. "Amazon bites off even more monopoly power." *New York Times*, June 21.

Khan, Lina M. 2016. "Amazon's antitrust paradox." *Yale Law Journal*, 126: 710–805.

Khan, Shamus Rahman. 2010. *Privilege: The Making of an Adolescent Elite at St. Paul's School*. Princeton, NJ: Princeton University Press.

Kiatpongsan, Sorapop, and Michael I. Norton. 2014. "How much (more) should CEOs make? A universal desire for more equal pay." *Perspectives on Psychological Science*, 9 (6): 587–593.

Kiely, Eugene. 2012. "'You Didn't Build That,' Uncut and Unedited." November 7, 2018. https://www.factcheck.org/2012/07/you-didnt-build-that-uncut-and-unedited/.

Kiley, Jocelyn. 2018. "Most continue to say ensuring health care coverage is government's responsibility." *FactTank*. Washington, DC: Pew Research Center.

Kitzmueller, Markus, and Jay Shimshack. 2012. "Economic perspectives on corporate social responsibility." *Journal of Economic Literature*, 50 (1): 51–84.

Klein, Naomi. 2014. *This Changes Everything: Capitalism vs. the Climate*. New York: Simon & Schuster.

Knott, Anne Marie, and Bill McKelvey. 1999. "Nirvana efficiency: A comparative test of residual claims and routines." *Journal of Economic Behavior and Organization*, 38 (4): 365–383.

Kochan, Thomas, ed. 2008. *Symposium: Kaiser Permanente Labor Management Partnership, Industrial Relations*, 47 (1): 1–96.

Kochan, Thomas A. 2013. *The Kaiser Permanente Labor Management Partnership: 2009–2013*. Cambridge, MA: MIT Sloan School Institute for Work & Employment Research.

Kochan, Thomas A., Eileen Applebaum, Jody Hoffer Gittell, and Carrie R. Leana. June 7, 2013. "The Human Capital Dimensions of Sustainable Investment: What Investment Analysts Need to Know." *Sustainable Investment Research Initiative Sustainability and Finance Symposium*. University of California, Davis, accessed January 29, 2019. Available at: http://www. cepr. net/index.php/publications/reports/human-capital-dimensions-ofsustainable-investment.

Kochan, Thomas A., Adrienne E. Eaton, Robert B. McKersie, and Paul S. Adler. 2009. *Healing Together: The Labor-Management Partnership at Kaiser Permanente*. Ithaca, NY: ILR Press.

Kochan, Thomas A., Duanyi Yang, William T. Kimball, and Erin L. Kelly. 2018. "Worker voice in America: Is there a gap between what workers expect and what they experience?" *ILR Review*, 72 (1): 1–36.

Koistinen, Paul, A. C. 1973. "Mobilizing the World War II economy: Labor and the industrial-military alliance." *Pacific Historical Review*, 42 (4): 443–478. doi: 10.2307/3638133.

Kolbert, Elizabeth. 2014. *The Sixth Extinction: An Unnatural History*. New York: Henry Holt.

Kornai, Janos. 1979. "Resource-constrained versus demand-constrained systems." *Econometrica*, 47 (4): 801–819.

Kornai, Janos. 1986. "The soft budget constraint." *Kyklos*, 39 (1): 3–30.

Kostakis, Vasilis, and Michel Bauwens. 2014. *Network society and future scenarios for a collaborative economy*. New York, NY: Palgrave.

Kotz, David M. 2002. "Socialism and innovation." *Science and Society*, 66 (1): 94–108.

Krones, Jonathan Seth. 2016. *Accounting for Non-Hazardous Industrial Waste in the United States*. Cambridge: Massachusetts Institute of Technology.

Kusnet, David. 2008. *Love the Work, Hate the Job: Why America's Best Workers Are Unhappier Than Ever*. New York: Wiley.

Lahti, Raimo. 2017. "Towards a more efficient, fair and humane criminal justice system: Developments of criminal policy and criminal sanctions during the last 50 years in Finland." *Cogent Social Sciences*, 3 (1): 1303910. doi: 10.1080/23311886.2017.1303910.

Laibman, David. 2002. "Democratic coordination: Towards a working socialism for the new century." *Science and Society*, 66 (1): 116–129.

Laibman, David. 2013. "Mature socialism design, prerequisites, transitions." *Review of Radical Political Economics*, 45 (4): 501–507.

Laibman, David. 2015. "Multilevel democratic iterative coordination." *Marxism 21*, 12 (1): 307–345.

Laliberte, Pierre, ed. 2013. "Trade unions and worker cooperatives: Where are we at?" Special issue, *International Journal of Labour Research*, 3 (2). Geneva: International Labour Office.

Lancaster, Roger. 2017. "How to end mass incarceration." *Jacobin*, November 7, 2018, accessed January 26, 2019. https://www.jacobinmag.com/2017/08/mass-incarceration-prison-abolition-policing.

Lane, Lee. 2009. *The Green Movement and the Challenge of Climate Change*. Washington, DC: American Enterprise Institute.

Lange, Oskar. 1938. "On the theory of economic socialism." In *On the Economic Theory of Socialism*, edited by Oskar Lange, Fred M. Taylor, and Benjamin Lippincott, 55–143. New York: University of Minnesota Press.

Langer, Gary. 2017. "Unwanted sexual advances: Not just a Hollywood story." *ABC News/Washington Post* poll. October 17, accessed January 26, 2019. Available at: https://www.langerresearch.com/wp-content/uploads/1192a1SexualHarassment.pdf.

Lazonick, William, and Mariana Mazzucato. 2013. "The risk-reward nexus in the innovation-inequality relationship: Who takes the risks? Who gets the rewards?" *Industrial and Corporate Change*, 22 (4): 1093–1128.

Lee, Joong-Jae. 2004. "Defense workers' struggles for patriotic control: The labor-management-state contests over defense production at Brewster, 1940–1944." *International Labor and Working-Class History* (66): 136–154.

Leung, Danny, Césaire Meh, and Yaz Terajima. 2008. *Firm Size and Productivity*. Ottawa, ON: Bank of Canada Working Paper 2008-45.

Li, Xiaoyang, and Yue M. Zhou. 2017. "Offshoring pollution while offshoring production?" *Strategic Management Journal*, 38 (11): 2310–2329. doi: doi:10.1002/smj.2656.

Lichtenstein, Nelson. 2000. "Class politics and the state during World War Two." *International Labor and Working-Class History* (58): 261–274.

Lieberman, H., and C. Fry. 2001. "Will software ever work?" *Communications of the ACM*, 44 (3): 122–124.

Lin, Ning, Robert E. Kopp, Benjamin P. Horton, and Jeffrey P. Donnelly. 2016. "Hurricane Sandy's flood frequency increasing from year 1800 to 2100." *Proceedings of the National Academy of Sciences*, 113 (43): 12071–12075. doi: 10.1073/pnas.1604386113.

Lincoln, William F., and Andrew H. McCallum. 2018. The Rise of Exporting by US Firms. *European Economic Review*, 102: 280–297.

Lindert, Peter H., and Jeffrey G. Williamson. 2016. "Unequal gains: American growth and inequality since 1700." https://voxeu.org/article/american-growth-and-inequality-1700.

Lister, Ruth. 2009. "A Nordic nirvana? Gender, citizenship, and social justice in the Nordic welfare states." *Social Politics: International Studies in Gender, State and Society*, 16 (2): 242–278.

Litwin, Adam Seth. 2010. "Technological change at work: The impact of employee involvement on the effectiveness of health information technology." *Industrial and Labor Relations Review*, 64 (5): 863–888.

Locke, Richard M. 2013. *The Promise and Limits of Private Power: Promoting Labor Standards in a Global Economy*. New York: Cambridge University Press.

Los Angeles Times. 1993. "Gallup poll finds 46% opposed, 38% in favor of NAFTA." *Los Angeles Times*. http://articles.latimes.com/1993-11-09/news/mn-54845_1_gallup-poll.

Lukasiewicz, Katarzyna, and Jakub Miler. 2012. "Improving agility and discipline of software development with the Scrum and CMMI." *IET Software*, 6 (5): 416–422.

MacKenzie, Ross, and Jeff Collin. 2012. " 'Trade policy, not morals or health policy': The US trade representative, tobacco companies and market liberalization in Thailand." *Global Social Policy*, 12 (2): 149–172. doi: 10.1177/1468018112443686.

Mackey, John, and Rajendra Sisodia. 2014. *Conscious Capitalism: Liberating the Heroic Spirit of Business*. Boston, MA: Harvard Business Review Press.

Macpherson, C. B. 1962. *The Political Theory of Possessive Individualism: Hobbes to Locke*. Oxford: Clarendon Press.

Maddison, Angus. 2007. *The World Economy, Volume 1: A Millennial Perspective; Volume 2: Historical Statistics*. New Delhi, India: Academic Foundation.

Maestas, Nicole, Kathleen J. Mullen, David Powell, Jeffrey B. Wenger, and Till Von Wachter. 2017. *Working Conditions in the United States: Results of the 2015 American Working Conditions Survey*. Santa Monica, CA: RAND Corporation.

Magdoff, Fred, and John Bellamy Foster. 2011. *What Every Environmentalist Needs to Know about Capitalism: A Citizen's Guide to Capitalism and the Environment*. New York: Monthly Review Press.

Malleson, Tom. 2013. "What does Mondragon teach us about workplace democracy?" In *Sharing Ownership, Profits, and Decision-Making in the 21st Century*, edited by Douglas L. Kruse, 127–157. Bingley, UK: Emerald.

Mandel, Ernest. 1986. "In defence of socialist planning." *New Left Review* (159): 5.

Mansbridge, Jane J. 1983. *Beyond Adversary Democracy*. Chicago: University of Chicago Press.

Margolis, Joshua D., Hillary Anger Elfenbein, and James P. Walsh. 2007. "Does it pay to be good . . . and does it matter? A meta-analysis of the relationship between corporate social and financial performance." Unpublished manuscript.

Margolis, Joshua D., and Hillary A. Elfenbein. 2008. "Do well by doing good? Don't count on it." *Harvard Business Review*, 86 (1).

Massey, Douglas S., Jonathan Rothwell, and Thurston Domina. 2009. "The changing bases of segregation in the United States." *Annals of the American Academy of Political and Social Science*, 626 (1): 74–90.

Matzler, Kurt, Johann Füller, Katja Hutter, Julia Hautz, and Daniel Stieger. 2016. "Crowdsourcing strategy: How openness changes strategy work." *Problems and Perspectives in Management*, 14 (3): 450–460.

May, Christopher. 2015. *The Global Political Economy of Intellectual Property Rights: The New Enclosures*. New York: Routledge.

Mazzucato, Mariana. 2015. *The Entrepreneurial State: Debunking Public vs. Private Sector Myths*. New York: Anthem Press.

McAlevey, Jane. 2016. *No Shortcuts: Organizing for Power in the New Gilded Age*. New York: Oxford University Press.

McClelland, D. 1961. *The Achieving Society*. Princeton, NJ: Van Nostrand.

McCreary, Lew. 2010. "Kaiser Permanente's innovation on the front lines." *Harvard Business Review*, 88 (9): 92, 94–7, 126.

McKibben, Bill. 2016. "A world at war." *New Republic*, August 15.

McKinnon, H., G. Muttitt, and K. Trout. 2017. *The Sky's Limit Norway: Why Norway Should Lead The Way in a Managed Decline of Oil and Gas Extraction*. Washington, DC: Oil Change International.

McWilliams, Abagail. 2015. "Corporate social responsibility." In *Wiley Encyclopedia of Management*, edited by C. L. Cooper, J. McGee, and T. Sammut-Bonnici, 1–4. Hoboken, NJ: John Wiley & Sons.

Meadow, D., and Jorgen Randers. 1992. *Beyond the Limits: Confronting Global Collapse, Envisioning a Sustainable Future*. Post Mills, VT: Chelsea Green Publishing.

Meidner, Rudolf. 1993. "Why did the Swedish model fail?" *Socialist Register*, 29 (29).

Michels, Robert. 1966 [1911]. *Political Parties*. New York: The Free Press.

Michie, Jonathan, Joseph R. Blasi, and Carlo Borzaga. 2017. *The Oxford Handbook of Mutual and Co-Owned Business*. New York: Oxford University Press.

Miles, Raymond E., and Charles C. Snow. 1978. *Organizational Strategy, Structure, and Process*. New York: McGraw-Hill.

Miller, Fred. 2017. "Aristotle's political theory." https://plato.stanford.edu/archives/win2017/entries/aristotle-politics/.

Minsky, Hyman P. 1980. "Capitalist financial processes and the instability of capitalism." *Journal of Economic Issues*, 14 (2): 505–523.

Minx, Jan, Kate Scott, Glen Peters, and John Barrett. 2008. *An Analysis of Sweden's Carbon Footprint*. World Wildlife Fund.

Mishel, Lawrence, and Josh Bivens. 2017. *The Zombie Robot Argument Lurches On*. Washington, DC: Economic Policy Institute.

Mishel, Lawrence, and Jessica Schieder. 2017. *CEO Pay Remains High Relative to the Pay of Typical Workers and High-Wage Earners*. Washington, DC: Economic Policy Institute.

Mishel, Lawrence, John Schmitt, and Heidi Shierholz. 2013. *Assessing the Job Polarization of Growing Wage Inequality*. Economic Policy Institute Working Paper. Washington, DC: Economic Policy Institute.

Moorhead, Molly. 2012. "Bernie Sanders says Walmart heirs own more wealth than bottom 40% of Americans." Accessed November 7, 2018. https://www.politifact.com/truth-o-meter/statements/2012/jul/31/bernie-s/sanders-says-walmart-heirs-own-more-wealth-bottom-/.

Morray, Joseph P. 1997. *Grand Disillusion: François Mitterrand and the French Left*. Westport, CT: Greenwood.

Moss, Michael. 2013. *Salt, Sugar, Fat: How the Food Giants Hooked Us*. New York: Random House.

Mouffe, Chantal. 1999. "Deliberative democracy or agonistic pluralism?" *Social Research*, 66 (3): 745–758.

Murrell, Peter. 1991. "Can neoclassical economics underpin the reform of centrally planned economies?" *Journal of Economic Perspectives*, 5 (4): 59–76.

National Center for Education Statistics. 2015. "2014 civics assessment." Accessed November 7, 2018. https://www.nationsreportcard.gov/hgc_2014/#civics/achievement.

National Law Center on Homelessness and Poverty. 2018. *Homelessness in America: Overview of Data and Causes*. Washington, DC.

Newman, Rick. 2009. "Why bank nationalization is so scary." *US News and World Report*. https://money.usnews.com/money/blogs/flowchart/2009/02/22/why-bank-nationalization-is-so-scary.

Nightingale, Paul, Tim Brady, Andrew Davies, and Jeremy Hall. 2003. "Capacity utilization revisited: Software, control and the growth of large technical systems." *Industrial and Corporate Change*, 12 (3): 477–517.

Nissenbaum, Dion. 2018. "Top U.S. diplomat backed continuing support for Saudi war in Yemen over objections of staff." *Wall Street Journal*, September 20.

Novak, William J. 2008. "The myth of the 'weak' American state." *American Historical Review*, 113 (3): 752–772.

Nove, Alec. 2004. *The Economics of Feasible Socialism Revisited*. London: HarperCollins.

Nussbaum, Martha C. 2011. "Capabilities, entitlements, rights: Supplementation and critique." *Journal of Human Development and Capabilities*, 12 (1): 23–37.

O'Mahoney, Siobhan, and Fabrizio Ferraro. 2007. "The emergence of governance in an open source community." *Academy of Management Journal*, 50 (5): 1079–1106.

OECD. 2016. *Country Note: Key Findings from PISA 2015 for the United States*. Paris: OECD.

OECD. 2018. *Geographical Distribution of Financial Flows to Developing Countries 2018*. Paris: OECD.

Oerlemans, Nastasja, ed. 2016. *Living Planet Report*. Gland, Switzerland: World Wildlife Fund.

Ofer, Gur. 1987. "Soviet economic growth: 1928–1985." *Journal of Economic Literature*, 25 (4): 1767–1833.

Olah, Rudolf. 2013. "What's with the aversion to documentation in the industry?" https://softwareengineering.stackexchange.com/questions/202167/whats-with-the-aversion-to-documentation-in-the-industry.

Ornston, Darius. 2014. "When the high road becomes the low road: The limits of high-technology competition in Finland." *Review of Policy Research*, 31 (5): 454–477.

Osterman, Paul. 2017. *Who Will Care for Us? Long-Term Care and the Long-Term Workforce*. New York: Russell Sage Foundation.

Ostrom, Elinor, Joanna Burger, Christopher B. Field, Richard B. Norgaard, and David Policansky. 1999. "Revisiting the commons: Local lessons, global challenges." *Science*, 284 (5412): 278–282.

Palley, Thomas. 2018. *Re-theorizing the welfare state and the political economy of neoliberalism's war against it*. FMM Working Paper, No. 16, Macroeconomic Policy Institute (IMK), Forum for Macroeconomics and Macroeconomic Policies (FFM), Düsseldorf.

Palmisano, S. 2004. "Leading change when business is good. Interview by Paul Hemp and Thomas A. Stewart." *Harvard Business Review*, 82 (12): 60.

Park, Haeyoun, and Iaryna Mykhyalyshyn. 2016. "LGBT people are more likely to be targets of hate crimes than any other minority group." *New York Times*, June 16.

Parker, Mike, and Jane Slaughter. 1988. *Choosing Sides: Unions and the Team Concept*. Boston, MA: South End Press.

Parkinson, John, and Jane J. Mansbridge. 2012. *Deliberative Systems: Deliberative Democracy at the Large Scale*. New York: Cambridge University Press.

Parreñas, Rhacel. 2015. *Servants of Globalization: Migration and Domestic Work*. Stanford, CA: Stanford University Press.

Pasurka, Carl. 2008. "Perspectives on pollution abatement and competitiveness: Theory, data, and analyses." *Review of Environmental Economics and Policy*, 2 (2): 194–218.

Pateman, Carole. 1970. *Participation and Democratic Theory*. Cambridge, UK: Cambridge University Press.

Paul, Mark, William Darity Jr., and Darrick Hamilton. 2017. "Why we need a federal job guarantee." *Jacobin*, December 29.

Pearl, Robert M. 2017. "What health systems, hospitals, and physicians need to know about implementing electronic health records." Accessed November 7, 2018. https://hbr.org/2017/06/what-health-systems-hospitals-and-physicians-need-to-know-about-implementing-electronic-health-records.

Pencavel, John, Luigi Pistaferri, and Fabiano Schivardi. 2006. "Wages, employment, and capital in capitalist and worker-owned firms." *ILR Review*, 60 (1): 23–44.

Perez, Carlota. 2015. "Capitalism, technology and a green global golden age: The role of history in helping to shape the future." *Political Quarterly*, 86: 191–217.

Pew Research Center. 2013. *The Rise of Single Fathers*. Washington, DC.

Pew Research Center. 2014. *Political Polarization in the American Public*. Washington, DC.

Pew Research Center. 2015. *Beyond Distrust: How Americans View Their Government*. Washington, DC.

Pew Research Center. 2016. *The State of American Jobs*. Washington, DC.

Pew Research Center, and Associated Press. 2006. *Who Votes, Who Doesn't, and Why: Regular Voters, Intermittent Voters, and Those Who Don't*. Washington, DC.

Plotnick, Robert D., Eugene Smolensky, Eirik Evenhouse, and Siobhan Reilly. 1998. *The Twentieth Century Record of Inequality and Poverty*. University of California at Berkeley and Public Policy Institute of California.

Polanyi, Karl. 1968 [1944]. *The Great Transformation: The Political and Economic Origins of Our Time*. Boston, MA: Beacon Press.

Population Reference Bureau. 2017. "Changing demographics reshape rural America." Accessed November 7, 2018. https://www.prb.org/changing-demographics-reshape-rural-america/.

Porter, Michael E., and Mark R. Kramer. 2011. "The big idea: Creating shared value. How to reinvent capitalism—and unleash a wave of innovation and growth." *Harvard Business Review*, 89 (1–2).

Porter, Michael E., Forest L. Reinhardt, Peter Schwartz, Daniel C. Esty, Andrew J. Hoffman, Auden Schendler, et al. 2007. "Climate business/business climate." *Harvard Business Review*: (October) 1–17.

Porter, Michael E., and Claas Van der Linde. 1995. "Green and competitive: ending the stalemate." *Harvard Business Review*, 73 (5): 120–134.

Porter, Michael E. 1985. *Competitive Advantage*. New York: The Free Press.

Posner, Richard A. 2009. *A Failure of Capitalism: The Crisis of '08 and the Descent into Depression*. Cambridge, MA: Harvard University Press.

Przeworski, Adam, and Michael Wallerstein. 1988. "Structural dependence of the state on capital." *American Political Science Review*, 82 (1): 11–29.

Public Citizen. 2018. "Trans-Pacific Partnership." http://www.citizen.org/our-work/globalization-and-trade/nafta-wto-other-trade-pacts/trans-pacific-partnership.

Pugh, Derek S., and David J. Hickson. 1976. *Organizational Structure in Its Context: The Aston Programme*. Vol. 1. Lexington, MA: Lexington Books.

Qu, Wen Guang, Yajing Ding, Yongyi Shou, Honggeng Zhou, and Hong Du. 2014. "The impact of enterprise systems on process flexibility and organisational flexibility." *Enterprise Information Systems*, 8 (5): 563–581.

Quilley, Stephen. 2000. "Manchester first: From municipal socialism to the entrepreneurial city." *International Journal of Urban and Regional Research*, 24 (3): 601–615.

Radford, Gail. 2003. "From municipal socialism to public authorities: Institutional factors in the shaping of American public enterprise." *Journal of American History*, 90 (3): 863–890.

Reardon, Sean F., Lindsay Fox, and Joseph Townsend. 2015. "Neighborhood income composition by household race and income, 1990–2009." *Annals of the American Academy of Political and Social Science*, 660 (1): 78–97.

Reinhart, Carmen M., and Kenneth S. Rogoff. 2009. *This Time Is Different: Eight Centuries of Financial Folly*. Princeton, NJ: Princeton University Press.

Rezai, Armon, Duncan K. Foley, and Lance Taylor. 2012. "Global warming and economic externalities." *Economic Theory*, 49 (2): 329–351.

Rhaman, Fifa. 2018. "Extended monopolies on biologic drugs—A warning to developing countries." Accessed November 1, 2018. http://www.ip-watch.org/2018/09/10/extended-monopolies-biologic-drugs-warning-developing-countries/.

Ritz, Adrian, Gene A. Brewer, and Oliver Neumann. 2016. "Public service motivation: A systematic literature review and outlook." *Public Administration Review*, 76 (3): 414–426.

Roberts, Nancy. 2004. "Public deliberation in an age of direct citizen participation." *American Review of Public Administration*, 34 (4): 315–353.

Roelfs, David J., Eran Shor, Karina W. Davidson, and Joseph E. Schwartz. 2011. "Losing life and livelihood: A systematic review and meta-analysis of unemployment and all-cause mortality." *Social Science and Medicine*, 72 (6): 840–854.

Rogers, Joel. 1990. "What does 'high road' mean?" University of Wisconsin-Madison, COWS. Accessed Jan 2, 2019. https://www.cows.org/what-does-high-road-mean.

Rogers, Joel. 2009. "Productive democracy." In *Renewing Democratic Deliberation in Europe: The Challenge of Social and Civil Dialogue*, edited by Jean De Munck, Isabelle Ferreras, Claude Didry, and Annette Jobert, 71–92. Brussels: Peter Lang.

Rogers, Joel. 2015. "Productive democracy: Why we need a new egalitarian politics—and why social democracy will never get us there." *The Nation*, 300 (14): 206–210.

Rolf, David. 2018. *A Roadmap for Rebuilding Worker Power*. Washington, DC: Century Foundation.

Romer, Paul. Forthcoming. "The trouble with macroeconomics." *American Economist*.

Rose, Stephen J. 2017. *Mismatch: How Many Workers with a Bachelor's Degree Are Overqualified for Their Jobs?* Washington, DC: Urban Institute.

Rose, Stephen J., and Heidi I. Hartmann. 2004. *Still a Man's Labor Market: The Long-Term Earnings Gap*. Washington, DC: Institute for Women's Policy Research.

Saad, Lydia. 2009. "Majority receptive to law making union organizing easier." Accessed November 7, 2018. https://news.gallup.com/poll/116863/Majority-Receptive-Law-Making-Union-Organizing-Easier.aspx.

Saad, Lydia. 2013. "In U.S., 71% back raising minimum wage." Gallup, last modified March 6, 2013, accessed November 7, 2018. https://news.gallup.com/poll/160913/back-raising-minimum-wage.aspx.

Saez, Emmanuel, and Gabriel Zucman. 2016. "Wealth inequality in the United States since 1913: Evidence from capitalized income tax data." *Quarterly Journal of Economics*, 131 (2): 519–578.

Sanders, Lynn M. 1997. "Against deliberation." *Political Theory*, 25 (3): 347–376.

Satz, Debra. 2017. "Feminist perspectives on reproduction and the family." Accessed November 8, 2018. https://plato.stanford.edu/archives/sum2017/entries/feminism-family/.

Schilling, Lisa, Alide Chase, Sommer Kehrli, Amy Y. Liu, Matt Stiefel, and Ruth Brentari. 2010. "Kaiser Permanente's performance improvement system, Part 1: From benchmarking to executing on strategic priorities." *Joint Commission Journal on Quality and Patient Safety*, 36 (11): 484–498.

Schilling, Lisa, James W. Dearing, Paul Staley, Patti Harvey, Linda Fahey, and Francesca Kuruppu. 2011. "Kaiser Permanente's performance improvement system, Part 4: Creating a learning organization." *Joint Commission Journal on Quality and Patient Safety*, 37 (12): 532–543.

Schilling, Lisa, Dennis Deas, Maile Jedlinsky, Deborah Aronoff, Juliette Fershtman, and Abdul Wali. 2010. "Kaiser Permanente's performance improvement system, Part 2: Developing a value framework." *Joint Commission Journal on Quality and Patient Safety*, 36 (12): 552–560.

Schlachter, Laura Hanson. 2017. "Stronger together? The USW-Mondragon union co-op model." *Labor Studies Journal*, 42 (2): 124–147.

Schmitz, James A., Jr. 2016. *The Costs of Monopoly: A New View*. Minneapolis: Federal Reserve Bank of Minneapolis.

Schneiberg, Marc. 2010. "Toward an organizationally diverse American capitalism: Cooperative, mutual, and local, state-owned enterprise." *Seattle University Law Review*, 34: 1409.

Schofer, E., and M. Fourcade-Gourinchas. 2001. "The structural contexts of civic engagement: Voluntary association membership in comparative perspective." *American Sociological Review*, 66 (6): 806–828.

Schor, Juliet. 2008. *The Overworked American: The Unexpected Decline of Leisure*. New York: Basic Books.

Schor, Juliet B., and Samuel Bowles. 1987. "Employment rents and the incidence of strikes." *Review of Economics and Statistics*, 69 (4): 584–592.

Schumpeter, Joseph A. 1976 [1942]. *Capitalism, Socialism and Democracy*. New York: Harper & Row.

Schweickart, David. 2011. *After Capitalism*. Lanham, MD: Rowman & Littlefield.

Scipioni, Antonio, Anna Mazzi, Marco Mason, and Alessandro Manzardo. 2009. "The dashboard of sustainability to measure the local urban sustainable development: The case study of Padua municipality." *Ecological Indicators*, 9 (2): 364–380.

Scott-Clayton, Judith. 2018. *The Looming Student Loan Default Crisis Is Worse than We Thought*. Washington, DC: Brookings.

See, L., F. Kraxner, S. Fuss, C. Perger, C. Schill, K. Aoki, et al. 2015. "The potential of crowdsourcing for the renewable energy sector." In *Handbook of Clean Energy Systems*, edited by J. Yan, 1–15. New York: John Wiley & Sons.

Sen, Amartya. 1993. "Markets and freedoms: Achievements and limitations of the market mechanism in promoting individual freedoms." *Oxford Economic Papers*, 45 (4): 519–541.

Sexton, Steve. 2011. "The inefficiency of local food." *Freakonomics*, November 7, 2018. http://freakonomics.com/2011/11/14/the-inefficiency-of-local-food/.

Shaffer, Harry G., ed. 1984. *The Soviet System in Theory and Practice: Western and Soviet Views*. New York: Frederick Ungar.

Shaikh, Anwar. 1978. "An introduction to the history of crisis theories." In *US Capitalism in Crisis*, edited by Union of Radical Political Economy, 219–241. New York, NY: URPE/Monthly Review Press.

Shaikh, Anwar M., and Jamee K. Moudud. 2004. *Measuring Capacity Utilization in OECD Countries: A Cointegration Method*. Working paper, The Levy Economics Institute. Annandale-on-Hudson, New York.

Shapira, Roy, and Luigi Zingales. 2017. *Is Pollution Value-Maximizing? The DuPont Case*. National Bureau of Economic Research. Cambridge, MA.

Shapiro, Sarah, and Catherine Brown. 2018. "The state of civics education." Center for American Progress. https://www.americanprogress.org/issues/education-k-12/reports/2018/02/21/446857/state-civics-education/.

Siaroff, Alan. 1999. "Corporatism in 24 industrial democracies: Meaning and measurement." *European Journal of Political Research*, 36 (2): 175–205.

Sibony, Olivier. 2012. "Collaborative strategic planning: Three observations." *McKinsey Quarterly*, 2: 12–15.

Silk, Ezra. 2016. *Victory Plan: The Climate Mobilization*. Accessed January 26, 2019 https://www.theclimatemobilization.org/victory-plan/.

Singer, Daniel. 1988. *Is Socialism Doomed? The Meaning of Mitterrand*. New York: Oxford University Press.

Slichter, Sumner H., James J. Healy, and E. Robert Livernash. 1960. *The Impact of Collective Bargaining on Management*. Washington, DC: The Brookings Institution.

Sloane, Peter J. 2014. "Overeducation, skill mismatches, and labor market outcomes for college graduates." *IZA World of Labor*, accessed January 26, 2019. https://wol.iza.org/uploads/articles/88/pdfs/overeducation-skill-mismatches-and-labor-market-outcomes-for-college-graduates.pdf?v=1.

Smillie, John G. 2000. *Can Physicians Manage the Quality and Costs of Health Care? The Story of The Permanente Medical Group*. Oakland, CA: Permanente Federation.

Smith, J. W. 1989. *The World's Wasted Wealth: The Political Economy of Waste*. Kalispell, MT: New Worlds Press.

Smith, Richard. 2016. *Green Capitalism: The God That Failed*. London: College Publications.

Standish Group. 1994. "Chaos study report." http://www.standishgroup.com.

Stanley, Marcus. 2003. "College education and the midcentury GI bills." *Quarterly Journal of Economics*, 118 (2): 671–708. doi: 10.1162/003355303321675482.

Stephens, Nicole M., Hazel Rose Markus, and Sarah S. M. Townsend. 2007. "Choice as an act of meaning: The case of social class." *Journal of Personality and Social Psychology*, 93 (5): 814.

Stevens, Mitchell L. 2009. *Creating a Class*. Cambridge, MA: Harvard University Press.

Stieger, Daniel, Kurt Matzler, Sayan Chatterjee, and Florian Ladstaetter-Fussenegger. 2012. "Democratizing strategy: How crowdsourcing can be used for strategy dialogues." *California Management Review*, 54 (4): 44–68. doi: 10.1525/cmr.2012.54.4.44.

Stiglitz, Joseph. 2017. Wealth before health? Why intellectual property laws are facing a counterattack. *Guardian*, October 19.

Stockholm Resilience Center. 2018. "The nine planetary boundaries." Accessed November 7, 2018. https://www.stockholmresilience.org/research/planetary-boundaries/planetary-boundaries/about-the-research/the-nine-planetary-boundaries.html.

Stolle, Dietlind, Stuart Soroka, and Richard Johnston. 2008. "When does diversity erode trust? Neighborhood diversity, interpersonal trust and the mediating effect of social interactions." *Political Studies*, 56 (1): 57–75. doi: 10.1111/j.1467-9248.2007.00717.x.

Stone, Brad. 2013. *The Everything Store: Jeff Bezos and the Age of Amazon*. New York: Random House.

Strauss, Benjamin H., Scott Kulp, and Anders Levermann. 2015. "Carbon choices determine US cities committed to futures below sea level." *Proceedings of the National Academy of Sciences*, 112 (44): 13508–13513. doi: 10.1073/pnas.1511186112.

Streeck, Wolfgang. 1983. *Co-Determination: The Fourth Decade*. Berlin: Wissenschaftszentrum.

Streeck, Wolfgang. 2014. *Buying Time: The Delayed Crisis of Democratic Capitalism*. London: Verso.

Sullivan, Tom. 2014. "Sweden's Dirty Secret: It Arms Dictators." *Business Insider*, May 20. https://www.businessinsider.com/swedens-dirty-secret-they-arm-dictators-2014-5.

Sundgren, Mats, Elof Dimenäs, Jan-Eric Gustafsson, and Marcus Selart. 2005. "Drivers of organizational creativity: A path model of creative climate in pharmaceutical R&D." *R&D Management*, 35 (4): 359–374.

Swamy, Dalip Singh. 1980. *Multinational Corporations and the World Economy*. New Delhi: Alps.

Swanson, David. 2018. "US wars and hostile actions: A list." Accessed November 7, 2018. http://davidswanson.org/warlist/.

Taibbi, Matt. 2013. "Secrets and lies of the bailout." *Rolling Stone*, 17.

Teixeira, Ruy. 2010. *Public Opinion Paradox: An Anatomy of America's Love-Hate Relationship with Its Government*. Washington, DC: Center for American Progress.

Thomé, Antonio Marcio, Luiz Scavarda, Nicole Suclla Fernandez, and Annibal José Scavarda. 2012. "Sales and operations planning and the firm performance." *International Journal of Productivity and Performance Management*, 61 (4): 359–381. doi: 10.1108/17410401211212643.

Thorne, Deborah, Pamela Foohey, Robert M. Lawless, and Katherine Porter. 2018. "Graying of U.S. bankruptcy: Fallout from life in a risk society." Accessed August 6, 2018. https://ssrn.com/abstract=3226574.

Thrall, A. Trevor, and Caroline Dorminey. 2018. *Risky Business: The Role of Arms Sales in US Foreign Policy*. Washington, DC: Cato Institute.

Timming, Andrew, and Juliette Summers. 2018. "Is workplace democracy associated with wider pro-democracy affect? A structural equation model." *Economic and Industrial Democracy*, accessed January 26, 2019. https://journals-sagepub-com.libproxy1.usc.edu/doi/pdf/10.1177/0143831X17744028.

Trujillo, Lourdes, Antonio Estache, and Sergio Perelman. 2005. *Infrastructure Performance and Reform in Developing and Transition Economies: Evidence from a Survey of Productivity Measures*. Washington, DC: The World Bank.

Turner, Bengt, and Stephen Malpezzi. 2003. "A review of empirical evidence on the costs and benefits of rent control." *Swedish Economic Policy Review* (10).

Union of Concerned Scientists. 2018. "What is hair-trigger alert?" Accessed November 7, 2018. https://www.ucsusa.org/nuclear-weapons/hair-trigger-alert.

United States Bureau of the Census. 1975. *Historical Statistics of the United States, Colonial Times to 1970*. Washington, DC: US Department of Commerce, Bureau of the Census.

United States Department of Agriculture. 2018. "Food security status of U.S. households in 2017." In *Key Statistics and Graphics*. Washington, DC.

Urban Institute. 2018. "The cost of affordable housing: Does it pencil out?" http://apps.urban.org/features/cost-of-affordable-housing/.

Vagins, Deborah J., and Jesselyn McCurdy. 2006. *Cracks in the System: Twenty Years of the Unjust Federal Crack Cocaine Law*. New York: American Civil Liberties Union.

Vidal, Matt. 2013. "Low-autonomy work and bad jobs in postfordist capitalism." *Human Relations*, 66 (4): 587–612.

Vilà, Joaquim, and J. Ignacio Canales. 2008. "Can strategic planning make strategy more relevant and build commitment over time? The case of RACC." *Long Range Planning*, 41 (3): 273–290.

Vine, David. 2015. *Base Nation: How US Military Bases Abroad Harm America and the World*. New York: Metropolitan Books.

Von Mises, Ludwig. 2008 [1920]. *Economic Calculation in the Socialist Commonwealth*. Auburn, AL: Ludwig von Mises Institute.

Vucetic, Srdjan 2018. "The uneasy co-existence of arms exports and feminist foreign policy." In *The Conversation*.

Accessed January 26, 2019. http://theconversation.com/
the-uneasy-co-existence-of-arms-exports-and-feminist-foreign-policy-93930.

Wainwright, Hilary. 2003. *Reclaim the State: Experiments in Popular Democracy*.
London: Verso.

Wall Street Journal. 2009. "The Obama Motor, Inc." https://www.wsj.com/articles/
SB124381255295170405.

Wallace-Wells, David. 2018. "The Uninhabitable Earth, Annotated Edition." *New York
Times Magazine*, accessed November 7, 2018. http://nymag.com/intelligencer/
2017/07/climate-change-earth-too-hot-for-humans-annotated.html.

Wallerstein, Immanuel M. 2004. *World-Systems Analysis: An Introduction*. Durham,
NC: Duke University Press.

Weinstein, James. 1967. *The Decline of American Socialism, 1912–1925*.
New York: Monthly Review Press.

Whippy, Alan, Melinda Skeath, Barbara Crawford, Carmen Adams, Gregory
Marelich, Mezhgan Alamshahi, et al. 2011. "Kaiser Permanente's performance
improvement system, Part 3: Multisite improvements in care for patients
with sepsis." *Joint Commission Journal on Quality and Patient Safety*, 37 (11):
483–495.

Whittington, Richard, Ludovic Cailluet, and Basak Yakis-Douglas. 2011. "Opening
strategy: Evolution of a precarious profession." *British Journal of Management*,
22 (3): 531–544.

Whittington, Richard, Julia Hautz, and David Seidl, eds. 2017. "Open
strategy: Transparency and inclusion in strategy processes." Special issue, *Long
Range Planning*, 50 (3).

Wilde, Oscar. 2007 [1891]. *The Soul of Man under Socialism and Selected Critical Prose*.
London, UK: Penguin.

Williams, Heidi L. 2013. "Intellectual property rights and innovation: Evidence from
the human genome." *Journal of Political Economy*, 121 (1): 1–27.

Williamson, Oliver E. 1975. *Markets and Hierarchies*. New York: Free Press.

Wilson, Duff, and Janet Roberts. 2012. "Special report: how Washington went soft
on childhood obesity." *Reuters*, April 27, accessed January 26, 2019. Available
at: https://www.reuters.com/article/us-usa-foodlobby/special-report-how-
washington-went-soft-on-childhood-obesity-idUSBRE83Q0ED20120427.

Wilson, Mark R. 2016. *Destructive Creation: American Business and the Winning of
World War II*. Philadelphia: University of Pennsylvania Press.

Winters, Jeffrey A., and Benjamin I. Page. 2009. "Oligarchy in the United States?"
Perspectives on Politics, 7 (4): 731–751.

Witherell, Rob, Chris Cooper, and Michael Peck. 2012. *Sustainable Jobs, Sustainable
Communities: The Union Co-op Model*. Ohio Employee Ownership Center. Kent,
OH, Kent State University.

Wodtke, Geoffrey T. 2016. "Social class and income inequality in the United
States: Ownership, authority, and personal income distribution from 1980 to
2010." *American Journal of Sociology*, 121 (5): 1375–1415.

Wolff, Edward N. 2013. "The asset price meltdown, rising leverage, and the wealth of
the middle class." *Journal of Economic Issues*, 47 (2): 333–342.

Wolff, Edward N. 2017. *Household Wealth Trends in the United States, 1962 to 2016: Has
Middle Class Wealth Recovered?* Cambridge, MA: National Bureau of Economic
Research.

Wolff, Richard D. 2012. *Democracy at Work: A Cure for Capitalism*.
Chicago: Haymarket books.

Woll, Cornelia. 2016. "Politics in the interest of capital: A not-so-organized combat." *Politics and Society*, 44 (3): 373–391.

Wooldridge, Bill, and Steven W. Floyd. 1990. "The strategy process, middle management involvement, and organizational performance." *Strategic Management Journal*, 11 (3): 231–241.

Wooldridge, Bill, Torsten Schmid, and Steven W. Floyd. 2008. "The middle management perspective on strategy process: Contributions, synthesis, and future research." *Journal of Management*, 34 (6): 1190–1221.

Woolhandler, S., and D. U. Himmelstein. 2017. "Single-payer reform: The only way to fulfill the president's pledge of more coverage, better benefits, and lower costs." *Annals of Internal Medicine*, 166 (8): 587–588. doi: 10.7326/M17-0302.

World Wildlife Fund. 2014. *Living Planet Report 2014*. Gland, Switzerland: World Wildlife Fund for Nature.

Wright, Erik O., ed. 1996. *Equal Shares: Making Market Socialism Work*. London: Verso.

Wright, Erik O., and Joel Rogers. 2011. *American Society: How It Really Works*. New York: Norton.

Yaun, David. 2006. "Driving culture change by consensus at IBM." *Strategic Communication Management*, 10 (3): 14.

Yeates, Nicola. 2005. "Global migration perspectives." *Global Commission on International Migration*. Geneva, Switzerland.

Yeates, Nicola. 2012. "Global care chains: A state-of-the-art review and future directions in care transnationalization research." *Global Networks*, 12 (2): 135–154.

Yoder, Eric. 2014. "Government workforce is closing the gender pay gap, but reforms still needed, report says." *Washington Post*, April 13. https://www.washingtonpost.com/politics/government-workforce-is-closing-the-gender-pay-gap-but-reforms-still-needed-report-says/2014/04/13/59281484-c1b2-11e3-b574-f8748871856a_story.html.

Young, Kevin A., Tarun Banerjee, and Michael Schwartz. 2018. "Capital strikes as a corporate political strategy: The structural power of business in the Obama era." *Politics and Society*, 46 (1): 3–28.

Yülek, Murat. 2015. *Economic Planning and Industrial Policy in the Globalizing Economy*. Switzerland: Springer.

Zider, Bob. 1998. "How venture capital works." *Harvard Business Review*, 76 (6): 131–139.

Zijdeman, Richard, and Filipa Ribeira da Silva. 2015. *Life Expectancy at Birth (Total)*. IISH Dataverse, accessed January 26, 2019. https://datasets.socialhistory.org/dataset.xhtml?persistentId=hdl:10622/LKYT53.

Zucman, Gabriel. 2015. *The Hidden Wealth of Nations: The Scourge of Tax Havens*. Chicago: University of Chicago Press.

INDEX

limitations on, 110
matrix authority structure, 84
national economic councils
and, 85–86
open strategy model and, 85,
179n25, 180n34
participative centralization and, 80–81
values-based goals and, 84
Collaborative Working, 99–108, 184n12
Computer Science Corporation (CSC)
(example), 107
ethos of interdependence, 99, 100–2,
108, 133, 182n56
evaluation and pay systems supportive
of ethos of interdependence, 101
IBM and IBM Research
(example), 105–7
Kaiser Permanente (example),
102–4, 183n63
limitations on, 111
meaningful employee goals, 101
New United Motor Manufacturing,
Inc. (NUMMI) (example), 104–5
specialization of tasks vs., 99–100
structured discussion forums, 101
360 degree staff evaluations, 103–4
T-shaped skills, 101–2, 104, 108
Computer Science Corporation (CSC),
Government Services division, 97–
98, 107, 109–10
conscious capitalism. *See* ethical-
capitalism model: limitations of as
solution to crises
consumer banks under socialism, 128
Cooper, Daniel, 160n10
cooperatives. *See* worker-owned
cooperatives
corporate social responsibility.
See ethical-capitalism model:
limitations of as solution to crises
corporatism, 173n24
Costco, 60
Cottrell, Alan, 189
criminal-justice system
in democratic-socialist system, 139–40
racism and punitive sentencing, 18
recidivism, 18
CSC. *See* Computer Science
Corporation (CSC)
cynicism, 15

Davenport, Thomas H., 177–78n13
Davis, Mike, 162n3
decommodification of basic needs
resources, 150
deep capture of government, 166n47
Defense Advanced Research Projects
Agency, 90, 130
democracy
challenge facing socialism,
77–78, 79–80
deliberative, 108, 135–36
as plutocratic in US, 35
restoration of confidence in, 3–5
techno-utopianism and, 73
Democracy Collaborative, 115
democratic management of the
economy, 75–111
Collaborative Innovating, 86–91
Collaborative Learning, 91–99
Collaborative Strategizing, 79–86
Collaborative Working, 99–108
from high-road capitalism to
democratic socialism, 108–11
lessons from capitalist enterprises,
78–79, 175–76n4
management of whole
economy, 76–78
democratic socialism, introduction,
1–7, 67
argument for, 1–3
democratic decision making, 5
overcoming limitations of neoliberal
capitalism, 2–3, 4–5, 6–7
public ownership of enterprise, 3
restoration of confidence in
democracy, 3–5
socialist utopia, 6–7
strategic management for the public
good, 5–6
wide participation in enterprises, 5–6
democratic-socialist model, feasibility
of, 145–56
climate change scenario and, 149
common platform for proponents
of, 150
communities as arenas of
contestation, 154–55
economic crisis scenario and, 148–49
gradual social-democratic reforms
scenario and, 149, 152–53

democratic-socialist model, feasibility
of (cont.)
  international solidarity, 150
  motivation for transformation, 147
  opportunity for control over the
    economy, 145–46
  political sphere as arena of
    contestation, 151–53
  schools as arenas of contestation, 154
  strengthening capabilities, 147–48
  workplaces as arenas of
    contestation, 153–54
democratic-socialist society, as solution
  to crises, 113–43. See also national
  economic councils; regional
  economic councils
  economic irrationality, overcoming
    of, 121–30
  enterprise, beyond hired hands, 131–33
  environmental unsustainability,
    overcoming of, 136–37, 191–92n48
  finance, beyond profitability, 127–28
  government unresponsiveness,
    overcoming of, 134–36
  illustrations of, 114–16
  imperialist domination, overcoming
    of, 141
  innovation, beyond venture
    capitalism, 129–30
  international conflict, overcoming
    of, 141–43
  municipal socialism, in early
    1900s, 117
  production, beyond growth at all
    costs, 128–29
  public ownership of enterprise, 121–25
  regional economic councils, 141
  small-scale and family enterprises,
    123, 129
  social disintegration, overcoming
    of, 137–41
  strategic management of the
    economy, 125–27
  work and income, beyond
    insecurity, 133–34
  workplace disempowerment,
    overcoming of, 131–34
  World War II, and strategic
    management of the
    economy, 117–20

Democratic Socialists of America, social
  and economic Bill of Rights for the
  21st century, proposed, 150
dictators, US support for, 20
digital technologies, in democratic-
  socialist system, 130, 131–32,
  134, 148, 191n316 See also techno-
  utopianism: limitations of as
  solution to crises
discounting concept, 163n12
domestic workers, 42, 167n59
Dupont, as willful polluter, 166–67n48

economic insecurity, 10
economic irrationality, 9–12. See also
  private enterprise and profit motive
  capacity underutilization,
    11–12, 160n14
  democratic-socialist society as
    solution to, 121–30
  economic down-cycles, 10–12
  food insecurity, 10
  root causes of, 21–22
  waste generation, 12, 160n17
  wealth inequality, 1, 9–10
economies of scale, defined, 24
economies of scope, defined, 24
education
  Advanced Placement/US Government
    exam scores, 154
  civics courses, 154
  cost of higher education, 19
  democratic-socialist system and, 133,
    138, 154
  global ranking of US student
    performance, 19
  higher education, 19
  impact on health, 18
  role in productivity, 52
  socialization of production and, 52,
    55, 170n12
  student debt, 19
  wage gap for teachers, 44
efficiency. See also Collaborative Learning
  assured under socialism, 132–33
  challenge facing socialism, 75–76,
    77–78, 91
  innovation, and, 182n56
  monopoly under capitalism and, 24
elections participation, 15, 151

individualism. *See also* interdependence, ethos of
collectivism and, 30, 99
ethos of, 30, 99, 182n54
industrial banks, 128, 129
industrial-conversion economic councils, 149
industry councils, 122–23, 124
Inglehart, Ronald, 182n54
innovation, 23, 28–29, 39, 129–30, 165n91, *See also* Collaborative Innovating
challenge facing socialism, 77–78, 86–87
Innovation Learning Network, 88
intellectual property rights, 28–29, 66, 116, 165n22
interdependence, ethos of, 99, 100–2, 108, 133, 182n56
interdependencies. *See* capitalism and expansion of interdependencies
international conflict, 19–20. *See also* hierarchical world economy; imperialism
civilian assistance, 20
democratic-socialist society as solution to, 141–43
foreign military interventions by US, 20
in Nordic social democracies, 68
nuclear arsenals and threat, 20, 46–47
regulated capitalism and, 66
root causes of, 21–22
socialization of production and, 56–57
US role in, 19–20
US international arms sales, 20, 66
international governance system, 142–43
Internet retail sales, 24–25
Internet service providers, 34–35
invisible hand (Adam Smith), 26–27
iron law of oligarchy, use of term, 177n10

job loss risk, 10
job satisfaction, 13, 92, 160n19
Jordà, Òscar, 171n16

Kaiser Permanente, 82–85, 88–89, 94–95, 102–4, 109–10, 148, 178n14, 181n45, 183n63

kaizen. See Collaborative Learning
Katz, L. F., 170n12
Kaysen, Carl, 160n17
Keynes, John Maynard, 64–65
Kiely, Eugene, 170–71n15
Kitzmueller, Markus, 172n9, 172–73n14
Knott, Anne Marie, 180n38
Kornai, Janos, 190n29
Kusnet, David, 160n19
Kyoto Protocol, 19

labor unions. *See also* Service Employees International Union (SEIU); United Auto Workers (UAW); United Steelworkers (USW)
as counterweight to employer power, 31
commitment to high-road and, 109
in democratic-socialist system, 131–32, 153–54
during World War II mobilization, 119, 184–85n20
historical achievements of, 22, 31, 93, 119, 184–85n20
incidence of in US, 13
Kaiser Permanente and, 83, 84, 88–89, 178n18, 178–79n23
partnerships with management, cases of, 161n23
proposed Employee Free Choice Act and, 14
in regulated capitalism, 65
role in organizing for socialist transformation, 153–54
in social democracy, 67
Swedish Meidner plan and, 192–93n5
teachers and, 154
Laibman, David, 160n13, 161n27, 189
land, and supply-and-demand imbalances, 168n66
Lange, Oskar, 190n28
legislation, influence on, 35
Levine, David I., 181n43, 182n56
Levine, David K., 165n25
life expectancy
differences based on residential location, 44
differences based on wealth and race, 18
increases in, 23, 162n4
unemployment and, 11
Lindert, Peter H., 165–66n33

Parker, Mike, 180–81n41
Parreñas, Rhacel, 167n59
participation, use of term, 177n9
  in high-road capitalist firms, 80–81
  limited under capitalism, 13, 34, 108–
    9, 110, 147–48
  in socialist economic management,
    123, 125–26, 131, 132–33
Patagonia, 51–52, 60, 61, 172n8
patents, 28–29, 66, 165n22, 165n25
peer production networks, 69, 71
Pencavel, John, 172n12
Perez, Carlota, 191n35
pharmaceutical industry patents, 28, 66
Pistaferri, Luigi, 172n12
plan-do-study-act model, 95
planned economies, debates
    over, 190n28
planned obsolescence, 160n17
planning, indicative, 183n1
Polanyi, Karl, 192–93n5
Posner, Richard, 173n18
poverty, in single-parent households, 42
private enterprise and profit motive
  competition leads to
    concentration, 24–25
  discounting concept, 163n12
  financial market instability,
    27–28, 164n19
  growth imperative and, 22–29
  inequality, disruption and destruction
    of communities, 23, 162n3
  market share of four largest
    firms, 24
  patent costs and wastefulness, 28–29,
    165n22, 165n25
  recessions and, 26–27, 164n16
  as root cause of crisis, 22–29
  short-term myopic decision making,
    25–26, 38–39
productive capacity, 11–12, 160n14
Ptaskiewicz, Mark, 179–80n31
public ownership of enterprise, 3, 121–25
public-private partnerships, 122

Qu, Wen Guang, 177–78n13
Quidsi, 24–25

racial discrimination, 17, 139
racism
  hate crimes and, 17

legacy of slavery and, 43
punitive criminal-justice system
    and, 18
skewed viewpoints on, 162n50
Reagan, Ronald, 9
recessions. *See also* Great
    Recession (2008)
  ethical-capitalism model and,
    62–63
  profit motive and, 26–27, 164n16
  regulated capitalism and, 64–65
recidivism, 18
Recreational Equipment, Inc.
    (REI), 114
reformed capitalism, promise and limits
    of, 59–73
  ethical-capitalism model, 60–64,
    172n9, 172–73n14, 173n17
  regulated capitalism, 64–66, 173n19
  social democracy, 67–68,
    174n26, 174n28
  socialization of property in, 59
  techno-utopianism, 69–73, 174n40
regional economic councils, 122–23,
    139, 141
regulated capitalism
  common struggles with proponents
    of, 152
  limitations of as solution to crises,
    64–66, 173n19
renewable energy, 136–37, 191–92n48
rent controls, 140, 192n57
rents, rise in, 18–19
research and development. *See also*
    Collaborative Innovating
  in capitalist firms, 86
  in democratic-socialist system, 139
resource depletion, environmental
    unsustainability and, 15
restorative justice, 139–40, 141
Reuther, Walter, 184–85n18
revolving door jobs, 35–36, 166n42
Rezai, Armon, 191–92n48
Ribeira da Silva, Filipa, 162n4
richest one percent
  power asymmetry and, 32
  stock ownership by, 25
  wealth held by, 10, 32, 159n3, 165–66n33
Ritz, Adrian, 184n12
robotics, 72
Roosevelt, Franklin D., 117

legacy of slavery and racism, 43
recent immigrants, 43
regional competition for jobs, 44
soft budget constraint, 190n29
software development and
standardization, 95–97
Software Engineering Institute (SEI),
Carnegie Mellon University, 96
sortition system, ancient Greece,
134–35, 179n26
Southwest Airlines, 60
Spain, Mondragon confederation, 114–
15, 183n5, 183–84n7
Speaking up, 103
species extinctions, 15
SRI. *See* socially responsible investment
(SRI) funds
standard of living
improvements due to capitalism, 23
in Nordic social democracies, 67
standardization. *See* Collaborative Learning
standardized work, 93, 94
stock ownership, by richest 1%, 25
strategic management. *See* democratic
management of economy
stress levels, 17
student debt, 19
Sweden
arms sales, 68
failure of Meidner plan, 193
intergenerational mobility in, 174n28
rate of civilian assistance, 20
recessionary takeover of banks, 124–25

Taibbi, Matt, 166n43
Taylor, Lance, 191–92n48
teachers, wage gap for, 44
Tech industry, 54–55
technical efficiency, 24
techno-utopianism
common struggles with proponents of, 153
limitations of as solution to crises,
69–73, 174n40
Thatcher, Margaret, 9
Theodore, Nik, 167n59
Thomé, Antonio Marcio, 177–78n13
360 degree evaluations, 103–4
Total Quality Management, 96
Toyota, 93, 96, 104–5, 109, 164n15,
180–81n43
Toyota Production System, 93

trade, based on environmental and social
criteria, 142
transaction costs, 175n2
Trump, Donald, 4, 7, 19

UAW. *See* United Auto Workers (UAW)
underemployment, 10–11,
159n7, 161n46
undocumented workers, 42
unemployment
calculation of, 10–11, 159–60n9
as disciplinary device of business
sector, 65
due to 2008 Great Recession, 10, 11
employment precariousness and,
159–60n9
impact on health/life expectancy, 11
long-term effects on earnings,
11–12, 160n10
regulated capitalism and, 64–65
techno-utopianism and, 72–73
threat of in capitalism, 31–32
underutilization and, 10–11, 159n7
Unilever, 60
United Auto Workers (UAW), 93, 109,
180–81n43, 184–85n18
United Nations, 44–45
United States, statistics
criminal-justice system, 18
defense spending, 142
ecological footprint comparisons, 137
funding for research, 52
government expenditures,
52–53, 170n13
high-school graduation rates, 52
homelessness, 18–19
households with food insecurity, 10
projected displacement due to sea-
level rises, 15–16
resource depletion rates, 15
rural vs. urban populations during
1800s, 50–51
SRI funds, 173n15
unemployment due to 2008 Great
Recession, 10
United Steelworkers (USW), 114–15
universal basic income, 72–73, 174–75n42
universal healthcare, 14
unresponsive government. *See*
government unresponsiveness
US Food and Drug Administration, 130